WAR AND DIPLOMACY ACROSS THE PACIFIC, 1919-1952

Edited by
A. HAMISH ION and BARRY D. HUNT

This collection of papers addresses the special problems the Pacific poses for policy makers, strategists, and historians alike. *War and Diplomacy Across the Pacific, 1919-1952* examines the technical operational issues that were discussed by those intent on the exercise of influence over the enormous distances the region entails, as well as conceptual issues concerning the relevance or utility of military applications in regions where the protagonists differed even in their most fundamental cultural and philosophical values. The authors address the issues of the Pacific from the points of view of the major naval powers—Great Britain, the United States, Germany, Japan—and Canada as an emerging power.

Contributors include James Leutze, Peter Lowe, John Chapman, Nobuya Bamba, Thomas Buell, and Arthur Menzies.

The editors, A. Hamish Ion and Barry D. Hunt, teach in the Department of History at the Royal Military College of Canada, Kingston.

WAR AND DIPLOMACY ACROSS THE PACIFIC, 1919-1952

WAR AND DIPLOMACY ACROSS THE PACIFIC, 1919-1952

Edited by
A. Hamish Ion and Barry D. Hunt

Wilfrid Laurier University Press

Canadian Cataloguing in Publication Data

Main entry under title:

War and diplomacy across the Pacific, 1919-1952

Conference held Mar. 17-18, 1983.
Includes bibliographical references and index.
ISBN 0-88920-973-1

1. Pacific Area - Foreign relations - Congresses.
2. Pacific Area - History, Military - Congresses.
I. Ion, A. Hamish.   II. Hunt, Barry D. (Barry
Dennis), 1937-   .   III. Military History
Symposium   (Canada) (10th: 1983: Royal Military
College).

DU29.W37 1988   327'.09182'3   C88-093959-1

59,262

CONTENTS

ACKNOWLEDGEMENTS

THE TENTH Military History Symposium held at the Royal Military College of Canada on March 17–18, 1983, would not have been possible without the financial support of the Department of National Defence and the Social Sciences and Humanities Research Council of Canada. We are also indebted to the College's Commandant, Brigadier F.J. Norman, for his continuing interest in and encouragement of our efforts. Similarly, the support and whole-hearted co-operation of his officers and staff were critical to this conference's highly successful outcome. As always, Mrs. Karen Brown of the History Department played the key role in looking after the many details of organization and of the welfare of all who participated.

CONTRIBUTORS

Nobuya Bamba is Professor of Political Science at Osaka University.

Thomas B. Buell is a former Commander, United States Navy, and naval historian who has taught at the Naval War College and U.S. Military Academy. His books include *The Quiet Warrior: A Biography of Admiral Raymond A. Spruance* (1974) and *Master of Sea Power: A Biography of Fleet Admiral Ernest J. King* (1980).

John W.M. Chapman lectures in international relations in the School of African and Asian Studies at the University of Sussex. He is the author of *The Price of Admiralty: The War Diary of the German Naval Attaché in Japan 1939-1943* (3 vols., 1980–83).

James R. Leutze is Bowman and Gordon Gray Professor of History, University of Carolina at Chapel Hill. Among his publications on U.S. foreign policy and national security affairs are *Bargaining for Supremacy: Anglo-American Naval Collaboration 1937-1941* (1977) and *A Different Kind of Victory: The Biography of Admiral Thomas C. Hart* (1981).

Peter C. Lowe is Senior Lecturer in the History Department at the University of Manchester and a past secretary of the British Association for Japanese Studies. His publications include *Great Britain and Japan 1911-1915: A Study of British Far Eastern Policy* (1969), *Great Britain and the Origins of the Pacific War: A Study of British Policy in East Asia 1937-1941* (1977), and *Britain in the Far East: A Survey from 1819 to the Present* (1981).

Arthur R. Menzies, now retired from the Canadian diplomatic service, first entered the Department of External Affairs in July 1940 and therefore had the opportunity to observe Canadian-U.S. relations

xii   *War and Diplomacy Across the Pacific, 1919-1952*

during the period 1941–1952. He was directly involved with Far Eastern affairs in the Department in 1944-1945 and again from 1946 to 1950 when he went to Japan as Head of the Canadian Liaison Mission to General MacArthur's headquarters. From 1952 to 1953 he was Chargé d'Affaires in Tokyo.

Barry D. Hunt is Professor of History at the Royal Military College of Canada. His publications include *Sailor Scholar: Admiral Sir Herbert Richmond, 1871–1946* (1982).

A. Hamish Ion is an Assistant Professor of History at the Royal Military College of Canada. He is Secretary-Treasurer of the Canadian Asian Studies Association and has written on various aspects of Japanese and Korean history and on Canadian-Japanese relations.

INTRODUCTION

A.H. ION

THROUGHOUT MOST of their history Canadians have looked out upon the world around them mainly across their southern and Atlantic frontiers. Only in fairly recent times has the Pacific loomed large in their collective consciousness. Indeed, as the 1982 Bruk Report on the creation of an Asia-Pacific Foundation[1] suggests, Canadians are still in the process of discovering their neighbours to the west. The pattern of Canadian-Pacific history since Confederation may best be explained within a framework of the discovery and rediscovery of this reality. Throughout the nineteenth century periodic Russian "war scares" did excite regional West Coast concern. But for Canadians generally, especially those in Ottawa, it was the opening of World War II in the Pacific, dramatically underscored by the tragedy of Hong Kong, that marked the beginning of the Pacific's rediscovery. As Japan is now Canada's major trading partner after the United States, and as our links and interests across the Pacific grow more complex, the need for fuller understanding of Canada's connections with the trans-Pacific region and of American, British, and European interests in the area will continue to take on heightened significance.

Previous RMC history symposia have reflected the Eurocentric predispositions of our national tradition.[2] It seemed appropriate, therefore, that this, the Tenth Symposium, turned our attention westward towards the Pacific. "War and Diplomacy Across the Pacific" is of course a broad and open-ended theme; yet by restricting the focus of the six papers that form this volume to the relatively short but crucial period that spans the years between the end of World War I and the conclusion of the Allied occupation of Japan in the early 1950s, the events of the Pacific War (1941–45) can be put into the context of the ideas and forces that continued from the pre-war into the post-war era.

---

[1] John Bruk, *Asia Pacific Foundation. A Study Prepared for the Secretary of State for External Affairs* (Ottawa, 1982).

[2] Past symposia have dealt with Military Reconstruction in Post-War Societies (1974), Soldiers as Statesmen in the Twentieth Century (1975), War Aims and Strategy: The Great War 1914-1918 (1976), General Staffs and Diplomacy: The Decade Before the Second World War (1977), Regular Armies and Insurgency (1978), Limits of Loyalty (1979), Total Mobilization for War (1980), Coalition Warfare (1981), and Armies of Occupation (1982).

Like Canada, the Great Powers generally have viewed their Asian policies in terms of their impact on European affairs. Still the Pacific remained the wavy frontier along which many of their important international interests met. The Pacific has also posed special problems for policy makers, strategists, and historians alike—problems of a technical-operational nature that had to be addressed by those intent on the exercise of influence over the enormous distances of the region, as well as conceptual issues concerning the relevance or utility of military applications in regions where the protaganists differed even in their most fundamental cultural and philosophical values. The central role of maritime-based power in resolving many of these questions also presented the opportunity to highlight the naval dimensions of the Pacific, in contrast to our previous symposia, which have been land-bound.

Until the early nineteenth century, the sheer physical immensity of the Pacific precluded extensive contact between Western nations and the peoples of East Asia. Since then, the Pacific and continental East Asia have been the focus both of continuous international rivalry and of persistent efforts to arrive at some international accommodation which would preserve peace in that region. That condominium evolved through the *Pax Britannica* and Open Door policies enforced by the Royal Navy throughout the nineteenth century to a new equilibrium after 1902 based on the Anglo-Japanese Alliance. This in turn was superceded by yet another diplomatic system following the Washington Conference of 1921–22. The search for a framework or mechanism that might accommodate international order in the Pacific has been, therefore, a persistent theme in the history of trans-Pacific Great Power relations. The collapse and reconstruction of those mechanisms during the years 1919–52 is a central concern of this study.

Other contemporary international issues trace their roots to the developments that preceded and flowed from World War II. Many of the problems addressed in these papers—cultural ignorance, racial prejudice, general assumptions and illusions concerning power relationships, disparities between political ends and military capabilities, evolving national and Allied goals, and the impact of individual personalities—concern us to this day. Our object, therefore, has been to reassess such issues in terms of their historical significance and their implications insofar as the "lessons" of these years continue to make an impact on the perceptions of Westerners and Asians alike.

I

THE PAPERS that follow address these questions from the points of view of the major naval powers—Great Britain, the United States, and Japan (as well as Germany, the latter's ally during the Pacific War)—and Canada as an emerging Pacific nation. Unfortunately, the dictates of space and budget precluded any direct examination of the major continental land powers—China and the USSR—or of other nations such as India, Australia, and the Netherlands, whose land and naval forces made important contributions to the outcome of World War II. A comprehensive treatment, therefore, had to give way to an approach that emphasized the problems and policies employed by those nations for whom direct involvement in the Pacific region between 1919 and 1952 implied a major trans-oceanic dimension—the employ-ment of sea power in both peace and war—and whose successful appli-cation of maritime-based diplomacy was constrained by limitations imposed upon them by the sheer distance at which it was conducted from the centre of their power.

During this period, the successful use of diplomacy to maintain a Pacific system and the effective utilization of force in war depended upon an appreciation of military strength in order to ensure the achievement of specific political goals. A major theme which is brought out by many of the papers is the disparity between perceived interests and commitments and the military capabilities to maintain and protect them. Indeed, what stands out clearly in all the papers is that the outbreak of war in the Pacific in 1941 was a leap into the dark for all of the combatants. They entered the war conceptually, if not also militarily, unprepared for what was to follow.

In his far-ranging keynote address, James Leutze analyses the broad issues of the Pacific system and the impact of the Pacific War upon United States policy. Peter Lowe, in his paper on British policy during the inter-war years, is concerned with the Pacific system from the point of view of a power whose military strength was on the decline. Nobuya Bamba, in his investigation of Japan on the road toward the Pacific War, explains Japanese actions in terms of Japan's split national identity resulting from the tensions between traditionalism and modernism seen in the personalities of key policy makers. John Chap-man, in dealing with German naval views of the Pacific, stresses the continuity of German naval thought about the Pacific from the late nineteenth century until the outbreak of the Pacific War. While distance prevented the Germans from deploying significant forces in the Pacific, the region nonetheless remained an important subsidiary sphere because of its potential for drawing Allied forces away from European waters. Further, German U-boats and armed merchant cruisers did operate with success against British shipping in the Indian Ocean before and after 1941. In investigating United States naval policy before and during the Pacific War, Thomas Buell questions the foundations of American thinking and the inability of the United States to evolve a single coherent strategy during the war. Arthur Menzies analyses American policies during the occupation of Japan from the standpoint of Canada, a junior partner in the wartime coalition which had defeated Japan. Menzies deals astutely with the issue of the role of a junior ally in the post-war settlement with Japan, and the creation of a new Pacific system under United States leadership as witnessed by a diplomat who was intimately involved in the formulation of Canadian policy toward Japan during the occupation.

II

JAMES LEUTZE persuasively suggests that American strategy in the Pacific after 1952 was based on mistaken perceptions about the defeat of Japan. In part this stemmed from the fact that a final verdict about the "lessons" of the conventional war against Japan was never fully rendered as it was obscured by the atomic bombings. Indeed, the success of the United States in the Pacific War may well have masked the realities and limits of military "power" and created an illusion of real strength. Despite this, as a result of the defeat of Japan in 1945 and the success of the occupation, policy makers in Washington did not question whether conventional military force would continue to be an effective tool in bringing about desired political ends in East Asia. Further, they did not doubt that the United States possessed the ability to turn erstwhile enemies into compliant friends. In adopting policies which led to military confrontation in the Pacific after 1952, albeit in the name of the containment of global communism, Washington may have overrated the utility of military might in solving East-West rivalries in East and South-east Asia. To a considerable extent this tendency evolved from the changed status of the United States in the Pacific as a result of the Second World War.

The emergence of an American-dominated Pacific system after 1945 should, however, also be seen in the context of the continuation of international concern for stability and order in the Pacific region. This international concern was intensified by changes taking place in East Asia following the First World War. Far from inaugurating an era of peace in the Far East, the 1919 Peace Conference at Paris heralded the beginning of a new period of revolution and political chaos in continental East Asia. This period saw the former Allied Powers grappling with new problems unleashed by the Bolshevik Revolution and created by the intensified desire for self-determination inspired by an Asian interpretation of President Wilson's Fourteen Points.

Yet the First World War brought changes other than those related to the emergence of national liberation and social emancipation movements. One of the most important of these for the future of international relations was the fact, as Fujiwara Akira has noted, that "during the First World War the fundamental aim of Japanese imperialism was confirmed as aggression in China."[3] This brought Japan into conflict with Britain and the United States, and with the emerging peoples' movements in China and the rest of Asia. Nevertheless, during the years from 1919 to 1941, the key to peace in East Asia was seen by Great Britain, Japan, and the United States to be in the creation and maintenance of a system that would accommodate the emergence of a new China and satisfy the aspirations for influence and prestige in the Pacific region of these three dominant powers. This Pacific system, which emerged out of the 1922 Washington Conference, was essentially an agreement of maritime nations, as the abiding concern with naval disarmament attested. The "New Diplomacy" was employed by powers in the Pacific who shared a similar problem of how to project influence at great distance from the centre of their power. While this Pacific system was directed toward peace in East Asia, it failed to take into account the continental interests of the Soviet Union. Similarly, the failure of the United States and its Western allies to create a new Pacific system after the Second World War in which the USSR and, until recently, the Peoples' Republic of China had a viable role undoubtedly exacerbated the Cold War in Asia and increased regional instability after 1945.

As in the period after 1945, so too after 1919, European linkages and imperial concerns outside of the Pacific were major factors in determining British attitudes to Pacific problems. Despite the loss of markets as a result of the First World War, British commercial interests in East Asia still far outstripped those of the United States. Yet as Peter Lowe points out, the British, aware of their relative if not real decline in military strength, were forced to rely heavily upon diplomacy to compensate for their military weakness. The British situation in the 1920s was in many ways similar to that of the United States after 1952, but the response was different. After 1918, when the defence of the Empire and its sea routes once again became the first priority of the Royal Navy, the Admiralty found itself in difficulty meeting all of its commitments, especially as it was economically and politically unrealistic to embark on a process of major naval expansion. Unfortunately for the Royal Navy, Canada, Australia, and New Zealand were unprepared to make substantial contributions to "imperial defence"needs in the Western Pacific at this time.

This unwillingness on the part of the Pacific dominions to contribute to their naval defence coupled with the inability of Britain to bear

[3] Fujiwara Akira, *Nihon kindaishi III* (Tokyo: Iwanami Shoten, 1977), p. 12.

the cost of a threatened naval building race with the United States was a prime reason why Whitehall agreed to the naval limitations of the Washington Conference. Prior to that time, when the British government reluctantly decided on its abrogation, the Anglo-Japanese Alliance, as Dennis Smith has argued, had served as "a palliative both real and psychological" to the fact that since the end of the nineteenth century British naval power had been largely inadequate to defend its interests east of Suez.[4] Arms-limitation agreements did not alter this fact. Indeed, Admiralty planners felt as the result of article 19 of the Five Power Naval Treaty (the non-fortification clause that forbade all military building within the Central and Western Pacific zone), which prevented the United States from building a first-class naval base west of Hawaii, that the Royal Navy was left as the sole force to counter aggressive tendencies on the part of Japan. Even though Japanese planners before and after the Washington Conference did not include Britain on their list of potential enemies,[5] the British from Jellicoe in 1919 onwards regarded Japan as the major threat.

The Royal Navy's prognosis of Japan's strategic options led the British to design the naval base at Singapore, for without it the Royal Navy felt that it could not strike a serious strategic posture east of Suez. Though the Singapore strategy might have been sound, by the late 1930s it had fallen victim to the axiom that "the degree to which seapower can be employed in the interests of Far Eastern policy must necessarily depend upon the demands made upon British naval strength in other parts of the world."[6] By 1941 the assumptions underlying the "main fleet to Singapore" policy had been greatly compromised by events in the Atlantic and Mediterranean waters. In the final event Britain could only spare the ill-fated *Repulse* and *Prince of Wales* in an effort to rescue Singapore.

In contrast to the Singapore strategy, the Orange Plan of the United States represented a different approach. While the British relied on their main fleet coming from the Atlantic or Mediterranean to Singapore, Plan Orange envisaged the speedy relief of the Philippines by naval and army units from Hawaii, without fully appreciating the ability of the Japanese fleet to interdict the long lines of communications between the Philippines and Pearl Harbor. Although allowance must be made for the fact that the formulation of the Orange Plan had to do with creating grounds for increasing the naval budget as well as providing a strategy, it is clear that there was a grave disparity

---

[4] Dennis Smith, "The Royal Navy and Japan: In the Aftermath of the Washington Conference, 1922-1926," in *Proceedings of the British Association for Japanese Studies*, III, I, ed. Gordon Daniels, (Sheffield: Sheffield University Press, 1978), pp. 69-86, 70.

[5] Ibid., p. 71.

[6] Ibid., p. 75.

between the reality and the illusions of strength and security that both British and American planning gave. This was further compounded by the lack of pre-war consultations between British and American planners with respect to the possibility of a war with Japan that would involve them both. One reason why more was not done to co-ordinate Pacific strategies, until the last moment, must be put down to a failure, on the British side at least, to appreciate the ability of the Japanese Navy to do the Royal Navy significant harm. In part this was a result of deficiencies in the way in which information concerning the Japanese Navy was collected and interpreted by the Directorate of Naval Intelligence (DNI).[7] Undoubtedly misplaced trust in DNI's assessments of Japan added to the feeling of security which pre-war planning gave and greatly contributed to the demoralizing effect that the early reverses of the Pacific War had upon British forces.

Faulty intelligence was not only a British problem. James Leutze asserts that part of the lack of success which has attended the American military in East Asia before and after the Pacific War has been due to a lack of understanding of the area and its peoples. This points to the fact that in addition to information collection, analysts of raw intelligence need to have some understanding of the culture and history of the region with which they are dealing. It is a paradox that of all the countries in East Asia, Japan was the one about which the West knew the most, and yet Allied military understanding of it remained so limited.

It can be argued that the high point of military knowledge about Japan was reached in the decade after 1905 when the British and Indian Armies conducted a fairly extensive programme of language training in Japan for officers (which was never fully revived after 1918). However, there remained in the 1930s men such as the naively Japanophile Major-General Piggott or the astute Colonel Wards who had the deepest knowledge of the Japanese military. There were also the readily available accounts written by such peripatetic teachers as the Master of Semphill and Bullock. Available too, though less open to the general public, were the order reports of Vickers Maxim and a myriad of other companies who had supplied the Japanese military over the years. Further, there were the academic assessments of the hundreds of Japanese who had studied at the technical colleges and universities of the West. This was merely the public edge of technical knowledge about Japan and does not take into account the steady

---

[7] See Geoffrey Till, "Perceptions of Naval Power Between the Wars: The British Case," in *Estimating Foreign Military Power*, ed. Philip Towle (London: Croom Helm, 1972), pp. 172-93, especially pp. 179, 191-92.

stream of military attaché reports and diplomatic analyses which flowed into the bureaucratic paper mills of London and Washington.

Imperial Japan was also a favoured stopping place for travellers. MacArthur, Stilwell, Marshall, and Stimson (whose liking for Kyoto it has been argued prevented it from being selected as a target for the atomic bomb) were only some of the many Western leaders, military and civilian alike, who had visited Japan and East Asia. For their part, many of the Japanese leaders were also well-travelled. As intelligence gathering and foreign experience was seen as an important part of a General Staff officer's training, many leading Japanese commanders including Tōjō, Yamamoto, Nagumo, Kondō, and Yamashita had held postings abroad. In sum, it was not lack of knowledge about Japan or on the Japanese side about the West that was wanting. As Arthur Menzies shows, much of the success of the Allied occupation of Japan after 1945 resulted from the effective marshalling of this knowledge in North America and elsewhere while the Pacific War was still going on. What was lacking prior to Pearl Harbor was an effective system of military intelligence analysis which could digest, synthesize, and put into practical form that which was already known. In the place of adequate objective intelligence, what there was for the Allies (especially the Americans, as James Leutze argues) was prejudice, preconception, xenophobia, and smug superiority.

Racial prejudice, which had played a large part in bringing about such British defeats as those at the Dardanelles and Kut-el-Amarah in the First World War, also contributed to the Allied defeats in the Second. Racial hatred fuelled the belief that the Japanese would fight to the last man. If racial prejudice was a significant factor in the perception of the European soldier of the Japanese enemy, which also extended to his Nationalist Chinese ally, it has to be remembered that the Pacific War was not simply a war of one colour against another. Much of the fighting in South-east Asia was done by the volunteer Indian Army, and Slim's forces in Burma included fighting men from virtually all parts and all races of the British Empire. Racial prejudice was directed against the enemy, yet did not mar the relations of men of a multitude of different races and cultures who gave their lives in the service of the same King-Emperor. The campaigns in South-east Asia could not have been won had it been otherwise.

The Pacific War, partially justified by the Japanese as a war to rid Asia of white imperialistic dominance, unleashed pent-up Japanese racist feelings. The massacre of innocent Koreans and Chinese in the aftermath of the Great Kantō Earthquake in 1923 was merely one harbinger of what was to occur during Japan's Fifteen Years War (1931–45). In an emotional attack on Japanese imperialism written in 1938, Amleto Vespa warned that "if the Japanese succeed in enslaving

China, as they have enslaved Manchuria, that system of loot, pillage, murder, kidnapping, brigandage, racketeering and degradation of a great people, which they call 'the ways of the gods', will then proceed in earnest."[8] Later events in Nanking, Shanghai, and countless other places bore these predictions out. The war in China was not simply a "holy war" for political supremacy over that country, but an opportunity for the Japanese Army to engage in plunder. The high-handed treatment of the local population in areas conquered by the Japanese Army stemmed from a racial contempt for weaker peoples. The concept of a Greater East Asia Co-Prosperity sphere was developed primarily for home consumption and had little basis in reality in most of the area which the Japanese wrested from Western control.

Although the Western idea of the "Yellow Peril" had its counterpart in the Japanese concept of the "White Peril," what was especially shocking for Westerners was that the Japanese treated them in war little differently from Chinese or Filipinos. Allied racial hatred for the Japanese was certainly intensified by the Japanese treatment of POWs. Some Japanese historians have tried to explain Japanese actions in regards to white prisoners by attempting to show that the British meted out the same brutality to Japanese POWs, and that more Japanese died in British camps during and after the War than did Allied captives in Japanese camps.[9] While this contention is highly suspect, the issue of the treatment of POWs by both sides is an area in which much research remains to be done. In fact many Allied deaths stemmed not from any deliberate callousness on the part of the Japanese, but from shortages of goods and medicines because of the Allied sinking of merchant shipping. The Japanese, who had not expected to take so many prisoners in the early stages of the war, did not have the organizational infrastructure or supplies in Malaya and elsewhere in South-east Asia to care adequately for the POWs, which outnumbered Japan's soldiers. The treatment of Allied civilians who chose for one reason or another to remain in Japan throughout the war showed that not all Japanese were brutal to white aliens. The Juganji temple near Osaka, where the ashes of over 1,000 POWs were enshrined during the Pacific War, remains another example of a different and compassionate attitude toward those who were prisoners. Nevertheless, racial prejudice infected both sides before and during the War and this altered their conduct of it.

---

[8] Amleto Vespa, *Secret Agent of Japan: A Handbook to Japanese Imperialism* (London: Victor Gollancz, 1938), p. 286.

[9] Louis Allen, "Not So Peculiar—A Footnote to Ienaga on Malaya," in *Proceedings of the British Association for Japanese Studies*, V, 1 ed. John W.M. Chapman and Jean-Pierre Lehmann (Sheffield: Sheffield University Press, 1980), pp. 113-26.

Racial prejudice contributed before 1941 to the Allies's under-estimation of the fighting qualities of the Japanese armed forces. Certainly the Japanese Army had in the past its fair share of disasters, as the incident that involved the 2nd battalion 5th Hirosaki Infantry Regiment in January 1902 or the later catastrophes at Nikolaievsk in March 1920 and at Nomonhan in May 1939 attest. Yet the Russo-Japanese War had shown that the "human bullets" of the Japanese Army were capable of enduring great hardships and sustaining very heavy losses in order to gain victory. While the Siberian Intervention of 1919–21 did little to enhance the reputation of the Japanese either at home or abroad, the counter-insurgency operations in Manchuria during the early 1920s and in the 1930s revealed that the Japanese Army had lost none of its tenacity. However, as Peter Lowe points out, many observers misread Japan's inability to defeat China deci-sively as a sign of military weakness and incompetence. It was deemed bad for the morale of British troops if contrary views were entertained. Indeed, it would appear that senior British officers in Malaya were impervious to repeated warnings by more junior officers who had a greater knowledge of Japanese military capabilities. The myth of the invulnerability of Singapore had already taken hold.

III

AS IT was, war with Japan was by no means inevitable, especially when viewed in the larger context of East-West and Asian relations. With the major exception of the Russo-Japanese War (1904–05), peace, however tenuous, had been maintained between Japan and the Great Powers since the shelling of the Shimonoseki Straits in 1864. Peace had existed in large part because the framework of international rela-tions had proved flexible enough, despite changing circumstances, to accommodate the different aspirations of the Great Powers toward China. To a considerable extent this was because the activities of the Great Powers in metropolitan China, from the time of the Treaty of Tientsin onwards, were directed toward exacting the greatest benefit for themselves from China with the least possible amount of effort or impact. Further, in the late nineteenth century the *Pax Britannica* was enforced by the power of the Royal Navy in Far Eastern waters. It was only in the twentieth century that Japan and the United States were powerful enough to challenge this.

The *Pax Britannica* gave way to a period of transition in the balance of power in East Asia after Japan emerged as a significant power following the Sino-Japanese War of 1894–95. Yet despite the *Dreibund* of 1895, it still remained clearly in the interest of Japan to co-operate with the Great Powers. When, after 1905, a new equilibrium was created based on the Anglo-Japanese Alliance, Japan was in a much more powerful position in the Pacific than it had ever been. While the Anglo-Japanese Alliance placed a heavy military burden on Japan, the Alliance helped to prevent foreign intervention in the Russo-Japanese War. Further, the Anglo-Japanese Alliance allowed Japan to annex Yi Korea in 1910 without international opposition. By 1914 Japan was well on the way to achieving the twin goals of democracy at home and imperialism abroad that had emerged from the domestic political debate after 1905.

The Twenty-One Demands of 1915 marked the first real failure of Japanese diplomacy since the turn of the century, even though the Japanese were later able, at the Paris Peace Conference, to exact concessions over Tsingtao and Shantung province, which they had wanted since 1915. Despite the debacle of the Siberian Intervention, Japan remained willing to co-operate with the Western Powers in the "New Diplomacy" of the post-Washington Conference years, to attend the naval disarmament conferences in Geneva and London, and to participate in the League of Nations. Japan's undoing resulted from its inability to accommodate a nationalistic China within the framework of a new balance of power in East Asia. This was something that the other Great Powers, albeit grudgingly, were prepared to do. The Pacific War was precipitated because the Japanese leadership was, for domestic political reasons, unable to extricate itself from the war in China, which by 1941 was clearly not going to be won quickly.

At one level, as Akira Iriye has noted, a sharp difference in the perception of international relations existed between the United States and Japan by the 1930s, a difference which saw the Americans believing that international stability and peace could be built on "economic interdependence among the industrial nations and their cooperation to develop other regions of the globe."[10] The Japanese, on the other hand, viewed the future in terms of a pan-Asianist regional order with themselves at its head. From the 1850s Japan had seen itself as having a special role and position in East Asia. This had been manifested in a steady expansion overseas, beginning with the annexation of the Ryūkyū Islands shortly after the Meiji Restoration. Within this expansion there was a strong element of altruism, but more obvious was Japanese self-interest.

As Nobuya Bamba shows, the ruling elite in Japan during the 1920s and 1930s entertained differing perceptions of Japan's national goals in East Asia, differences which had their roots in the conflict between modernism and traditionalism within Japan's national identity. This conflict had contributed a cyclical nature to Japanese history since 1868 in which periods of openness to Western influences gave

[10] Akira, Iriye, *Power and Culture: The Japanese-American War 1941-1945* (Cambridge, Mass.: Harvard University Press, 1981), p. 34.

way to periods of exclusiveness. The period from the Hibiya Park riots in 1905 to the Mukden Incident of 1931 was characterized by a genuine openness to outside influences on the part of Japanese society. The Depression, the decline of parliamentary democracy, concern over the decline of moral standards in society, and the unsettled state of world affairs all contributed to the rise of traditionalist feeling, which revealed itself in the form of militarism and Japanese fascism. Even so, it was not until the late 1930s, after the commencement of the Sino-Japanese War in 1937, that the "military clique" gained control of Japanese politics.

A major part of the responsibility for the rise of militarism lay with the inability of parliamentary political parties to stamp out the terrorism of the early 1930s, and to unite effectively to resist the pressure of the Army. Furthermore, the failure of the socialist movement to join with liberals and social democrats in a national united front against fascism gave unintended aid to the rise of militarism. It was the lack of organized opposition, rather than its own strength, that allowed the government to embark upon the disastrous war in China after 1937. Once involved in the war, regardless of its wider perception of international affairs, the Japanese government found itself boxed into a corner. It had to continue that war, even if it meant conflict with the Western Powers, because the government would lose political power otherwise. The growing unpopularity of the China War might well have brought a change in government by 1941. In that sense, the United States embargo on oil exports to Japan was unfortunate, for it was an ultimatum that did not allow time for a gradual withdrawal from China, which might have allowed some face-saving. As a result the Japanese felt that they had no alternative but to go to war with the United States and Great Britain.

While war with the Western Powers was not unexpected, it has to be pointed out that until shortly before the beginning of the Pacific War, the Japanese Navy was opposed to making war against the United States because "a war with the latter was practically regarded as a catastrophe."[11] However, it was also clear as early as the summer of 1940 that the Navy was solidly behind any attempt to take the oil fields of the Dutch East Indies if the United States imposed an oil embargo.

Prior to 1941 Japanese naval operational planning had been confronted with the imponderables of how to cope with combined Anglo-American naval power in the advent of war. As John Chapman has pointed out, the capture by the Germans in August 1940 of secret

---

[11] John W.M. Chapman, "Forty Years On: The Imperial Japanese Navy, The European War and the Tripartite Pact," in *Proceedings of the British Association for Japanese Studies*, V, 1, pp. 72-86.

British despatches intended for the political and military authorities in Singapore, which were passed on to the Japanese Navy, revealed the weak state of the British garrison there. This allowed the Japanese to reduce the size of their forces allocated against Singapore and to concentrate the bulk of the Fleet against the United States Pacific Fleet. German support of Japan was not only important in the form of a shift in the European and global balances of power, which gave Japan the opportunity to strike against the Allies, but also in the provision of vital intelligence which helped form the Japanese Navy's war strategy.

While Japan's strategy proved successful in achieving the immediate goal of securing oil supplies for the Navy and home industries by the occupation of the Dutch East Indies, the underlying weakness of Japan's strategy was soon revealed. While it might be said that ultimate Japanese success was dependent on a German victory in Europe, which was not forthcoming, Japanese strategy in the Pacific was fatally flawed. That situation was aggravated by their failure to develop any comprehensive system of trade defence. The dramatic loss of merchant bottoms as a result of unrestricted Allied submarine activity quickly nullified the original intent of the southern strategy and meant that after the first year of the war the Japanese Navy was desperately short of fuel oil. Even in the early months of the war, so scarce was fuel for the Japanese that, John Chapman notes, German offers of commerce raider and U-boat assistance were rejected unless the Germany Navy could provide its own tankers. Long before bombing took its toll, war production in Japan had begun to slacken because of the shortage of raw materials owing to the sinking of shipping. The apparent lack of foresight on the part of the Japanese in terms of convoying merchant shipping reveals that the Japanese were not prepared for extended total war. However, for three years the Japanese Navy was able to protect their main islands from attack. For the Japanese the Pacific War was not as it was for the American Admirals "merely a replay of a strategy learned at the Naval War College."[12] Japanese strategy was almost entirely opportunistic and open-ended, and was swiftly revealed to be flawed.

However, it is not the failings of the Japanese strategy but the weaknesses of Allied strategies against Japan which are important in explaining why the Pacific War continued for so long. A major flaw in the Allies' war effort against Japan was their inability to co-ordinate their plans and actions against Japan before and during the war. In

---

[12] Paul R. Schratz, "The Orient and U.S. Navy Strategy," in *The American Military and the Far East,* Proceedings of the Ninth Military History Symposium USAF Academy, 1980, ed. Joe C. Dixon (Washington: U.S. Government Printing Office, 1981), pp. 127-38.

that respect the Pacific War stands in sharp contrast to the European War in which co-ordination was a marked feature. Indeed, the Pacific War had ended before the Allies had decided upon a single strategy on how to defeat the Japanese by conventional means. As Arthur Menzies points out, in Canada's case much effort was expended in the northern Pacific but no offensive against the Japanese was attempted via a northerly route. While the stationing of Canadian troops on the Pacific coast did not hasten the defeat of Japan, it did serve to take manpower away from more important areas.

IV

DURING THE Pacific War, the American military gained relatively little knowledge in fighting drawn-out campaigns on Asian soil. The ground fighting that the United States's soldiers and marines did was largely restricted to fierce, short-lived battles for small islands. In that sense, the Pacific War gave little clue to what might be expected once the Americans found themselves fighting an extended campaign in Asia, as they did in Vietnam. Island campaigns did reveal the importance of combined operations, an art which had fallen into disrepute following the failure at the Dardenelles in 1915. Some 600 combined operations took place during the Second World War, the majority of them in the Pacific. In the island-hopping operations in the Pacific, the United States could bring to bear the full weight of organization, technology, and firepower on narrow fronts close to the shore. Aircraft-carriers and naval air power as well as the artillery support provided by warships were crucially important to these operations.

As Thomas Buell argues, the great emphasis placed on the importance of the aircraft-carrier has continued since the Pacific War in the stress put on the development of fast carrier flotillas. The aircraft-carrier supplanted the battleship as the premier heavy unit in the United States Navy. Since 1945 the retention of bases in the Philippines, Guam, South Korea, and Japan from which United States aircraft could strike against potential enemies on the Asian mainland has raised legitimate doubts about whether the continued reliance on carrier forces has been either necessary or worthwhile. For behind the continued existence of fast carrier flotillas is the Mahanian assumption that war is decided by big battles. This has not been the case in recent wars in East Asia.

During the Pacific War, the United States saw in the carrier a tool which helped to overcome the problem of supplying air support to forces waging war at a great distance from their home bases of support. The problem of distance has now largely been overcome by the acquisition of forward bases ringing the Asian mainland, by the long-distance capability of aircraft and underway replenishment, and by better communications. It would be wrong, nevertheless, to assume that the advent of nuclear weapons should change conventional strategic assumptions about the Pacific. While the use of nuclear weapons in any future conflict in East Asia cannot be discounted, certain factors mitigate against their use and relevance. As Mao Tse-t'ung has stated, the atom bomb is a paper tiger. Again, the simple fact that the Pacific and East Asia have always been of secondary interest to the great nuclear powers implies that there would have to be a strong European reason for the use of nuclear weapons in Asia. A strong and reasonable fear is that any use of nuclear weapons in Asia could well force a nuclear response in Europe. Barring an accident, it is logical to assume that the Superpowers, out of fear of the possible response in Europe, would not be prepared to use nuclear weapons in Asia. This does not mean to say that Asian powers might not be prepared to use nuclear weapons in defence of their own national existence, but such use by an Asian power would be less likely to precipitate a world nuclear war. Given the finality of the use of nuclear weapons by the Superpowers, their strategic assumptions in terms of Asia should still rest on the use of conventional forces. Fortunately, for the Allies in the Pacific War, the Japanese fought their war in the same European style as the Allies in that their military thinking was based on Clausewitzian-Jominian models. However, the war against Japan did not prepare the United States to face a foe in Asia whose style of warfare did not reflect Western orthodoxy.

The Allied occupation of Japan saw the military perform a very different role from the one which had engaged its attention during the previous four years. While the occupation was an undoubted success, it must be remembered that the occupation of South Korea was a failure. The success of the occupation in instituting reforms in Government, agriculture, and industry depended upon their being accepted by the occupied peoples. In contrast to South Korea, the occupation of Japan was a success because the Japanese wanted it to be a success. To an extent also the success of the occupation depended upon the goodwill of the American allies, which was engendered by a consensus among them as to what the goals of the occupation should be. Arthur Menzies reveals the close identification of Canadian views with those of the United States over policies for Japan. While the Allied partners might disagree with the United States on some of the details of occupation policy, the success of MacArthur undoubtedly aided the creation of a new Pacific system under American auspices. It was the task of bringing Japan back into the comity of nations that was the motive behind the reforming policies of the Supreme Commander for the Allied Powers. As Grant Goodman has noted:

The atomic bombings of Hiroshima and Nagasaki had both alienated and embarrassed much of American opinion, and one answer
was, of course, to blot Japan from our consciousness. Thus, had it
not been for the incomparable figure of MacArthur himself, who
had become so identified with Japan and with America's commitment to Japan, the Japan-US alignment of today might never have
developed with the seeming ease and naturalness with which it did.[13]

It is not the least of MacArthur's qualities as a leader that he was able
to overcome the bitterness left by the events of the war and view the
problems of Japan and the Japanese after 1945 with compassion.
Imperfect though it is, the new Pacific system after 1945 could not
have come into being if SCAP's actions in Japan had alienated the
United States's Western allies. The success of the occupation, however,
did contribute to an illusion that the United States possessed the ability
to solve all other problems in East Asia. The failure in South Korea
was overlooked.

V

IT IS clear from the period 1919 to 1952 that there were no easy
solutions to the problems of the nations across the Pacific. If stability
and peace are to be maintained, the events of this period suggest that
such requires the creation of a Pacific system which encompasses all
the major continental and maritime powers in the region. They
emphasize also that, for the military to be successful both in peace
and in war, great attention should be paid to the problem of how
intelligence can be applied in a practical way to achieve aims. More
importantly, what the Pacific War and later Vietnam have revealed is
that the results of military intervention in East Asia are limited, and
for military intervention to be successful its aims must be defined and
the military tasks must not be too great.

Canada played a minor role in Pacific affairs until the end of this
period. However, one of the legacies which Canada has from the occupation era is the high reputation which E.H. Norman, the Canadian
diplomat and historian of Japan, has enjoyed in Japan. Much of this
derived from his genuine sympathy for the Japanese intellectual
community, which had suffered greatly during the Fifteen Years War.
As Nobuya Bamba reveals, there were two sides to the Japanese national
personality in the 1920s and 1930s—one of which was modernistic,
liberal, and pro-Western in outlook. While the success of MacArthur

---

[13] Grant K. Goodman, "MacArthurian Japan: Remembered and Revised," in *The British Commonwealth and the Occupation of Japan*, ed. Ian Nish (London: ICERD, 1983), pp. 1-14.

lay in reviving this side of Japan, the example of E.H. Norman shows the value of understanding at an individual level in helping to sustain the confidence of Japanese, albeit academicians, whose *Weltanschaunng* was broadly akin to his own and his fellow Canadians. As a result of Norman's presence in Tokyo, Canada had a greater influence on Japanese affairs than Ottawa might have expected, and his humanitarianism and sensitivity were accepted by many Japanese intellectuals as the touchstones of Canadian foreign policy toward Japan. In playing a greater role in the Pacific in the future, Canadians should realize from the history of this period that good relations with their western neighbours entailed not only mutual economic benefit but also responsibility to ensure peace through a viable Pacific system and the maintenance of a humanitarian outlook that transcends cultural and ideological differences.

CONTINUITY AND CHANGE IN AMERICA'S SECOND OLDEST FOREIGN POLICY COMMITMENT

JAMES LEUTZE

I HAVE set myself a rather formidable task: to survey the course of United States military and diplomatic policy in Asia in the years between 1920 and 1970. As if that were not enough, I will violate that time frame at both ends, that is, I will consider, if only briefly, developments preceding 1920 and coming after 1970. Inevitably, in any such sweeping assessment, I cannot devote the time and attention required by each of the important events of this period. And I will surely overlook events that should receive as much attention as those I have chosen to single out. Finally, it is certain that many will find themselves at odds with my conclusions.

Despite these reservations, I am determined to forge ahead under the general assumption that you can not make an omelet without cracking eggs. It seems to me entirely appropriate to make some re-evaluations, some new interpretations, and some generalizations about this important era and this critical geographic area. In short, I begin with the conviction that some previous assumptions need to be turned on their heads. It is also my hope that this survey will provide some new perspectives, stimulate new research, and produce further re-evaluations.

After surveying this period, I have come to two modest conclusions. One is that, taken in aggregate, American policy in Asia between 1920 and 1970 has fallen short of its goals. It did not keep Japan from building a formidable naval force in the 1920s and 1930s; it did not keep Japan from an expansionist policy in the 1930s and early 1940s; and it did not preserve the political integrity of the Chiang Kai-shek regime during the late 1930s and 1940s. To be sure, Commonwealth and American forces won the Pacific War against Japan but, as will become clear, I do not believe they did so in the wisest or most prudent manner. They unnecessarily encouraged the Soviets to enter the war in Asia. They were successful in fostering democracy and helping recreate an economically viable Japan after the war, but a costly war had to be fought to maintain the artificial division of Korea. The United States was unable to keep the Chinese from entering the Korean War, and may have unwisely provoked them into partaking; and most recently America entered and fought an even more costly and unsuccessful war in South-east Asia. If not a catalogue of total failure, this is something far short of success.

23

The other conclusion is that this lack of success stems in part from a lack of understanding of, or a lack of sympathy for, Asian history, culture, and national diversities. As has been suggested: "cultural differences and misunderstandings have always placed Western and Eastern politics in what is essentially an adversary role."[1] This fact has been so well established in previous conferences and in other scholarly endeavours that I suggest that it can be accepted as a given.

These "cultural differences and misunderstandings" go a long way to explain the lack of success I alluded to initially; however, it seems to me that there is much more that is needed by way of explanation. In looking for additional reasons I propose to walk through this period chronologically, identifying instances where we have fallen short; however, I should point out that I do not intend to give equal treatment to every era or every error. I am particularly interested in the period 1920 to 1970 and I will devote primary attention to that time. After completing this survey I will make some observations regarding the continuity of the American experience and attempt to explain why it fell short.

One final caveat before we begin our progress through time: If one wishes to argue that my proposition regarding the failure of American policy overlooks the possibility that it was not a failure but simply an inability to keep things from happening the way they were normally going to happen—to argue, in other words, in the way Tolstoy did, that events were foreordained and that the interference of human actors was inconsequential—I would quibble only with the term "over-look." I have considered that possibility, find it impossible to argue with someone holding that conviction, and fear that should any such explanation of history ever become widespread there will seldom be meetings like this one.

One of the major thrusts of U.S. diplomatic and military policy after World War I was to head off a naval arms race between the maritime powers. The explanation for this was partly military—arms races caused wars—and partly economic. The focus for discussion of this issue was the Washington Naval Conference of 1921–22. In many ways this conference ended as a success for American diplomats. The participants reached agreement on nine treaties—the most important of which set ratios for the world's major navies and provided for a ten-year holiday in capital ship building. Another treaty guaranteed China's territorial integrity and reiterated the Open Door principle. In still another the U.S., Britain, France, and Japan agreed to respect each other's rights over Pacific island possessions.[2] It is generally agreed

---

[1] *The American Military and the Far East:* Proceedings of the Ninth Military Symposium, U.S.A.F. Academy, 1980; Washington: U.S. Government, 1980, p. 246.

[2] For an excellent summary, see Stephen Roskill, *The Period of Anglo-American*

that this conference was a short-term success, but a long-term failure. The agreed upon ratios gave Japan a smaller navy; this, coupled with the abrogation of the Anglo-Japanese Alliance and the 1924 Oriental Expulsion Act in the United States, served to humiliate the Japanese and accentuate their feelings of international inferiority. Just how real this bitterness was is evident in the way the Japanese hastened to build up to treaty limits as soon as the construction holiday was over, and to do so at a time when the U.S. was economically and politically constrained by isolationist sentiments from doing likewise. Soon after Japan reached treaty limits, it served notice that it was abrogating the treaty, and then proceeded to build rapidly during the remainder of the 1930s. Less commonly known was the personal irritation and loss of face which many senior Japanese naval officers felt they suffered as a result of the Washington Treaties.[3] Taking account of these feelings is critical when one tries to determine *why* the Japanese chose to go to war with the U.S. in 1941. After a lecture at Duke University in the early 1970s I had the pleasure of hearing Colonel Genda, one of the chief planners of the Pearl Harbor attack, discuss the process by which he and his associates planned and prepared it. After his informative lecture I asked Colonel Genda *why* Japan attacked. His answer went something like this: "I asked many senior officers that same question. Their answer often was 'I have lived all my life under the stigma of inferiority forced upon me by the British and the Americans. I know that our chance for surprising and defeating them may not be very good—but if I am ever to have the chance to regain my pride and our country's stature, it must be now!'"

I do not wish to put too much emphasis on this particular account; I do mean to suggest that U.S. disarmament policy in the Far East, while well intentioned, bore bitter fruit.

The same is clearly true regarding American policy concerning the territorial integrity of China, which was also incorporated into the Washington treaties. The first erroneous assumption here was that some power acceptable to the U.S. could bring order out of the chaos into which China had fallen. By the late 1920s the U.S. had decided that this someone was Chiang Kai-shek and the Kuomintang.[4] More will be said about this choice later; the important thing to note here is that, despite American policy, the Japanese occupied Chinese terri-

---

Antagonism, 1919-1929, Vol. I of *Naval Policy between the Wars,* (London, 1968), Chapter VIII.

[3] Akira Iriye "1922-1923," in *American East Asian Relations: A Survey,* ed. Ernest R. May and James C. Thomson, Jr. (Cambridge, Mass. 1972), p. 233.

[4] Michael Schaller, *The U.S. Crusade in China, 1938-1945* (New York, 1979), pp. 4-5. See also Barbara Tuchman, *Stilwell and the American Experience in China, 1911-1945* (New York, 1971), p. 105.

tory and created the puppet state of Manchuko barely ten years after the Washington Conference. The U.S. countered with the thoroughly decent and totally ineffectual Stimson Doctrine of non-recognition. Well-intentioned, but with no standing in international law, the Stimson Doctrine proved as effective in the 1930s as a similar policy toward the communist government of China proved eighteen years later. Secretary of State Stimson followed his doctrine with the so-called Borah Letter, which he considered the most important state document issued during his tenure as his country's chief diplomatic representative.[5] The letter matched the doctrine in its utter lack of effectiveness. Here I might pause to state one of my convictions; I oppose generally the policy of diplomatic non-recognition, and I am very dubious about the wisdom of issuing sweeping public statements which condemn the motives of other nations while praising one's own. The latter is only wasteful of time and effort, the former simply underlines a nation's inability to influence a situation and to make it difficult to alter that inability by narrowing the range of diplomatic manoeuvre.

The inability of the United States to influence Japanese actions in China and elsewhere in South-east Asia only became more apparent as the 1930s moved on and the 1940s began. But after 1937, when co-ordination with the British began, American problems were compounded. Not only was the U.S. unable to deter its potential adversary, but it was unable to influence its potential allies to any significant degree. The issue was, and is, complex, but it bears a moment's consideration because it helps explain why the United States was so ill-prepared for war in the Far East when it finally came. When U.S. officials first entered into co-ordinated war planning with their British allies, they were convinced that they had to "tie them down" so that perfidious Albion would not leave the U.S. "in the lurch."[6] For some of the more bellicose American planners, the problem initially was doubt that the British would "stick" with any plan for co-ordinated action once the going got tough; this attitude evolved into a more generally held view that the British would prefer to cave in rather than stand up to the Japanese. Part of the problem, as the U.S. planners saw it, was that British defection or lack of resolution would leave the U.S. defending British "colonies"—a most distasteful fate.[7] However, not all American policy makers agreed on a "get tough" policy toward Japan, as Admiral Thomas Hart, Commander of the Asiatic Fleet, found to his disgust. When it came to being tough regarding Japanese "outrages" in Shanghai, Hart favoured the mailed

---

[5] Robert H. Ferrell, *American Diplomacy: A History* (New York, 1969), p. 591.

[6] See James Leutze, *Bargaining for Supremacy* (Chapel Hill, 1977), p. 15.

[7] For general suspicions about British Far Eastern policy, see Leutze, *Bargaining*, especially p. 210 and pp. 243-44.

fist (even though there was precious little mail). The Department of State, in his view, favoured appeasement; and in June 1940 the British favoured "turning tail" and running.[8] It is only fair to note that the British were in a terrible bind at this time and that they were not entirely pleased with American plans or policies in the Far East.

The point here is not that either policy was demonstrably correct; it is just that some co-ordinated, consistent policy would, in all likelihood, have been more effective. Criticism of the war plans that evolved, both for the Americans and for the Allies, can be more specific.

The basic plan for a U.S. war in the Pacific was a variation of the Orange Plan evolved after World War I. It called for holding the Philippines while the U.S. Pacific Fleet fought its way West from Hawaii.[9] There have been too many critiques of this Plan to merit going into the issue here, but suffice it to say that when war came there was no fleet left to fight its way West. Furthermore, although the very dubious premise of holding the Philippines had become more theoretically possible by the addition of air power to the shield, Lieutenant-General Douglas MacArthur vitiated any chance he might have had for a successful defence by adopting a thoroughly unrealistic forward-based, aggressive response to the Japanese landings, contributing in the process to the loss of his Far East air force.[10] Thus by December 9, 1941, the U.S. was virtually back to square one regarding its own plans.

As far as Allied plans were concerned, they, too, came to naught. But they did so for more complex reasons and not nearly as quickly. Contingency planning is never easy, but there is much evidence to suggest that co-ordinated Allied planning for the Pacific could hardly have been worse. Part of the problem was priorities, as Churchill suggested in his "Sinister Twilight" allusion. Once the Atlantic was given priority the Pacific regressed to the back of the collective mind. While that retrogression is easily understood, it obviously should not have happened. Then there was the matter of mutual suspicion. Originally the Americans had not wanted to get drawn into a war for Britain's colonial possessions; subsequently, it was Britain's turn not to want to get drawn into any war in the Pacific unless the Americans were thoroughly committed to come to its aid.[11] As I will suggest later,

---

[8] James Leutze, *A Different Kind of Victory* (Annapolis, Md., 1981), pp. 167-71.

[9] For information on War Plan Orange see Louis B. Morton, "The War in the Pacific: Strategy and Command," in *U.S. Army in World War II* (Washington, 1962), Chapter I.

[10] See William Manchester, *The American Caesar* (Boston, 1978), p. 206. See also Morton, *Fall of the Philippines*, Chapter 5-9, and Clayton James, *The Years of MacArthur*, Vol. II (Boston, 1970), Chapter I.

[11] See Christopher Thorne, *Allies of a Kind: The United States, Britain, and the War Against Japan, 1941-1945* (Oxford, 1978), p. 71 ff. The Chiefs of Staff had suggested

this American (and Commonwealth) anti-colonialism cast a long shadow. The British concern, considering their involvements elsewhere, was prudent. But firmly held prejudices and prudence hardly justify the shambles that was Allied "planning" for the Far East. The picture of Tommy Hart and Vice-Admiral Sir Tom Phillips, the new British naval commander Far East, standing on the dock on December 6 improvising deployments is all too vivid and all too sad.[12] Three days later Phillips would be dead and Hart would bemoan the fact that he had been misled by MacArthur's confidence and Washington's lack of decisiveness.

When war came little remained of Allied war plans but some generalized "Plenaps," which had not been formally approved in London or Washington, and a vague concept for co-operation via "mutual co-ordination."[13] The ABDA (American, British, Dutch, Australian) combined headquarters that was slapped together bore all the imprints, and suffered all the defects, of improvisation. Before considering some of those imprints and defects, let me say a final word about the coming of the war in the Pacific. There is a natural and understandable tendency to assume that things would have followed the course that they did no matter what had been done differently. In a broader sense it can be insisted that history should concentrate only on what did happen, and that historians should not bother themselves with what might have been. While I generally accept both of these admonitions, I have two observations that apply here. First, if we only concentrate on what happened, without even considering the options, we close off a whole variety of research opportunities that might produce results if we keep an open mind. This observation is particularly appropriate in a subject area that has been so pawed over that it approaches intellectual pablum. Secondly, I associate myself with the historian, A.J.P. Taylor, who said, "history is what happened within the context of what might have happened."

To return to the point, I wonder what would have been the effect of an open, public enunciation of an Allied mutual security pact in the Far East. I wonder whether more could have been done to support those diplomats and elements within the business community and the Navy who made up the moderate group in Japan.[14] I wonder whether

---

as early as May 1940 that "we must rely on the United States of America to safeguard our interests in the Far East."

[12] Leutze, *A Different Kind of Victory*, p. 226.

[13] Leutze, *A Different Kind of Victory*, pp. 210-11 and p. 254. "Plenaps" was the name given to these generalized plans. Washington had disapproved the latest version because they contained too many political undertakings and were not offensive enough. Hart thought the only way to operate effectively was through "unified control" rather than "mutual co-operation."

[14] One of the more hopeful endeavours in this regard that came to naught was

the witch-hunt for a conspiracy regarding Pearl Harbor did not distract attention from a far more productive criticism of MacArthur's policy in the Philippines. I can state with certainty that preoccupation with the issue of whether Roosevelt did or did not know the Japanese were going to attack Pearl distracted criticism then, and now, from the resulting disaster. Whatever else may be said about it, Roosevelt's policy in the Far East was an abysmal failure. We can argue whether the Japanese were wise or foolish, whether their strike was a tactical or a strategic success, but we cannot argue that the opening of the war was anything other than the kind of disaster that would have marked the end of many governments. In other circumstances I can just hear a Senator Arthur Vandenburg saying: "You have sat too long here for any good you have been doing. Depart, I say, and let us have done with you. In the name of God go!"[15]

Now to the issue of Allied actions and tactical moves in the early months of the Pacific War. I have already alluded to the improvised way in which ABDA began to function. Things did not get better. In the matter of strategic and tactical reaction to the Japanese drive south and west, the common assumption is that nothing could have been done and the issue is merely one of which filigree you like around the outlines of failure. I am not quite so sure. There are two things I can say about what was wrong. First, diverting supplies and escorts to Singapore was ill-advised, and as wasteful as sending Canadian reinforcements to Hong Kong.[16] Secondly, on the whole issue of escorting convoys, Hart, who favoured a more offensive role for naval forces, was right and the British and the Australians, who favoured convoy escort, were wrong. Was it an impossible dream to have stopped the Japanese juggernaut? One often hears that it was. But let me remind you of a few dates: ABDA collapsed on March 15, 1942; Corregidor fell on May 6; the Battle of the Coral Sea was fought over the next two days, and Midway came one month later. By most assessments, Midway was the turning point in the Pacific War. The timing is too close here for me to accept without question the concept that miracles were impossible in January and February but became common in May and June. Obviously a change anywhere along the line would have had totally unforeseeable consequences, but can we not at the

---

a proposed meeting between Roosevelt and Prince Konoye in the fall of 1941. See William Langer and S. Everett Gleason, *The Undeclared War, 1940-1941* (New York, 1953), pp. 719 ff.

[15] Leo Amery used these words, used first by Cromwell to dismiss the long Parliament, in reference to Neville Chamberlain in May 1940. See Iain MacLeod, *Neville Chamberlain* (New York, 1962), p. 289.

[16] Hart consistently argued against wasting ships in escort duty; he preferred that they play a more offensive role. See Leutze, *A Different Kind of Victory*, p. 265.

same time accept at least the possibility that better co-ordination, better planning, a different strategy, and possibly a little luck just might have upset the Japanese advance in the early months of 1942?[17]

Whatever might have been the "may-have-beens," my most serious reservations concern the way the authorities framed their strategy for fighting the war. The strategy of Europe First or Atlantic First, although it may have been arrived at by dubious reasoning, was basically sound. America's primary interests were in the European theatre and Hitler was far and away the most formidable opponent. Therefore, securing those interests and countering the Nazi threat first was logical.[18] Unfortunately, for a variety of reasons, including public indignation over Pearl Harbor, pressure by the Navy Department and General Douglas MacArthur, the difficulty of agreeing over the timing of the Second Front, and, eventually, the suction of the Guadalcanal campaign, that strategy was modified. By 1943, the U.S. was devoting almost the same level of resources to the Pacific and to the Atlantic area. Weaponry with mutual applicability, such as landing craft, were being shared between the two theatres, to the detriment of the primary theatre.[19] To gain American agreement to Operations Husky (Sicily) and Avalanche (Italy), the British agreed, at Casablanca, to give the U.S. a free hand in the Pacific.[20] What this implied was an agreement to disagree over the way the war for Asia would be fought, and a

---

[17] Even with the poor planning, confusion, and disagreements, in the decisive battle of the Java Sea in February 1942 the Allies were not overwhelmingly outweighed or outgunned by the Japanese. This is not to argue that the Japanese did not have superiority in this battle, just to suggest that their advantages were not theoretically insurmountable. See F.C. Van Oosten, *The Battle of the Java Sea* (Annapolis, 1976).

[18] For the Europe First decision see, among others, Samuel Eliot Morison, *Strategy and Compromise* (Boston, 1958). Ironically, in view of later decisions, Eisenhower argued in the spring of 1942 that in view of the logistical difficulties of supplying efforts in the Pacific, fighting Germany first conformed to the strategic maxim of engaging the lesser foe first. See Richard M. Leighton and Robert W. Coakley, *Global Logistics and Strategy, 1940-1943* in *U.S. Army in World War II* (Washington, 1970), p. 355.

[19] By December 1943 America had deployed 125 LSTs against Japan, 92 against Germany; 34 Attack transports (ADAs) against Japan, 10 against Germany. There were a total of 1,810,367 American personnel in the Atlantic area and 1,878,152 in the Pacific area. Maurice Matloff, *Strategic Planning for Coalition Warfare, 1943-1944* (Washington, 1973), p. 398.

[20] See Louis Morton, *Strategy and Command: The First Two Years* in *United States Army in World War II* (Washington, 1962), pp. 438-39. See also Morison, *Strategy and Compromise*, pp. 75-7. Morton makes it clear that all parties, King, MacArthur, and others, did not agree on precise strategy in the Pacific, rather they agreed on giving the Pacific a higher priority and on having the U.S. call the tune. There were extensive attempts to see that the South-west Pacific receive a higher priority, and even become the "Second Front" against Germany, see "United States Armed Forces in the Far East" (USAFFE), War Department Files, especially Record Group 4, General Douglas MacArthur Archives, MacArthur Memorial Library, Norfolk, Virginia.

victory for those Americans who wanted to see the Pacific accorded a higher priority: a victory in short for the Navy, the Marine Corps (for which this was the only war), Admiral Ernest King, MacArthur, the Australians, and those trying to rescue China.

The Atlantic would always receive the highest priority, but I believe that increasing the priority assigned to the Pacific was a mistake which encouraged a waste of lives and materiel in that theatre. The basic problem was that the American planners, partly because of the shock of Pearl Harbor, consistently overestimated Japanese capabilities. Added to the "logistical snowball," which was started downhill with the Guadalcanal campaign, was an unwillingness to simply hold a defensive perimeter against the Japanese while vigorously prosecuting the war in Europe.[21] American planners believed that if the Japanese were given any respite they would rebuild, refit, dig in, and possibly become virtually impossible to dislodge. On this matter I side with the British Chiefs of Staff and their planners who argued consistently, and were consistently rebuffed, that an active defence was sufficient to hold the Japanese, who could be effectively dealt with once Germany was brought to its knees.

Not content with assigning the Pacific a higher priority and exaggerating the Japanese threat, American strategists soon began to argue over how to carry out the mandate they had received. I do not want to re-open the whole debate over which was better, MacArthur's New Guinea–Mindanao axis, or Nimitz's Central Pacific drive. What I do want to suggest is that the compromise arrived at—pursuing both courses simultaneously—was a mistake which compounded the error in the assignment of priorities. Surely confronting a dual advance complicated the problem for the defenders of the Japanese Empire, but just as surely such an advance was the least cost-effective manner of handling the offensive task.[22]

Now some readers are no doubt thinking, "O.K., let's say the initial strategy had been adhered to, and let's say instead of diverting all the manpower and resources to the Pacific, those men and those resources had been available in the Atlantic, what difference would it have made?" If you are thinking that, I am pleased, because that is just the kind of effect I hope to have. If, on the other hand, you expect me to answer that question, I am going to disappoint you. It is not that I do not think that it is a fair question to ask, it is simply that

---

[21] Admiral Henry Eccles, *Logistics in the National Defense* (Harrisburg, Pennsylvania, 1959), Chapter 7. See also Leighton and Coakley, *Global Logistics*, Chapter 15.

[22] For Japanese reaction to the problem see Hayashi Shigeru, *Taiheiyō Sensō* (*The Pacific War*) (Tokyo, 1971) and Saburo Hayashi, *Kōgun: The Japanese Army in the Pacific War* (Quantico, Virginia, 1959), Chapter IX.

within the compass of my topic, to attempt to answer would be similar to the diversion I suggest took place during World War II. Let me, however, make one observation. Some might suggest that there was no effective way to absorb more manpower and more resources in the Atlantic than were being utilized there in 1942 and 1943. That is to say, until 1944, it is doubtful if more would have made much difference. That might be, but what effect would potential availability have had on the Second Front discussions and what might additional lift capacity have meant on D-Day? Bear in mind that Overlord was a "moderate" cross-Channel assault rather than the "massive" assault initially contemplated.[23] Remember as well that, as carried out it, was a very close-run thing. Could the war in Europe have been ended in 1944? Perhaps much of what went west could not have been smoothly accommodated in the European area, but to argue that what was utilized and put into the pipeline was the absolute maximum that could be accommodated or utilized is too doctrinaire for me.

When it came to ending the war in Asia the United States again, it seems to me, followed a familiar path. Because the Americans over-estimated Japanese strength they strongly encouraged the Soviets to enter the war in Asia. As I think most would accept, when August 1945 came they did not need Soviet forces. Nor was this only because of the atomic bomb. By this point in the war Japan was already being forced to contemplate surrender as a result of losses inflicted by conventional weapons. I do not wish to get into the argument regarding use of the atomic bombs, but I will assert that American officials did not exhaustively explore all other avenues of securing Japanese capitulation. The most obvious avenue was to offer to consider the retention of the Emperor. Might it have been possible to avoid Russian entry, the dropping of the bombs, and Operation Olympic by expressing willingness to consider conditions under which Hirohito would renounce his deity yet remain in the Royal Palace?[24]

One final note on American strategy in Asia in World War II: it would be charitable to categorize U.S. policy toward China as a blunder. According China Great Power status and naming Chiang one of the Big Four was indicative of Roosevelt's misconceptions. Sending

---

[23] Original discussions of the proposed return to France posited an assault of from 10 to 25 Anglo-American divisions. In fact, Overlord landed five divisions with a backup in England of 16 by D + 90. Matloff, *Strategic Planning*, pp. 131 ff. For a follow-up see Leighton and Coakley, *Global Logistics*, p. 371. For the general strategic shift from a large scale to a medium scale cross channel assault, see Sir Arthur Bryant, *The Turn of the Tide* (New York, 1957), p. 803.

[24] For a recent discussion of American unwillingness to consider a "conditional" Japanese surrender which allowed retention of the Emperor, see Ronald Lewin, *The American Magic* (New York, 1982), Chapter 13.

General Joseph Stilwell to China compounded the error, despite his knowledge of the area and his military brilliance. The various plans put forward for fighting the war from China and India all came a cropper. The Anglo-American estimates of the internal conditions throughout Asia were consistently wide of the mark. The denouement would not come until later, but American policy toward China during the war was poorly conceived, poorly administered, and ultimately unsuccessful.[25]

In the immediate post-war period we happily came upon one of the rare success stories in our survey—the occupation of Japan. In this case one sees an instance of an unique combination of circumstances and personality. For a humiliated Japan the acceptability of a new form of government imposed by the victors was made more acceptable by the Olympian presence of their humiliator General Douglas MacArthur. It is almost as though they substituted one Emperor for another. This is in no way meant to detract from MacArthur's success, which in my view exceeds most of his fabled triumphs on the battlefield. Through his wise guidance, peace, representative democracy, a new educational system, improved health and sanitation, and the foundation for economic recovery, was established on the ruins of the Japanese Empire. The U.S. occupation of Japan must be one of the most successful occupations of modern times. Ironically, it may have influenced the Americans' view of their ability to dictate political forms to other Asian countries.

Hard on the heels of this success came another, more controversial one. The determination by the Truman Administration that it could not and should not do more to support the Chiang Kai-shek regime was wise and prudent. By 1948 the Americans had done all that was possible, indeed probably much more than they should have done, to prop up a discredited and disintegrating government. For this determination by the Truman Administration they have to thank, though not exclusively, General George C. Marshall. General Marshall was sent to China in 1946 to try to mediate between the Kuomintang and the Communists, while at the same time recognizing the KMT as the legal government of China. It was a thankless and essentially impossible task that signified the basic contradiction at the heart of the U.S. policy. Marshall returned in January 1947 having failed in his mission, but having arrived at the conviction that the U.S. should do no more to prop up Chiang Kai-shek. While serving as Secretary of State, Marshall would have occasion to hedge on that conviction, but not because he had changed his mind. Political sensitivity told him that to get his programmes for Europe approved, some gesture would

---

[25] See Tuchman, *Stilwell.*

have to be made toward China. That gesture took the form of the economic and military aid package known as the China Aid Act of 1948. However, Marshall's settled conviction remained that the U.S. should not become further involved in China, and should not offer its good offices as a mediator between the contending parties.[26]

These two successes would be followed by the Korean War (1950-53). The first thing to emphasize in this case is the way in which what was called "our [U.S.] loss of China" influenced action in Korea. China finally fell to the Chinese Communist forces in 1949. So politically traumatic was that collapse, for which the Republicans promptly blamed the Democrats, that when North Korean forces rolled into South Korea in June 1950 Truman had virtually no other course than to act forcefully. There is an old military axiom which says "don't reinforce failure," but in the case of Korea and then Vietnam the United States would be acting, in part at least, in the shadow of the loss of China. I am not going to argue here whether entering that war was a good idea. What I will argue is that insisting that it be a U.N. war was wise, but that the way in which the war was waged was unwise. The value of the first decision, making it a U.N. conflict, even though that was, to some extent, a sham, is obvious. Despite the fact that it may have hampered the Americans in some ways, it was a recognition that the conflict had political and diplomatic ramifications far outside the boundaries of Korea, and that recognition provided an element of restraint which I believe was positive.[27] On the matter of how the war was waged, my basic argument is that the United States blundered in bringing the Chinese into the war. Just as it was a serious miscalculation to have left Korea outside the boundaries of the announced defence perimeter, so too was it a miscalculation to ignore warnings of China's sensitivity about the U.S. advance toward its border.[28] Probably the first error was in deciding, without much consultation, to advance across the 38th parallel and unify Korea by force—a significant departure from the initial strategy of simply driving back the North Korean invaders and preserving the territorial integrity of South Korea.[29] In retrospect this first bold move may well have been the initial step down the slippery slope of military adventurism in Southeast Asia. In any case, the problem did not assume its full proportions until the advance northward prompted the Chinese to enter the war.

---

[26] For an excellent account of the Marshall Mission see the officially published two volume report with commentary.

[27] For a good general discussion of the Korean War, see David Reese, *Korea: The Limited War* (Baltimore, 1964).

[28] See Roy E. Appleman, *South to Naklong, North to the Yalu* (Washington, D.C., 1961), p. 608.

[29] Appleman, pp. 607-9.

I would submit that greater prudence might well have avoided that unfortunate development. At the very least the Americans could have been better prepared had the provocativeness of the U.S. advance not been compounded by an appalling misinterpretation of field intelligence and American willingness to ignore not only Chinese but also Korean and Indian warnings. But perhaps some, including General MacArthur, so overestimated American power and the will to apply it that they accepted, or even welcomed, the entry of China. Any who felt that way, I would hope, came to view the situation differently by 1952. By that point it had become obvious that to "win" the war militarily in Korea would take an effort that was beyond the will of the American public. A negotiated settlement was the only practical way out.

That brings us to the final, and most recent, conflict in Southeast Asia, the Vietnam War. There has been so much written recently on this war, so many reassessments, so many memoirs, so many retrospectives, that I am very hesitant to advance more than a tentative analysis.[30]

However, there are three relevant points to be made. First, there is absolutely no question that the current consensus about America's war in Vietnam—on the tenth anniversary of the American departure from that sad land—will be significantly altered ten years from today. One thing that makes me certain of this is the smug unanimity within the academic community that the war was immoral and that the war was unwinnable. In my experience with historical events and those who interpret them, I have rarely found unanimity to last for long, and certitude, particularly on moral questions, inevitably turns to doubt. I am not suggesting that in ten years the academic community will agree that Vietnam was a winnable crusade; merely that within a generation after its end there will be less unanimity and less certainty about its cause and the manner in which it was fought.

Secondly, I do not believe that anyone will come to question this premise: America failed in Vietnam in part because it did not understand the people with whom it was dealing in either the North or the South.[31] This premise harks back to one of my original points about

---

[30] The proceedings of a conference held at the Woodrow Wilson Center of the Smithsonian Institution in November 1982 on the "Lessons of Vietnam" is a valuable addition as is Col. Henry Summers, *On Strategy: A Critical Analysis of the Vietnam War* (Novato, California, 1982); and George C. Herring, *America's Longest War* (New York, 1979).

[31] See former President Nguyen Van Thieu's comments at the Woodrow Wilson Center meeting. Note also the reports of the conversation between an American officer and a North Vietnamese officer during the Paris Peace Conference. The American pointed out that the United States had never lost a military engagement in the whole

the activities of the United States in Asia; that is, its lack of understanding of, and its lack of sympathy for, Asian history and culture.
In this instance it is difficult to know in which geographical area of
Vietnam this lack of sensitivity had the greatest effect. From my
perspective it seems that the U.S. was equally inept in dealing with
friend and with foe.

Thirdly, and on this point I do anticipate considerable research
and possible modification: in Vietnam the United States relied far too
heavily on an assumed capacity to influence the situation militarily. I
am not arguing here the question of whether it could have won the
war by the earlier, and possibly more timely, use of military muscle.[32]
I am arguing that there was an overestimation of what could be done
with military muscle in the instances where that muscle was applied.

Fourthly, Lyndon Johnson's actions in Vietnam can only be
understood in the context of the Democrats' presumed "loss" of China
fourteen years earlier and the lack of Congressional mandate Truman
had laboured under during the Korean War. The Gulf of Tonkin
Resolution provided Johnson with the Congressional acquiescence,
still short of a declaration of war mind you, that Truman never had.

With those modest conclusions on a still highly emotional topic,
I would like to stop and go back over the historical terrain we have
traversed to see what stands out from the mass of detail. One remarkable thing is the *continuity*, not just in the pattern of falling short of
announced goals, but also in terms of the policy itself. American
commitment to Asia comes second only to the Monroe Doctrine in
terms of continuity and longevity. Since the enunciation of the Open
Door in 1899 the United States has sought to influence events in Asia.[33]
In the case of the Open Door the object was to head off a partition
of the Manchu empire by outside forces and the anticipated further
exploitation of the Chinese people that partition was expected to bring.
Although the original policy was couched primarily in economic terms,
the principle of maintaining territorial integrity and containing outside
influences remained little changed as a goal of U.S. foreign policy
from 1899 through 1973. It is this principle that constitutes the basis
of the Americans' support for arms control in Asia, their love affair

---

course of the war. "Ah, that is true," replied the Vietnamese, "but totally irrelevant."
For general coverage see Fitzgerald, *Fire in the Lake*.

    [32] Some of the most provocative new work on Vietnam suggests that, in fact, the
Johnson Administration knew the limits of U.S. power in Vietnam, but maintained an
optimistic posture for political reasons. See Leslie Gelb and Richard K. Betts, *The Irony
of Vietnam: The System Worked* (New York, 1979). For an alternate view, see David Halberstam, *The Best and the Brightest* (New York, 1972).

    [33] For an excellent treatment of the early years of relations between the United
States and China, see Michael H. Hunt, *The Making of a Special Relationship: The U.S.
and China to 1914* (New York, 1983).

with Chiang Kai-shek, the Stimson Doctrine, their opposition to Japanese expansionism, and their involvement in Korea and Vietnam. True, in the case of China, Korea, and Vietnam, the outside force the Americans were trying to contain was communism not mercantilism, but the principle was similar nonetheless. Another way of looking at this policy is to see the traditional U.S. role in terms of anti-colonialism. The continuity here is that the U.S. opposed the colonial exploitation of Asia by European powers in 1899, by Japanese power in 1940, and by Russian (read communist) power in 1950.

Here, of course, we come to an interesting paradox. Clearly the U.S. has had a long-term policy of anti-colonialism in Asia, but the situation becomes very complicated when the U.S. tries to balance that anti-colonialism with the relative priority it assigns to Europe and to Asia. As I have already suggested, that anti-colonial prejudice complicated, and ultimately contributed to, fatal flaws in American pre-war planning and early war fighting in the Pacific. The Americans did not want to support British or Dutch colonialism; on the other hand they could not allow Britain to collapse in Europe. The result was the strategic compromise that the U.S. would shift forces to the Atlantic to replace those forces Britain withdrew to protect its Asian colonies. I see that as the definitive military acceptance of the United States as a Great Power in the European theatre.[34] The problem was, of course, that the Japanese did not wait for this passing of the torch or changing of the guard to be completed; they attacked when they were ready. This led to their being confronted by the stumbling, sputtering, "allied" command called ABDA.

The next evidence of paradox came in the way in which the war was fought. The U.S. had secured acceptance of its military primacy in the coalition, and had in turn accepted the Europe First strategy. What the U.S. did not have were the forces in being to effectuate that strategy. The British did have the forces and, since they did, they called the tune in terms of Torch, which in my view set the strategy for the entire European war, and largely dictated the timing of the opening of the Second Front.[35] The place where the U.S. could fight a war largely on its own terms was in the Pacific and there it did, while never really changing its conviction that Europe was the centre ring.

America's schizophrenic, love-hate relationship with Europe and the influence it had on U.S. Asian policy was next evinced in Indo-China. The reason the U.S. allowed the French back into Indo-China and ultimately adopted their war effort there was that the U.S. wanted to keep European France from falling to the communists.[36] So the

---

[34] See Leutze, *Bargaining for Supremacy*, Chapters 14 and 15.
[35] See Mark Stoler, *The Politics of the Second Front* (Westport, Connecticut, 1977).
[36] See Herring, *America's Longest War*, p. 10.

U.S. swallowed its anti-colonialism regarding Asia in deference to its anti-communism in Europe. One could argue that Europe was always the ultimate falling domino. Maintaining the territorial integrity of Western Europe—first Britain, then France, then Berlin and West Germany, and ultimately NATO—has become the United States's third longest foreign policy commitment. Furthermore, that commitment is in almost continuous conflict with its more elderly, yet less important, cousin—America's commitment to Asia. The way in which the war in Korea and the war in Vietnam were fought can be understood only if seen against the backdrop of America's other commitments.[37] Europe was the ultimate falling domino, and one could argue that the United States finally withdrew from Vietnam because it was becoming too great a diversion of attention and resources from the major task— protecting Europe by confronting the Soviets strategically.

But that is another story. The point here is that, for good or ill, there has been a significant degree of continuity in American policy toward Asia. Good historians should not have been surprised that the United States would want to keep Korea or South Vietnam from being exploited by outside forces, although they might have been struck by the difference between how that desire was expressed in 1900 and 1950. Nor would historians have been surprised at the complexities which arose when the United States tried to sort out its responsibilities and priorities between Asia and Europe. The commitment to Asia was undertaken when that was the only foreign sphere, outside the Western Hemisphere, where it seemed conceivable that the U.S. could assert its influence. And interestingly enough Britain was the midwife and shield of this policy just as it had been midwife and shield for the Monroe Doctrine. By the time World War II came along it had become apparent that the Americans had matured enough to make their will manifest in Europe as well. American confusion arose in trying to balance the varied and sometimes conflicting goals of its Asiatic and European policies.

That is all I intend to say on the subject of continuity. Now let me conclude by speaking briefly about the issue of change. Clearly World War II is the watershed. Regarding Asia, during the 1921–41 period, Americans were more realistic and less involved; during the

---

[37] One of the earliest Intelligence Estimates of the developing situation in the summer of 1950 cited the attack by the North on the South as fitting into "Soviet global strategy" in several ways. First among them was: "It offers a test on grounds militarily most favorable to the Soviet Union of the resolution of the United States in its announced policy of 'total diplomacy.' Such a test would probably be considered important in connection with possible Chinese moves in support of Ho Chi Minh, Burmese Communists, or Malayan Communists, and possible Soviet moves in Germany or Iran." *Foreign Relations of the United States* (1950), Vol. III (Washington, D.C., 1976), p. 150.

1945–73 period, Americans were most involved and less realistic. Something other than the assumption of greater responsibilities occurred between 1941 and 1945. My conclusion is that the way in which Americans looked at that war and interpreted their role in it significantly influenced their conduct in the post-war world. It is my distinct impression that Americans generally, and specifically some American policy makers, misinterpreted the lessons of that war and overestimated the American military contribution to the victory. In terms of the victory in Europe I would rate America third behind Russia and Britain, in terms of military contribution to victory.[38] Most Americans I believe would say first, or at worst, second. Rankings are terribly difficult to arrive at—and to sustain. In the Pacific War, the United States was clear and away the primary contributor to the defeat of Japan. But how great a victory was it? Let me here say that I do not wish to detract from the brave men who fought on either side in this war, but I would simply make some observations. The turning point in the naval war came in June 1942. After the battle of Guadalcanal the Japanese were definitely on the defensive everywhere.[39] The United States never confronted the major portion of the Imperial Japanese Army.[40] The relatively small U.S. submarine force sank the great bulk of merchant and combatant shipping.[41] The point is that, while winning the war in the Pacific was a vast enterprise that cost 41,322 lives out of 170,596 casualties, it was not a war that was seriously in question after the first eight months. It was not a war that required the full or even the major forces of either combatant. It was not a war in terms of casualties or men engaged that ranks ahead of the British war in the Middle East, 1915–18, the Italian war against the Austrians, 1914–18, or the Japanese war against the other Allies in the 1937–45

---

[38] One, of course, can argue about measurements in this area, but in terms of casualties the Soviets suffered 7,500,000 military dead, 14,000,000 military wounded, 10-15,000,000 civilian dead; the United Kingdom, 397,762 military dead, 475,000 military wounded, 65,000 civilian dead; the United States, 292,100 military dead, 571,822 military wounded. Churchill goes to great pains to point out that until June 1944 the United Kingdom had more divisions in contact with the enemy than did the U.S. See Churchill, *History of the Second World War*, Vol. III.

[39] E.B. Potter, *Nimitz*, p. 208. See also John Miller, *Guadalcanal: The First Offensive* (Washington, D.C., 1971), p. ix and p. 350.

[40] Total strength of the Japanese Expeditionary Army in China was 1,050,000 men at the end of the war. Total strength in the Home Islands was 2,350,000. Total strength in Manchuria was 780,000. Total strength in Korea was 260,000. For comparison, the largest number of Japanese troops engaged by the U.S. in a single operation was in the Philippines where the garrison numbered something over 200,000. For figures, see Saburo Hayashi, *Kōgun: The Japanese Army in the Pacific War* (Quantico, Virginia, 1959).

[41] For a chart of submarine inflicted losses, see Theodore Roscoe, *United States Submarine Operations in World War II* (Annapolis, Maryland, 1958), pp. 523-24.

war in Asia. In terms of modern land wars it ranks far down the list.[42] In actuality it was a vast naval and air war ended in part by the ultimate weapon.

To return to the American role in the whole of World War II, let me now define what I mean by "military contribution." What I mean is what most people commonly think of—combat troops, combat air, combat shipping in contact with the enemy. It is here that the U.S. ranked in Europe behind its allies. America's greatest contribution to the success of the Allied cause was the vast productive effort that allowed it to supply its own huge army (the U.S. mobilized 14.9 million, the Russians only five million more) as well as providing much needed equipment to the British, French, Russians, and Chinese. The Americans overwhelmed their enemies with the products of their factories and ultimately with the firepower their technology made possible.[43]

In the flush of victory and the warm afterglow that suffused the American vision for many years, this mundane, undramatic logistical success tended to be pushed further into the background, overshadowed by the concept that the U.S. was the world's most technologically advanced military power.[44] The Americans overestimated the efficacy of sheer mass multiplied by mobility and their past and present ability to express it on the battlefield. The commonly held view was that America had won World War II, and if there were other problems in the world that proved intractable, they might—reluctantly—bring their military power to bear on them as well. (In this regard I am reminded of General George Patton and his numerous fans who, apparently in all seriousness, thought we might just push the Russians out of Eastern Europe.) And if the U.S. ran into a problem that its army and navy could not handle, there was always the bomb.

What I intend to suggest here is that the Americans were drawn into two wars in Asia in part because they thought World War II implied that they could make their will *fiat* simply by the use of enough military power. Unfortunately, a careful analysis of the 1941–45 conflict would have shown that the military power that had played the greatest

---

[42] The *Japanese Statistical Year-Book* says the Japanese lost 485,717 men in American battle zones and 700,000 against British, Dutch, Australian, Chinese, and Russian forces. See Hayashi, *Kōgun*, p. 219.

[43] The economic cost of the war to the U.S. was 350 billion dollars, that equals the cost to the United Kingdom and the U.S.S.R. For the U.S. production figures, see *The Statistical History of the United States* and Leighton and Coakley.

[44] For a contemporary view of American power and responsibility, see *Vital Speeches, Public Opinion Quarterly* and the *Annual Reports* of the Service Secretaries and later the Secretary of Defense.

role in World War II was not applicable to Korea or Vietnam. The U.S. did not need more supplies, there were not appropriate areas for large scale naval war, and the ultimate technology—nuclear weapons—was politically unacceptable. It is in the area of air power that my general thesis has its clearest applicability. There is a clear line, it seems to me, between the overestimation of the efficacy of bombing in World War II and the overestimation of its efficacy in Korea and Vietnam.[45] Now, if some air power advocates take umbrage at this suggestion, let me try out a more modest one. There was an obvious error in assuming that air power or any kind of mechanized power would have the same effect when applied against an underdeveloped country as it did against a highly developed nation *and* in assuming that air power would be allowed the same latitude in a limited war that it had been allowed in an unlimited one.

So, contributing to American failures in Asia was a failure to interpret World War II with sufficient rigour. Interestingly enough there were instances in the post-war period where sound interpretations of World War II did influence U.S. policy. My first example is when Marine Corps General David Shoup walked into a meeting to discuss the possibility of invading Cuba.

When talk about invading Cuba was becoming fashionable, General Shoup did a remarkable display with maps. First, he took an overlay of Cuba and placed it over the map of the United States. To everybody's surprise, Cuba was not a small island along the lines of, say, Long Island. It was about 800 miles long and seemed to stretch from New York to Chicago. Then he took another overlay, with a red dot, and placed it over the map of Cuba. "What's that?" someone asked him. "That, gentlemen, represents the size of the island of Tarawa," said Shoup, who had won a Medal of Honour there, "and it took us three days and eighteen thousand Marines to take it."[46]

The next example of a sound interpretation of the United States' World War II experience has already been noted, but I think it useful to underline the point; it was George C. Marshall in his civilian reincarnation as Special Ambassador and then as Secretary of State who

---

[45] I am very familiar with the controversy surrounding the *United States Strategic Bombing Survey* and what David MacIssacs has to say about David Halberstam's views on bombing. However, I still would argue that the impact of bombing came too late to affect the outcome of World War II in Europe, and that the Air Force goes too far in claiming that air power was the "decisive factor" in the Pacific War. For the prior argument, see David MacIssacs, *The U.S. Strategic Bombing Survey*, Vol. I, vii-xvii. For claims of decisiveness, see W.F. Craven and J.L. Cate, *The Army Air Forces in World War II* (Chicago, 1953), Vol. V, 739. The Military Analysis Division estimated that "defeat had been assured as early as the spring of 1944."

[46] Halberstam, *Best and the Brightest*, p. 85.

advised against further involvement in China. I cannot but believe that Marshall was harking back, at least in part, to his World War II experience as Chief of Staff. He had a realistic view of U.S. capabilities and priorities. Finally, it was another U.S. general who gave one of those all-too-rare exhibitions of prudence regarding Vietnam. At the time of Dien Bien Phu (1954) it was Dwight Eisenhower who vetoed the commitment of American military power—explicitly American air power. Eisenhower had a professional view nurtured during World War II about the efficacy and applicability of military force. His first doubts about the establishment of the base at Dien Bien Phu had been expressed in World War II terms. "Bastogne" he said "was a far different story." There beleaguered troops had to be resupplied by air. But Bastogne was an episode in a large campaign; it was far from being a contrived and semi-isolated manoeuvre.[47]

Paradoxically, it was another World War II veteran who set the United States on the course to stalemate in Korea. Could it be that MacArthur had an unrealistic view of the applicability and appropriateness of military force gained from a misreading of the history of World War II? In his mind's eye was MacArthur simply continuing in 1950 the glorious land campaign begun in 1944? (In all of his campaigns, from Australia to V-J Day, MacArthur lost only 90,437 men; the Battle of the Bulge alone cost 106,502.)[48] Perhaps, but in this case the enemy was not the beleaguered Japanese garrison in the Philippines, cut off from support by the interdiction of their sea lanes. To be sure, in Korea once again he faced a dispirited foe; but this time their supply lines could not be interdicted by the application of sea power, and the euphoria induced by the precipitate retreat northward should have been tempered by the realization that the North Koreans were actually retreating toward the ultimate redoubt, the Chinese Army. Moreover, MacArthur should have remembered that when it came time to prepare for the final push against the Japanese home islands in the summer of 1945, Europe seemed, for the moment at least, secure. And irony of ironies, America's nemesis, the Russians, were fully occupied battering the Japanese defences in mainland Asia.

In conclusion, I would like to return to the points made at the outset: first, American policy in Asia has been marked primarily by what it has failed to achieve; and second, its lack of success has derived in part from American lack of understanding of the area and its people. What I have tried to do in the body of this paper is to provide support for those two conclusions while raising the following relatively unexplored issues or approaches. (1) The witch-hunt over Pearl Harbor

[47] Dwight Eisenhower, *The White House Years* (New York, 1963), Vol. I, 339.
[48] William Manchester, *The American Caesar* (Boston, 1978) p. 4.

distracted attention from the defeats suffered elsewhere—most notably in the Philippines—and in a broader sense sent reporters and congressmen off looking for an unlikely conspiracy while they had clear and obvious evidence of an unprecedented military disaster. (2) It is very possible that better planning and more co-ordination could have stopped the Japanese advance before May 1942. (3) The strategy of Europe First was not followed nearly rigorously enough. (4) There was a consistent tendency to overestimate Japanese offensive potential and use that as a rationale for diverting supplies and manpower to the Pacific. (5) The "loss" of China cast a long shadow and in Korea and Vietnam Americans were reinforcing that failure. (6) The U.S. bears considerable responsibility for bringing China into the Korean War. (7) In Vietnam the U.S. overestimated what could be done with military power. (8) The American policy of trying to maintain the territorial and political integrity of Asia has a long history, only the provocateurs have changed. (9) However, once the U.S. became powerful enough, the Americans undertook a new commitment—to Europe—and once undertaken that commitment received priority. Hence the U.S. was left with a strong, but secondary, tie to Asia. Policy makers gave lip service to this reality, but in practice allowed themselves to be drawn into Asian adventures. (10) Finally, I suggested that an unrealistic concept of the U.S. contribution to victory in World War II helped provide the rationale for military involvement in Asia.

Obviously, one of the lessons is that correctly interpreting history is vitally important for policy makers. They must know where they are in time, but they must also have a realistic sense of what the past implies about various courses of action.

Finally, the U.S. must learn more about areas and peoples it considers to be vital to its security. It is obvious to me that the American attitude toward Asia has been affected by a narrowness that can realistically be called racism. A nation that aspires to greatness in today's pluralistic world cannot afford such prejudice toward other peoples. If the United States is to avoid further failures in Asia, or in other distant corners of the world, it must recognize that truly enlightened self-interest must be just that—enlightened and as free as possible of prejudice, preconception, xenophobia, and smug superiority.

RETREAT FROM POWER: BRITISH ATTITUDES TOWARDS JAPAN, 1923–1941

PETER LOWE

Britⓘsh ATTITUDES towards Japan from 1923 to 1941 offer valuable insights into the dilemmas facing a declining power attempting to rationalize commitments and to defend interests in a period of accelerating strain and tension. The most important questions to be asked are how the British Foreign Office, the Committee of Imperial Defence, and the Chiefs of Staff perceived the problems facing them and how accurately they gauged Japan's capacity to inflict grave damage and Britain's ability to postpone or outmanoeuvre the Japanese challenge. This paper is divided into two sections, in the first the overall defence problems in the Far East are assessed; the second considers some of the personalities involved among the ambassadors and the military attachés of the period and the nature of their appraisals of Japan.[1]

In August 1923 the Anglo-Japanese Alliance formally came to an end. From the British viewpoint this brought to a head issues concerning the defence of British interests which had been looming for a generation and which had been deferred through the existence of the Alliance. Anglo-Japanese relations had experienced increasing strain from approximately 1911 onwards as a result of the diverging relationship between the two powers, resulting from economic rivalry in China and difficulties involving the United States and the British dominions.[2] The decision to terminate the Alliance did not necessarily mean that Japan would become antagonistic and it was hoped that the cluster of treaties concluded at the Washington Conference in 1921–22 would reconcile the interests of the powers principally involved in the Pacific region. However, the possibility of Japanese hostility now had to be recognized: Britain's vast territorial interests in South Asia and South-east Asia, and the strategic interests of the dominions, particularly Australia and New Zealand, required the formulation of

---

[1] For a valuable reassessment of Anglo-Japanese perspectives before the outbreak of the Pacific war, see *Anglo-Japanese Alienation: Papers of the Anglo-Japanese Conference on the History of the Second World War*, ed. Ian Nish (Cambridge: Cambridge University Press, 1982).

[2] On these aspects see Peter Lowe, *Great Britain and Japan, 1911-15* (London: Macmillan, 1969) and Ian Nish, *Alliance in Decline: Anglo-Japanese Relations, 1908-23* (London: Athlone Press, 1972).

a policy that would afford some protection to those interests. The "Singapore strategy" constituted this policy or, to express it more accurately, constituted the facade of this policy. It was decided that Britain must pursue a new approach, concentrating on the construction of a large naval base at Singapore, which would meet the needs of a fleet capable of challenging the Japanese Fleet. The strategy put heavy emphasis on maritime factors: the Royal Navy would be responsible for defending the area and the roles to be played by the Army and the Royal Air Force were viewed as subordinate and minimal. It was understandable that the stress should be placed on the Navy at a time when air power was relatively undeveloped and when a Japanese military threat to British possessions appeared extremely remote. It was clear in the early 1920s, however, that for financial reasons it would be impossible for Britain to station a significant naval force permanently in Far Eastern waters. Furthermore it appeared that there was small likelihood of Britain facing conflict in Europe following the defeat of Germany and the chaotic situation in Russia consequent upon the civil war. The "Ten Year Rule" symbolized this attitude of the remoteness of war. Considerable doubts were voiced contemporaneously as to the viability of the Singapore strategy and whether the risks inherent in the despatch of a fleet from European waters would actually be taken. These doubts were reflected in the attitudes of General Smuts, Vice-Admiral Richmond, and the influential Liberal M.P., George Lambert.[3] It is fair to state that while the Singapore strategy was theoretically viable in the 1920s, it was not wise to devise policy on a "best situation" scenario. Reiteration of British willingness to send a fleet east was important in the context of imperial relations, for it met the demands from Australia and New Zealand for a policy that would assist them in their state of vulnerability. Suspicions of a justified character were developing in Australia, however, regarding the depth of the British commitment and those fears were not to be allayed by the passage of time.

The Manchurian Crisis of 1931 to 1933 demonstrated for the first time that Japan was pursuing a policy of more rapid expansion with scant regard for international conventions.[4] Britain had some sympathy for Japan on the grounds of Chinese provocation, and Brit-

---

[3] For the origins and nature of the Singapore strategy, see Paul Haggie, *Britannia at Bay* (Oxford: Oxford University Press, 1981); Ian Hamill, *The Strategic Illusion: the Singapore Strategy and the Defence of Australia and New Zealand, 1919-1942* (Singapore: Singapore University Press, 1981); and James Neidpath, *The Singapore Naval Base and the Defence of Britain's Eastern Empire, 1919-1941* (Oxford: Clarendon Press, 1981). For a lucid account of contemporary reservations, see Neidpath, pp. 73, 77, 88-91.

[4] For a comprehensive examination of the Manchurian crisis, see Christopher Thorne, *The Limits of Foreign Policy* (London: Hamish Hamilton, 1972).

ish policy makers had long held that if Japan had to expand anywhere, then Manchuria was the least dangerous region for such activity.[5] The existence of the League of Nations Covenant complicated matters and Sir John Simon, the Foreign Secretary, sought to incorporate this consideration as effectively as he could in his ceaseless endeavour to square the circle. In defence terms the most worrying feature was not what occurred in Manchuria but rather the subsidiary and related crisis that arose in Shanghai in January 1932. An incident, staged by the Japanese Military Attaché, was the pretext for decisive Japanese intervention in Shanghai, which gave rise to serious fighting. Much alarm was manifested in London, for Shanghai was the most important port in China and the principal centre of British investment. Officials in the Foreign Office drafted alarmist minutes, warning of the dire threat to Britain's position. In their judgement at the end of January and beginning of February 1932, Britain could soon be faced with a bellicose Japan, intent on expelling British interests from the Far East, which in turn could affect the British presence in India.[6] While such apprehension was exaggerated at that time, it was an accurate indicator of the way in which the situation would evolve over the ensuing decade. A reassessment of defence policy was called for and the immediate effect was to underline how tenuous British policy was. The Singapore base was only partially constructed, the armed forces were wholly inadequate (with the lowest defence estimates in the interwar period being introduced by Neville Chamberlain in 1932), and there was no possibility of Britain being able to risk confrontation with Japan. The Shanghai crisis was settled in May 1932 and the tension in Anglo-Japanese relations subsided. The European situation was deteriorating, however, and a new spirit was seen in Germany with Hitler's attainment of power in 1933.

Japan was now recognized as a potential adversary of major importance and one whose menace could materialize sooner rather than later. Britain had to prepare for the contingencies of conflict with Germany, Italy, and Japan, a combination that it was impossible to envisage handling successfully.[7] The Royal Navy was still regarded as the key to combating Japan and the decision was taken to proceed swiftly with the completion of the Singapore base. Neville Chamber-

---

[5] For the views of Sir Edward Grey before 1914, see Lowe, *Great Britain and Japan,* pp. 22-3.

[6] See *Documents on British Foreign Policy, 1919-1939,* hereafter cited as *DBFP,* Second Series, IX, 281-283, memorandum by Pratt, February 1, 1932, with minute by Vansittart, February 1, 1932.

[7] For a discussion of defence issues in the mid-1930s, see Ann Trotter, *Britain and East Asia 1933-1937* (Cambridge: Cambridge University Press, 1975), pp. 47-60, 88-114.

lain had argued in favour of developing air power in general rather than expanding the Navy. However, air strength was rudimentary in the Far East, despite persuasive arguments put forward by air personnel; the Chiefs of Staff regarded the Army and Air Force as having limited roles. Some attention was being given to the defence of Malaya, as illustrated in the experiment conducted by General Dobbie—ironically assisted by Colonel Percival—concerning the ability of an invading force to land on the Malayan coast.[8] The experiment proved that such landings were feasible, but no attention was paid to Dobbie's investigation in London. It is strange that Percival did not draw more conclusions from his experiences when heading the military command in Malaya in 1941-42.

The Sino-Japanese War began in July 1937. Britain now encountered the full repercussions of Japanese expansion. British nationals and property bore the brunt of foreign suffering in China: the Japanese army had no sympathy for occidentals and believed that Chinese resistance was fostered by British aid. While the British government and British public opinion certainly sympathized with China, Britain extended little direct assistance: paradoxically China derived more help from Germany and the Soviet Union in the period 1937 to 1939.[9] In Europe, the Spanish Civil War was raging and this involved additional complications and demands on British forces. Relations with Italy were bad as a result of the Abyssinian Crisis. Germany was becoming more menacing and the Czechoslovak Crisis of 1938 brought home the extent to which the situation had worsened. The Committee of Imperial Defence considered the implications of a new European appreciation by the Chiefs of Staff early in 1939. The Prime Minister, Chamberlain, drew attention to undertakings given to the dominions in the past and Lord Chatfield, former First Sea Lord and now Minister for the Co-ordination of Defence, emphasized that if the position justified it, a fleet should be sent to the Far East.[10] The trend of thinking in London was, however, towards greater stress on the Mediterranean as vital to British interests. Growing German activity in central and eastern Europe plus Italian ambitions and existing British commitments to defend Egypt and Iraq reinforced the view that it would be dangerous for Britain to neglect the Mediterranean. The Committee of Imperial Defence decided in May 1939 to endorse Vice-Admiral Cunningham's report that in the light of the greater complex-

---

[8] See S. Woodburn Kirby, *Singapore: the Chain of Disaster* (London: Cassell, 1971), pp. 31-2.

[9] See Peter Lowe, *Great Britain and the Origins of the Pacific War* (Oxford: Clarendon Press, 1977), p. 140.

[10] Lowe, *Great Britain and Origins of Pacific War*, p. 67.

ities now emerging in Europe, it was impossible to say categorically how rapidly a fleet could be sent to the Far East in the event of a grave crisis with Japan.[11] Efforts were made to conceal from Australia the implications of these developments but without success, and Australian apprehension increased.[12]

The first formidable test of British resolve occurred with the eruption of a serious confrontation in the northern Chinese treaty port of Tientsin in June to August 1939. The local Japanese military had long disliked the continuance of the treaty ports, since they symbolized the Western imperialism Japan was seeking to replace and the remaining obstacles to Japanese victory in China. The British authorities pursued a somewhat muddled policy towards Tientsin and had taken insufficient care to guard against a major clash developing. At the same time confrontation was inherent in the situation and pressure would have occurred sooner or later. The inability of the Consul-General in Tientsin to report clearly to London on what was happening compounded the difficulties. The Japanese imposed a rigorous blockade around the British concession in June 1939 and demanded significant concessions. There was a definite possibility of the two countries drifting into war. Anguished discussions took place in the Cabinet Foreign Policy Committee and in the Chiefs of Staff Committee. The latter warned of the perils associated with the despatch of a fleet east; it would not be possible to send more than two capital ships to assist the China squadron without leaving the Mediterranean inadequately defended.[13] The Cabinet endorsed the view that a diplomatic solution should be reached if possible. Ultimately the Tientsin Crisis was defused following talks in Tokyo conducted by Sir Robert Craigie and then by the dramatic effects of the Nazi-Soviet Pact and the beginning of the European war.

Hitler's astonishing victories in Europe in the spring of 1940 stimulated Japan into a new aggressive phase. The first major sign of this comprised the pressure on Britain in June to July 1940 to close the Burma Road and thus cut off supplies to China. Churchill was now Prime Minister and was initially unwilling to submit to Japanese intimidation. The Chiefs of Staff were so overwhelmed with European complications—the fall of France and the possibility of a German invasion of Britain—that they firmly recommended on July 1, 1940, a diplomatic arrangement with Japan. Indeed they went beyond this to

---

[11] Lowe, *Great Britain and Origins of Pacific War*, p. 68.

[12] Haggie, pp. 144-6, 153.

[13] Cabinet committee on foreign policy, June 19, 1939, F.P. (36) 52nd meeting, enclosed in F6110/1/10, F.O.371/23400, Public Record Office, Kew, London. Transcripts/translations of Crown-copyright records in the Public Record Office, London, appear by permission of the Controller of H.M. Stationery Office.

urge that Britain should do all possible to secure a peace settlement between Japan and China. The Cabinet decided to close the Burma Road for three months, during the wet season when it was more difficult to transport goods, on the understanding that during this period Japan would endeavour to terminate the war in China. While Japanese leaders wished to end the "China Incident," they had no intention of doing so on terms involving any significant concessions by Japan.[14] By October 1940, Britain's position was improving in the light of the outcome of the Battle of Britain and of the encouraging signs of President Roosevelt's willingness to adopt a more positive approach towards the European conflict. The Burma Road was accordingly reopened.[15] The Burma Road Crisis saw the appearance of a new British assessment of strategy towards Japan; this was the first thorough reappraisal of defence policy since 1937. It fully revealed the desperate position Britain faced in the Far East. The Japanese advance into French Indo-China and the threat to Thailand all increased the threat to Malaya. The bankruptcy of British strategy was encapsulated in the pathetic statement:

> In the absence of a Fleet our policy should be to rely primarily on air power. The air forces required to implement that policy, however, cannot be provided for some time to come. Until they can be made available we shall require substantial additional land forces in Malaya, which cannot in present circumstances be found from British or Indian resources.[16]

The most significant feature of the report was the statement that the whole of Malaya should be defended without concentrating narrowly on the defence of Singapore. The profound weakness in each of the armed services was recognized. In the air a strength of 336 aircraft was deemed necessary, that was about four times the existing air strength, which consisted largely of obsolete or obsolescent aircraft.[17] Churchill was critical of the report: he believed Japanese prowess had been exaggerated and that it would be wrong to divert resources from the "real wars" in Europe, the Middle East, and the Atlantic.[18]

In 1941 there was much activity comprising the exchange of views between Britain, the United States, the Netherlands government in

---

[14] For the development of Japanese policy towards China in 1940, see J.H. Boyle, *China and Japan at War, 1937-1945: the Politics of Collaboration* (Stanford: Stanford University Press, 1972).

[15] Lowe, *Great Britain and Origins of Pacific War*, pp. 172-4.

[16] "The situation in the Far East in the event of Japanese intervention against us," Report by Chiefs of Staff Committee, July 31, 1940, COS(40)592, also WP(40)302, Cab.66/10.

[17] *Ibid.*

[18] Lowe, *Great Britain and Origins of Pacific War*, p. 163.

exile, and the dominions on defence against Japan. The most tangible
outcome was the closer relationship being established between London
and Washington, except that no definite promise of American assistance was forthcoming until the beginning of December 1941. Roosevelt was preoccupied with the political complexities and did not wish
to advance too rapidly.[19] The most important single aspect for the
Far East resulted from the lengthy Allied ABC-1 discussions held in
Washington early in 1941. The talks were valuable for facilitating
mutual understanding and contact, and there was agreement on the
identification of Germany as the most dangerous antagonist.[20] The
chief area of disagreement involved the American attitude to Singapore, for the American Chiefs of Staff did not regard this as absolutely
fundamental to Allied strategy, as did the British. The Americans felt
that the British placed emphasis on Singapore for imperial instead of
strategic reasons and that while the loss of Singapore would be serious,
the blow need not be irreversible—"Its value as a symbol has become
so great that its capture by Japan would be a serious blow. But many
severe blows have been taken by these various nations and other severe
blows can be absorbed without leading to final disaster."[21] Neither the
British nor the Americans showed any depth of perception in weigh-
ing up the most appropriate strategy against Japan, and neither grasped
the full significance of the economic motives for holding Malaya. The
various conferences held at Singapore in October 1940 and then in
the first few months of 1941 between the British, Australians, and the
Dutch with the Americans present accomplished little that was tangible. Much needed co-operation in strategic planning was handicapped
by the absence of the necessary political understanding between those
involved. The Americans would give no guarantee of support to the
British until just before the start of the Pacific War, and the British
would give no promise of support to the Dutch until they received a
promise of support from the Americans. It is hardly surprising that
the catastrophe was so resounding in the first phase of the Pacific War
(December 7, 1941 to August 7, 1942).

I would like to turn now to the personalities and approaches of
the most important ambassadors and military attachés of the period;
focusing on three ambassadors—Sir Charles Eliot, Sir Francis Lindley,

---

[19] For discussion of Roosevelt's attitude, see J. Macgregor Burns, *Roosevelt: the
Soldier of Freedom, 1940-1945* (Weidenfeld and Nicolson, 1971) and R.A. Dallek, *Franklin
D. Roosevelt and American Foreign Policy, 1932-1945* (Oxford: Oxford University Press,
1979).

[20] For the full record of the talks, see "British-United States staff conversations,"
BUS(J)41, Cab.99/5.

[21] "Statement by the United States Staff Committee. The United States Military
Position in the Far East, February 19, 1941," BUS(J)(41)16, Cab.99/5.

and Sir Robert Craigie—and on two military attachés—Major-General
F.S.G. Piggott and Lieutenant-Colonel G.T. Wards.

Eliot was the Ambassador to Tokyo from 1920 to 1926. He was
the last ambassador to serve during the existence of the Anglo-Japanese
Alliance. His career had been unconventional, for he had resigned
from the Foreign Office in 1904 following a disagreement with Lord
Lansdowne. He had then pursued an academic career, which included
serving as Vice-Chancellor at the universities of Sheffield and Hong
Kong. He was one of the leading Western authorities on Buddhism.
Eliot returned to the diplomatic sphere in 1918, when he was appointed
High Commissioner and Consul-General in Siberia. In 1920 he went
to Tokyo and proved a capable representative at a time of flux in
Anglo-Japanese relations. Eliot conformed to the usual diplomatic bias
of sympathizing clearly with the country to which he was accredited.
He favoured the continuance of the Alliance and maintained that it
had benefited both partners. From the vantage point of Hong Kong
during the Great War, Eliot had appreciated how important Japanese
aid to Britain had been.[22] He castigated the anti-Japanese feelings
sometimes exhibited by British people, including some who should
have known better: "I have heard British military and naval officers
of high rank openly describe the Japanese by vulgarly abusive epithets
and such outbursts of course come to the ears of Japanese officials,
who take their revenge in petty tyranny and aggravating interference
when the opportunity offers."[23] The Foreign Office was more critical
of Japan, believing that it had exploited the Alliance for ulterior
reasons.[24] The leading politicians involved, Lloyd George and Curzon,
took a broader view and one similar to that of Eliot.[25] Eliot was well
aware of the evil of racial prejudice and of the miscalculations to which
it could give rise: he warned that the Japanese should not be made
to feel inferior.[26] The pressures to end the Alliance were too powerful
to combat and Eliot then reported that the Japanese had accepted the
results of the Washington Conference with good grace.[27] The humiliating circumstances of the end of the Alliance rankled with some
Japanese, however, including some service personnel.[28] Eliot worked
hard to preserve cordiality with Japan and, in the opinion of Piggott,

---

[22] *DBFP*, first series, XIV, 42-8, Eliot to Curzon, June 17, 1920.

[23] *DBFP*, Eliot to Curzon, p. 45.

[24] Lowe, *Great Britain and Japan*, p. 310.

[25] Lowe, *Great Britain and Japan*, p. 310.

[26] *DBFP*, first series, XIV, Eliot to Curzon, December 12, 1920.

[27] *DBFP*, 631-2, Eliot to Curzon, February 2, 1922.

[28] See M.D. Kennedy, *The Estrangement of Great Britain and Japan, 1917-35* (Manchester: Manchester University Press, 1969) p. 55 and F.S.G. Piggott, *Broken Thread*
(Aldershot: Gale and Polden, 1950), p. 196.

was not unsuccessful in so doing.[29] Eliot retired in 1926 having contributed much to smoothing over the inevitable difficulties of the transitional era in Anglo-Japanese relations. He then concentrated on his literary work and, perhaps fittingly, died in March 1931 on a Japanese steamer between Penang and Colombo while on his way home.[30]

Sir Francis Lindley served as Ambassador from 1931 to 1934. He was the son of a Scottish judge and a career diplomat; he had been in Tokyo before, from 1905 to 1908, as a junior member of the staff. Lindley was industrious and trenchant in his approach, if somewhat lacking in depth of perception. He was normally inclined to defend Japanese actions but was capable of rebuking them on occasion. An example of the latter is afforded by his response to the bombing of Chinchow in the early stages of the Manchurian Crisis: "I informed the Minister for Foreign Affairs that speaking without instructions I was impressed with the gravity of bombing of Chinchow. Japanese Government had given assurance that they would do nothing to aggravate the situation. This was most serious aggravation and could not fail to make the worst impression at Geneva and in America."[31] Lindley subsequently came to believe that it was impossible to prevent Japanese domination of Manchuria and that all that could be hoped for would be a form of compromise whereby the Japanese might acknowledge a concept of remote Chinese sovereignty. He reported in March 1932:

> It is worse than useless to try to persuade the Japanese that it is against their own interests to commit the country to vast enterprises in Manchuria. I do not know what Edward III of England and his Court would have said to anyone using similar arguments regarding the pursuit of his interests in France but I do know that the Japanese, practically without exception, regard these arguments merely as a proof that the speaker is personally hostile to them. For . . . it must be again emphasised that the whole nation looks upon success in the struggle for predominance in Manchuria as vital to the very existence of the country. Rather than give way in any particular of substance, Japan will, in our opinion, embark on war without hesitation.[32]

At around the same date Lindley forwarded the report of the Military Attaché, Colonel Simson, that the Japanese were displaying a greater interest in air power and that aircraft manufacture was being stepped up.[33]

---

[29] Piggott, p. 199. Note also, Kennedy, p. 66.

[30] Piggott, p. 203.

[31] *DBFP*, second series, VIII, 735-6, Lindley to Reading, October 9, 1931.

[32] *DBFP*, second series, X, 166, Lindley to Simon, March 21, 1932.

[33] *DBFP*, p. 215, Lindley to Simon, March 30, 1932.

In May 1932 Lindley commented on the aftermath of the assassination of the Prime Minister, Inukai Tsuyoshi. He fully appreciated the implications of this episode in which a number of young naval officers had been involved. Lindley reported Simson's opinion that if senior Japanese officers ordered the arrest of junior officers engaged in political activity, this would be obeyed. The deduction to be drawn was that some senior officers condoned the behaviour of the juniors.[34] Lindley was anxious that the consequences of the Lytton report on the Manchurian Crisis, completed in September 1932, should not involve Britain in taking the lead at Geneva. In this respect Lindley may justifiably be criticized for paying insufficient attention to the wider implications of the situation for Europe and the League. In February 1933, at the conclusion of the League's deliberations on the Lytton report and with Japan on the brink of leaving the organization, Lindley reflected on the likely trend of events and maintained that he had failed in one important objective of his mission:

> I am aware that these strong expressions of opinion may be thought as unbecoming as they are unusual in an official despatch. My excuse and I believe my justification, is that during my tenure of the post of Ambassador in Tokyo, with all its unique advantages for judging local events, I have entirely failed to bring home to His Majesty's Government the danger to the Empire of drifting into open antagonism with Japan over Manchuria. I have watched the position deteriorate steadily and always as foreseen by this Embassy . . . and I blame myself grievously for my failure to convince His Majesty's Government of the risks they were running by allowing matters to take their course according to the fixed and immutable principles of the League. I now find myself faced with the imminent danger, if not actual probability, of the supreme failure of not having prevented a disastrous and avoidable conflict with the country to which I am accredited.[35]

Anthony Eden and Sir Robert Vansittart held that Lindley had overstated the case and that Lindley had alleged that Britain had followed a policy more closely identified with the League than had been the position.[36] According to his American colleague, Joseph C. Grew, Lindley was not as sympathetic to the Japanese in private as he appeared to be in public.[37] However, he certainly left the Foreign Office with the impression of being strongly pro-Japanese. Lindley

---

[34] *DBFP*, p. 459, Lindley to Simon, May 26, 1932.

[35] *DBFP*, second series, XI, 373, Lindley to Simon, February 24, 1933.

[36] *DBFP*, p. 373, n6, minutes by Vansittart and Eden, March 27-28, 1933.

[37] Information from Grew's unpublished diary, as cited in Thorne, *Limits of Foreign Policy*, p. 99.

retired in 1934, apparently disillusioned with his government's response to the representations he had made.[38] He had been involved in a complex crisis in which his own ability to influence the course of events had been limited; unlike Sir Robert Craigie later in the 1930s, Lindley was usually not conducting discussions of central importance. He may be termed a reasonably competent ambassador but one who did not demonstrate great depth of perception.

The ambassador faced with the most daunting challenges and one whose contribution to postponing catastrophe has frequently been underestimated was Sir Robert Craigie. Craigie was the son of an admiral and possessed considerable interest in naval issues. Before going to Tokyo, Craigie had been head of the American Department at the Foreign Office and had functioned as the chief Foreign Office expert on matters concerning naval agreements and attendant negotiations. He served as Ambassador in Tokyo from August 1937 to the start of the Pacific War. Craigie was evidently not popular in the Foreign Office, and members of the Far Eastern Department drafted critical minutes on his assessment of developments and recommendations. They also believed that in the first half of his mission he was unduly influenced by his Military Attaché, General Piggott; this aspect will be discussed shortly. Craigie was a somewhat reserved man of aloof character; his wife was an American and sometimes sat in at his meetings with colleagues from other embassies. Craigie did not reveal a profound grasp of Japanese politics but he displayed an indomitable spirit of determination and tenacity in a situation that was almost wholly menacing. Craigie's formidable skills as a negotiator contributed to defusing confrontations that might easily have led to actual conflict. Craigie believed that the formulation of British policy in East Asia called for subtlety and appropriate speed of manoeuvre, qualities that were often sadly absent in a Foreign Office harassed by the demands of the European situation and with an inclination to underestimate Japan. The most challenging crises Craigie handled were those over Tientsin and the Burma Road. Craigie had been unhappy during the winter of 1938–39 at the trend in Tientsin. He could perceive the signs of Japanese impatience attaining dangerous proportions and believed that far more care was required if a collision was to be avoided. He supported the views of the Consul-General in Tientsin that four Chinese suspected of complicity in a political assassination should be handed over to the Japanese authorities and so recommended to London. Owing to confusion between the Foreign Office and the Consul-General, matters rapidly worsened and the Japanese blockade ensued. Craigie urged that he should be allowed to pursue informal

---

[38] Kennedy, p. 318.

discussions with the Foreign Minister on the chances of a settlement, including the lifting of the Japanese blockade of Tientsin. Neville Chamberlain knew Craigie personally and supported his suggestion that he be allowed to explore solutions. Craigie used Piggott to clarify Japanese reactions. The former believed that negotiations offered the best route but, at the same time, he recommended that retaliatory economic measures should be prepared in case the position became so grave that such action had to be taken.[39] Craigie and Arita Hachiro, the Foreign Minister, eventually agreed, on July 22, 1939, on the terms of a statement in which Britain gave recognition to the "special requirements" of Japanese forces in China in the course of "safe-guarding their own security and maintaining public order."[40] The statement has been criticized by some for going too far by way of recognizing Japanese aggression, but it was couched in general terms and did not restrict Britain's policy significantly. This statement diminished tension but did not constitute a solution to the specific problems involved in Tientsin. Craigie had, however, made a contribution of real importance to the diminution of strain at the most difficult point.

In 1939-40 Craigie had hoped that the breathing space afforded by the Nazi-Soviet Pact would allow him to effect genuine improvement in Anglo-Japanese relations by resolving problems in Tientsin definitively. He worked with patience and persistence and was rewarded ultimately with an agreement concluded in June 1940.[41] Sadly, this achievement was overshadowed by events in Europe, and Craigie's success in helping to terminate one source of aggravation was at once replaced with another. The Ambassador's role in the Burma Road controversy was very similar to his role over Tientsin. The position was now far more dangerous than in 1939, and the information obtained from the service attachés pointed to the Japanese Army's willingness to act unless Britain closed the Burma Road. He urged a diplomatic solution upon the War Cabinet at the beginning of July 1940:

> I feel that I am entitled to enquire whether in fact His Majesty's Government are prepared to risk drifting into a state of war with Japan on this issue? . . . This is of course for His Majesty's Government to decide but I should be failing in my duty if I did not state

---

[39] Lowe, *Great Britain and Origins of Pacific War*, p. 86. For a longer biographical assessment see Peter Lowe, "The Dilemmas of an Ambassador: Sir Robert Craigie at the Tokyo Embassy, 1937-41," in *Proceedings of the British Association for Japanese Studies*, Vol. II, Part 1, *History and International Relations* ed. Gordon Daniels and Peter Lowe (Centre of Japanese Studies, Sheffield University, 1977), pp. 34-56.

[40] *DBFP*, Third Series, IX, 313-14, Craigie to Halifax, July 23, 1939.

[41] Lowe, *Great Britain and Origins of Pacific War*, pp. 127-34.

in emphatic terms that the risk is considerable; that we shall be playing straight into the German hands, and that in the final analysis we shall be serving less our own vital interests than the interests of Chiang-Kai-shek [sic] and his Government.[42]

After initial doubts in the War Cabinet resulting from Churchill's reservations, plus uncertainties on Halifax's (the Foreign Secretary) part, Craigie was again instructed to negotiate with the Japanese authorities and secure the best agreement he could.[43] Craigie and Arita agreed that the Burma Road would be closed for three months. The Ambassador had again handled the delicate exchanges with finesse and dexterity.

In 1941 Craigie's position was less central, for with the growing involvement of the United States in the Pacific crisis, attention moved to Washington. Craigie was not closely consulted on developments in 1941, and the same was true of his American colleague, Ambassador Grew. There was much similarity in their reactions. Craigie consistently believed that a policy of firmness had to be tempered with realism. He was critical of the decision to enforce drastic economic sanctions against Japan on the grounds that this was bound to precipitate confrontation, for which British and American forces were not prepared. Craigie warned that a surprise Japanese attack was always possible and should be guarded against. He may legitimately be criticized for not appreciating the deeper implications of world events, in that American involvement in a world war (both in the Pacific and Europe) would be a gain of incalculable proportions. However, as regards Japan and its ability to inflict grave injury, Craigie was correct. In drafting his final report on his mission in Tokyo, he showed much courage in adhering to his opinions and criticized British and American policies for inconsistency in dealing with Japan in 1941. Churchill was incensed but Craigie stood by his assessment, which must command respect from the historian.[44] Sir Robert Craigie was a most conscientious, hard-working ambassador who ably represented his country during the most challenging phase of Anglo-Japanese relations in the twentieth century.

Of the military attachés of the period, only two stand out, in contrasting respects. Major-General F.S.G. Piggott twice held the post of Military Attaché, between 1921 and 1926 and from 1936 to 1939. Piggott's father was a barrister and acted as a legal adviser to the Japanese government; Piggott had been taken to Japan by his parents

---

[42] Tokyo to Foreign Office, July 4, 1940, F3544/43/10, F.O.371/24666.

[43] Foreign Office to Tokyo, July 11, 1940, F3568/43/10, F.O.371/24667.

[44] See Peter Lowe, "Great Britain and the Opening of the War in Asia," in *Anglo-Japanese Alienation*, ed. Nish, p. 119.

at the age of four.[45] His experiences in Japan in his formative years instilled a lifelong love of Japan and its people. He was most unusual for a military attaché in having such an extensive knowledge of the society to which he was accredited and, more significant, so many contacts of importance within it.[46] Piggott first became Military Attaché at the most sensitive time, when the Anglo-Japanese Alliance drew to a close. Piggott enjoyed close relations with the Japanese general staff and knew many of the senior officers personally.[47] He complemented the work of Ambassador Eliot in helping to smooth over the inevitable difficulties resulting from the end of the Alliance. Japanese resentment was not disguised, however. Piggott relates how a Japanese general known as an Anglophile summed up the situation; "You had an Alliance with us on Sunday; you broke it on Monday and started a Base [Singapore] on Tuesday. Surely the inference is obvious that you no longer trust us."[48] Piggott believed that the Japanese Army was not interested in foreign adventures in the middle of the 1920s, and that the Army would support the conciliatory approach of the Foreign Minister, Baron Shidehara Kijūrō.[49] Upon departing from Tokyo, Piggott saw the Prince Regent, shortly to become Emperor Hirohito; the Prince regretted that when he had visited London in 1921 his advisers would not let him ride on the underground.

In 1936, when he commenced his second tour as Military Attaché, Piggott again met Hirohito and, against a darkening background, the Emperor emphasized his hope for closer Anglo-Japanese relations.[50] Piggott had been sent back to Tokyo because it was believed that his unique range of contacts could be used to advantage in defusing confrontations that might otherwise become difficult to cope with. He was obviously then of higher rank than was normal for such a post, which accordingly increased his influence within the Embassy and over his fellow service attachés. The Foreign Office believed that Piggott had excessive influence over Craigie. The Far Eastern Department deemed sections of reports to be of an appeasing nature, what they termed "Piggotries," meaning that they had effectively been written by Piggott and should accordingly be viewed critically. One official wrote: "Tokyo Embassy have intimated to us privately that they know we can distinguish 'Piggotries' from serious reports and they evidently rely on us to prevent the former from receiving too wide publicity or reaching the eyes of those who have neither the experience nor the

---

[45] Piggott, pp. 1-3.
[46] Piggott, p. 171.
[47] Piggott.
[48] Piggott, p. 196.
[49] Piggott, p. 206.
[50] Piggott, p. 271.

time to sift the grain from the chaff . . . ."[51] Piggott arranged for Craigie to meet a number of top generals, including Prince Kanin, and
Generals Sugiyama, Terauchi, Hata, Umezu, and Homma.[52] Piggott
and Craigie sought to convey their sincerity in working to avert war.
Piggott was naive in the political sphere and sometimes failed to appreciate the implications of his recommendations to Craigie. It is unlikely
that Craigie simply endorsed the opinions of Piggott. More convincing
is the explanation that Craigie used Piggott's range of contacts for
political reasons in order to defuse some of the problems with which
he was dealing. The War Office and the Foreign Office concluded
that Piggott had outlived his usefulness and he was withdrawn in the
autumn of 1939. Piggott's final assessment of the Japanese Army was
that it was stronger than ever before in its history.[53]

Major G.T. Wards (afterwards Colonel) was Assistant Military
Attaché from 1938 to 1940 and afterwards Military Attaché. Wards
possessed excellent knowledge of the Japanese language resulting from
his having been attached to a Japanese regiment for a substantial period
after the First World War. According to Piggott, Wards shared "one
hundred per cent in the life of a Japanese regiment, both on and off
duty" and there was only one other officer who had equalled this
feat.[54] Wards was one of the few to grasp accurately the Japanese
potential for inflicting serious defeat on opposing forces. From what
he had seen of the Army, Wards had no doubt that it would prove a
most formidable foe. Unlike many diplomats and strategists, Wards
did not draw erroneous conclusions from the Army's inability to compel
China to accept Japanese terms in the fighting in the undeclared war
since 1937. Wards regarded Japanese soldiers as generally well trained,
resourceful, tenacious, and capable of enduring suffering in a spirit
of stoicism. He believed that the British Army seriously underestimated Japan and that senior generals too often showed complacency
when discussing the possibility of a Japanese attack. When he visited
Malaya in April 1941, Wards addressed the officers of the Singapore
garrison with the General Officer Commanding, General Lionel Bond,
in the chair. Wards pointed to the thorough training and excellent
morale of Japanese soldiers and castigated the views prevailing in
Malaya that the Japanese found it difficult to operate at night, that
they were poor pilots and drivers, and that in all they could pose no
grave threat to the British forces. He warned prophetically that it was
most foolish to underestimate the Japanese. At the end of his talk

---

[51] Minute by Nigel Ronald, July 19, 1939, F7163/6457/10, F.O.371/23527.
[52] Piggott, pp. 298-9.
[53] Piggott, p. 334.
[54] Piggott, p. 166.

General Bond expressed his disagreement, describing Wards's remarks as "far from the truth" and "in no way a correct appreciation of the situation."[55] Wards remonstrated privately with Bond afterwards and was told that "we must not discourage the chaps and we must keep their spirits up."[56] Wards must have reflected appropriately when he observed the events in Malaya between December 1941 and February 1942.

In retrospect, British policy towards Japan before the Pacific War was a combination of vacillation and error in strategic appraisal, coupled with some diplomatic skill in averting conflict for as long as it did. The former was the consequence of financial exigency, ignorance, and racial prejudice; the latter the product of the more experienced members of the Foreign Office and particularly of Sir Robert Craigie's work. Lack of resources and muscle may be replaced by political tactics and negotiations provided the requisite shrewdness and subtlety is present and deployed to maximum advantage. The use of political skills is itself dependent on precision in assessment of a potential enemy. Britain failed by this criterion but fortunately for it, when the Japanese blow was struck, the United States was wholly committed to resisting and defeating Japan.

---

[55] Kirby, pp. 74-5.
[56] Kirby, p. 75.

THE PACIFIC IN THE PERCEPTIONS AND POLICIES OF THE GERMAN NAVY, 1919-1945

JOHN W.M. CHAPMAN

$\mathbf{F}$ROM THE perspective of contemporary conditions, it requires an unusual degree of mental agility to imagine a time when European imperialism had reached its zenith and the Pacific region represented the farthest periphery of its impact. For the English-speaking peoples, the effort is perhaps not quite so difficult because individual and collective recollections, in Britain at least, have not quite yet been extinguished by the march of time and generations. For North Americans and Australasians, on the other hand, the Pacific has for some time come to represent a much more central facet of their political and economic consciousness than perhaps could ever be the case for any Europeans. The trend of the past decade and more for people in Britain to retreat *into* Europe has perhaps helped to emphasize with even greater acuteness the retreat *of* Europe from the global political involvement in the first half of the century. Such a narrowing of horizons in the German case, so far as the Pacific was concerned, occurred at a much earlier date, with the elimination of the quite extensive Imperial German presence in the region shortly after the outbreak of war in 1914. At first sight, it would appear that subsequent German activity, and therefore influence, in the Pacific region could be dismissed as non-existent or, at best, negligible. If visible and direct activity correlates with influence, then it will be difficult to explain British influence over U.S. policies in the Pacific after the fall of Singapore in 1942, when the British presence in the region virtually disappeared. No case can be made for direct power of major significance being exerted by Germany in the Pacific region after 1914, though the power that Germany exerted in Europe could and did have an impact on developments in the Pacific from the mid-1930s, especially in the period from 1940 to 1942.

Canadian awareness of the German threat was considerable because the bulk of the Canadian armed forces abroad were located in the European theatre, only a small number arrived at Pacific desti-

In the preparation of this paper, the author is pleased to acknowledge the help provided by the British Academy, London; the Japan Foundation Endowment, Sheffield; the Arts Research Support Fund, University of Sussex; and the Social Science Research Council, London.

nations.[1] The Japanese threat to Canada never loomed very large, although the seizure of some of the Aleutian Islands and the shelling of the Oregon and west Vancouver Island coasts by Japanese submarines served as rare reminders of it.[2] It is really only since the late 1950s that people on the North American continent have been realistically exposed to extra-continental dangers, though the alarms and despondencies of foreign conspiracies have undoubtedly exercised a clear influence on the behaviour of U.S. policymakers and public opinion on many earlier occasions. If alleged German conspiracies in 1917 and 1940 could influence the North American continent without any significant physical presence in the hemisphere of German forces, then the case for keeping an open mind about the relevance of German influence in the Pacific after 1914 is necessarily demonstrable. The important thing about influence is that it does not have to be openly demonstrated, indeed, it is much to be preferred that it is not openly demonstrated, otherwise it loses its effectiveness as a policy instrument. If the historian does not look out for it and its effects, he assuredly will not discover it, though it may be argued that there is a danger that in looking for it, it will assuredly be found, even when it does not exist. This suggestibility with regard to conspiracy is by no means the exclusive domain of historians. Its victims abound with every day that the Cold War persists, and it is not easy, often, to detect the difference between the cynical and the gullible, even at the highest levels of state power, among the societies sucked into its orbit.

In examining German influence in the Pacific between 1919 and 1945, it makes sense to proceed from an analysis of the role of the German Navy, because what direct activity there was on the part of the German state was most expediently projected through the resources available to the Navy. It also monopolized the coercive instruments

[1] On September 13, 1942, the German Naval Attaché in Japan was to provide "for the information of the Führer" details of British Empire troops in Japanese hands. On the following day, Berlin was informed that the number of Canadians was 1,732. The signal was intercepted and deciphered as Top Secret Ultra PPA 48 of September 14, 1942 and may be seen in the National Archives, Washington, D.C., Record Group 457, Records of the National Security Agency, SRGL No. 0551, declassified in 1981. The author is grateful to Mr. Stephen Howard (Warwick) and Mr. John E. Taylor (Washington, D.C.) for their assistance.

[2] At a discussion between the Chief of Staff of the German Naval War Staff, Admiral Schniewind, and the head of the Japanese Naval Mission in Berlin, Admiral Nomura Naokuni on June 22, 1942, the latter denied any intention on Japan's part "to pursue an offensive from the Aleutians against Alaska and in the direction of Canada." *OKM/SKL/1.Skl.Ib 15785/42 g. Kdos* of June 29, 1942, a copy of which was shown to Hitler on July 2 by Vice-Admiral Krancke, the Navy's permanent representative at Führer H.Q. *Oberkommando der Marine: 1.Skl.: Kriegstagebuch Teil C, Heft XV: "Zusammenarbeit mit Japan," Bd.2, (1942-1944)*. The author appreciates the assistance provided with German Navy sources by Mr. Bob Coppick (Ministry of Defence, London) and Mr. Harry Rilley (National Archives, Washington, D.C.).

of the German state in the region in times of crisis and especially of conflict. Especially at such times, other interest-groups and governmental agencies were obliged to seek the assistance of the Navy, and this tended to have the consequence that the channelling of their influence over the societies of the Pacific came to be substantially dependent on it. The abundance of historical evidence from the German Navy's communications was a not inconsiderable factor in the Anglo-American defeat of Germany and Japan, and the survival both of Anglo-American monitored evidence and of the original German sources provide the historian with a multiplicity of levels at which to assess international influence.

While it was at times of crisis and conflict that the need to monitor German influence in the Pacific became most acute, it is reasonable to argue that it is rare for influence of any substantial kind to be built up overnight. It will be important, therefore, in the first section of the paper, to establish a framework for understanding the relative significance of the German Navy in the setting of governmental policy-making in Germany throughout the period under review, as well as to make some comparisons both with the pre-1919 period and with the equivalent position in Japan especially. In the second section, the broader context of the German Navy's central framework of operational thinking and strategic planning has to be established in order to relate it to its Pacific dimensions. In the final section, the structure of interaction between the Navy's central organs in Europe and its representatives in the Pacific periphery has to be related to the parallel hierarchies and personnel of the Japanese Navy, government, and society. From a scrutiny of these levels and interactions, it may then be possible to demonstrate sufficiently the extent to which German navalist thinking and behaviour may have exerted a significant influence over the Pacific environment through the prism of the Japanese ruling elites.

THE NAVY AND GERMAN POLICYMAKING

BEFORE 1918, the Imperial German Navy was an organization with very limited traditions dating back only as far as 1848 and the foundation of the Prussian Navy. But its roots could also, to a considerable extent, be identified with the seafaring and commercial experience of the Hansa towns in the Middle Ages. It operated under the shadow of the German Army, which continued to provide many of its senior officers until 1889. Although the Army's general staff system was renowned and much imitated abroad, its infrastructure rested on the very diverse contingents drawn from the many princely states, which were not easily welded into an unified national force in time of emergency. This was paralleled in the civilian administrative structure in matters of foreign and economic policy, even after 1918. After 1889, the Imperial Navy emerged as the one truly centralized component in the German armed forces up to 1935, when the Air Force was formally established. Its comparative lack of complications made it all the more attractive to the individual policymaker, from a more superficial point of view at least.

In practice, under the Wilhelmine Constitution, however, there was the complication of dual control. Under it, there was a direct subordination of the High Command, with its responsibilities for operational matters, to the Emperor, while the Navy Ministry, responsible for administrative and technical matters, was indirectly accountable, via the Reich Chancellor and Reichstag, to the Emperor. This structure had a direct counterpart in Japan up to 1945, where the Meiji Constitution was modelled on the Wilhelmine, and the system of direct access (*iaku joso*) and independence of the Supreme Command from Cabinet and Diet was largely preserved long after it disappeared in Germany. It applied equally to the Japanese Navy, which was strongly influenced by British precedents, as to the Army, which modelled itself heavily, but not exclusively, on German methods and tactical thinking. Whereas in Japan the military acted in the name of the Emperor, in Imperial Germany the Emperor sought to play an active policymaking role; this became particularly marked after 1899 when significant resources began to be put into an expansion of the fleet. Direct access applied not only to the central organs in Berlin, but also to the naval stations at Kiel and Wilhelmshaven, to the fleet, and even to the officer commanding the Cruiser Squadron stationed in the Pacific.

After 1919, some curbs were placed on the independence of the Japanese Navy as a result of the insistence on a non-active admiral as Navy Minister to prevent the Minister from claiming he had to obey superior orders from the Chief of Naval Staff. The other main curbs lay on the size of the naval budget, which had been greatly inflated prior to 1921 as a consequence of the Japanese-American naval arms race. By contrast, the Weimar Navy suffered a drastic reduction following the scuttling of the fleet at Scapa Flow, and yet its share of the military budget was much lower than that of the Army. The Japanese Army, on the other hand, suffered more heavily than the Navy from post-war cuts.[3] Paradoxically, a fleet headquarters was estab-

---

[3] For information on the German defence budget, see *Auswärtiges Amt (Bonn): Abteilung II F-M: "Reichswehr — Etat," (1920-1935)*, and on cuts in the Japanese military budget in the 1920s, see *Auswärtiges Amt: Abteilung IV Ostasien: Akte Po. 13 Japan: "Militärische Angelegenheiten Japans," Bd.1, (1920-1926)*. The help of the late Mr. Ken Hiscock (Foreign & Commonwealth Office, London) and of Frau Dr. Maria Keipert (*Auswärtiges Amt*, Bonn) has been of great value.

lished at Wilhelmshaven as early as 1922, whereas a Combined Fleet headquarters did not emerge in Japan until about a decade later. In Japan, separate war and navy ministries persisted, while in Germany a major innovation was introduced in the form of an unified Ministry of Defence—a precedent subsequently followed by most major powers at much later dates. The military personnel of the Ministry came primarily from the Army, and the Army's influence over the defence decision-making system was strengthened by the election of an Army field marshal as President and C-in-C of the Armed Forces from 1925 to 1934.

Civilian control in Germany and Japan before 1918 was generally weak; but from 1918 onward, control by political parties, whether or not operating through a parliamentary assembly, increased, not least because the parties and the civilian bureaucrats in both countries had interests in common *vis-à-vis* the military. From 1931, and more particularly in the wake of the February Incident of 1936 (*ni-ni-roku jihen*) in Japan, the power of the Ministry of Finance was broken by assassination. In Germany, by contrast, Hitler and the Nazi Party, in conjunction with the police and secret police, eliminated all other parties, then extended their control over the civilian ministries and ultimately the armed forces in the course of the 1930s. The leadership characteristics of Japanese prime ministers, even of General Tōjō Hideki from 1941 to 1944, were very different from Hitler's, and in these differences of style, approach, and method lay deep-seated Japanese suspicions of Hitler's motives and intentions. Japanese prime ministers, who to this day have been drawn preponderantly from the ranks of the civil and military bureaucracy, tried to preserve some measure of civilian autonomy by exploiting Army-Naval rivalries; but this became decreasingly effective after 1936, when military harmony was achieved at civilian expense, and assassinations of military and naval personnel were virtually eliminated. Between 1926 and 1933, there was a swing back from party-political dominance in Germany as a result of the difficulties in managing coalition government, which placed greater responsibility and control in the hands of the civilian and military bureaucracies. General Gröner was drafted in as Defence Minister in 1928 in response to opposition demands for greater control of the activities of the Army in the Soviet Union, over the Navy budget, and the links between the Navy's intelligence services and right-wing extremist organizations.

Inter-service rivalry was not a serious problem in Weimar, Germany, unlike in Japan, because the Navy was not seen, as it was in Japan, as the country's principal guardian of national security. Prior to 1914, however, the Army had grumbled at the massive spending on the "luxury fleet" and the privileged position it obtained from the Emperor's personal interest and patronage. Hitler, even more than the Emperor, distrusted and resented the dominant position that the Army had built up in the troubled years from 1928 to 1933, even though it was thanks to the Army-supported *coup d'état* in Prussia in 1932 that he wrested control of Germany's most important *Land* away from the Social Democrats, and power was handed over to the Nazis. Before 1918, the Navy had looked to the Emperor for support, and after 1933, the Navy had high hopes of Hitler's support for a massive expansion of the fleet and increased influence with German heavy industry. In practice, however, the German economy was inhibited in the 1930s by severe balance-of-payments problems and low reserves of hard currency, and the political position of Göring as Prime Minister of Prussia, Minister of Aviation, and Head of the Four-Year Plan meant that the establishment of a separate Air Force was inevitable.[4] This consequently reduced the funds available to the Navy and contributed significantly to the inter-service frictions in Germany, which lasted until Göring fell from grace and the Navy C-in-C, Grand-Admiral Karl Dönitz, ironically displaced Göring as Hitler's successor in May 1945.

The independent position accorded to the Navy High Command in William II's day made it possible for the Emperor to make use of the Navy for foreign policy purposes, with little or no consultation with the Chancellor or Foreign Minister. William II made use of Admiral Paul von Hintze as his personal liaison with the Tsar before 1914, intervened to have him appointed German Minister in China, where he was given a very free hand, and arranged for his promotion to State-Secretary in the Foreign Ministry in the closing months of the war, much to the chagrin of the professional diplomats. Navy State-Secretary von Tirpitz denounced the Foreign Ministry as the "most indolent government agency in the Empire," and German naval attachés were encouraged to bypass the heads of diplomatic missions to make reports to him and other Navy chiefs as a natural extension of the independence of the Supreme Command. It was partly on their advice that the decision to go ahead with unrestricted submarine warfare was taken, with such disastrous effects on the already bad relations with the United States. On the other hand, the Foreign Minis-

---

[4] The establishment of a Reich Commissariat for Aviation was one of the first acts of the Hitler regime. The relevant ordinance was dated February 2, 1933 but backdated with effect to January 30, the date of Hitler's accession to power. The Commissariat was to be directly subordinate to the Chancellery and was to be given precedence over every other ministry, described as "the highest agency in the Reich" (*die oberste Reichsbehörde*). At first, no attention was paid to the upstart ministry as it complained in April 1933 that its officials were not being invited to inter-ministerial meetings. *Auswärtiges Amt: Abteilung II F — Luft: "Reichsverkehrsministerium (jetzt RLM),"* *Bd.1, (1931-1935)*.

try did not always keep von Tirpitz informed of its own foreign policy initiatives, even in areas like the Pacific where Navy interests were very substantial. It was not until 1923, for example, that von Tirpitz belatedly learned that the Foreign Ministry had made serious efforts in 1909-10 to persuade Japan not to renew the Anglo-Japanese Alliance. Other instances of parallel foreign policies being pursued by the military and the Foreign Ministry arose in the course of World War I, such as in the attempts of 1915-16 to make direct overtures to Japan to change sides and to help arrange a secret peace between Germany and Tsarist Russia.[5]

Feeling in the armed forces about the Foreign Ministry's inglorious handling of the peace negotiations and its acceptance of left-wing politicians as diplomatic representatives abroad scarcely increased friendly sentiments. Nevertheless, a number of former Navy officers were recruited into the Foreign Ministry after the war, the most notable being State-Secretary von Weizsäcker. On the other hand, rejected Navy officers such as Reinhard Heydrich lost little love for former comrades. An important early issue of contention was the refusal of the Foreign and Finance Ministries to agree to the funding of permanent naval attachés abroad, and there appears to have been a rather limited interaction with the Foreign Ministry during the tenure of the post of Chief of the Naval Command by Admiral Paul Behncke (1920 to 1924). His successor, Admiral Kurt Zenker, worked positively in support of the foreign policy of the Chancellor, Gustav Stresemann, and had frequent meetings with significant figures in the Foreign Ministry, such as Ambassador von Maltzahn (Washington) and Ambassador Solf (Tokyo), on the attaché issue and on Foreign Ministry assistance to German cruisers on training missions on all the oceans of the world. Zenker and Raeder, who succeeded in 1928, also made common cause with the Army to prevent or limit cutbacks in the military budget, though in some matters the Navy was in a less strong position to defend itself from such pressures than the Army. One such case was the persistent complaints by the Foreign Ministry about the activities overseas of the Navy's World Intelligence Service, which was closed down because it was too expensive and seemed to be duplicating some of the Foreign Ministry's functions. But in general, the Navy was able to ride on the coat-tails of the Army and the Defence Ministry in its efforts to interest and involve the Foreign Ministry after 1927 in its operational plans and fleet manoeuvres. After 1934, Hitler

---

[5] Unsigned minute of a discussion with Tirpitz on November 8, 1923 and Gartzke memorandum *RWM/ML/zu A II 9000 G.Stbs.* of August 26, 1921 in *Marine Archiv: Marinekommandoamt/Flottenabteilung: Akte AIIc.1: "Marinepolitische Angelegenheiten," Heft 1, (1923-1929).*

was not content to remain a mere figurehead on his election as President. The assassination of von Schleicher and von Bredow was a foretaste of his determination to limit the political influence of the Army. He was content to keep on the traditional leaders of the civil and military establishment (von Neurath, Schacht, von Blomberg) whom he inherited, but his impatience with their over-cautious attitudes to external policy came to a climax in the purge of 1938. Raeder was excluded from the purge because the general lines of Navy external policy preferences, dating from the 1920s, coincided remarkably closely with those of Hitler and the Nazi Party.

As crisis turned to war, Hitler appointed military leaders amenable to the implementation of his own strategic ideas. Raeder was one of the few people who felt able to put forward different views (such as over the decision to attack the Soviet Union), and it was as a result of growing differences of opinion about naval policy that Raeder chose in the end to resign early in 1943. In 1941, Raeder had insisted on rejecting Hitler's decision not to supply the Italian fleet with adequate fuel from German stocks; he resigned on the issue of the decommissioning of remaining heavy naval units in favour of an expansion of the U-boat campaigns. Dönitz as head of the U-boat arm was a natural choice as successor in these circumstances and briefly succeeded Hitler as head of state in the closing weeks of the war in Europe. No less than Stalin, or Roosevelt, or Churchill, Hitler imposed the tightest of civilian control over the military, though the price involved a magnification (as in the U.S.S.R.) of the power of the internal security organs, as well as Party appointees.

CENTRAL STRATEGIC PLANNING IN THE NAVY HIGH COMMAND

IT IS possible to identify three main strategic concepts employed by German naval planners in the century up to 1945: coastal defence, battle-fleet operations, and counter-blockade. These are not, of course, mutually exclusive concepts: they have to be located in the international, political, and economic contexts of those periods in which each formed a salient element in strategic thinking. In particular, there is a fundamental dependence on available military capabilities, as well as on the resources independently available to target states. In times when military expansion occurs, as in the Tirpitz era (1898 to 1916), it is possible to identify a tendency to over-emphasize German strength, self-confidence, and potential, and to play down, despise, or misconstrue the capabilities, but above all, the intentions, of target states. After the event, even Tirpitz recognized this when he observed: "The German only sins in exuberance of national feeling, because, an incorrigible political illusionist, he wavers between the two extremes, the fear of power and the intoxication of power."[6] A recent analysis of German Navy war planning against Britain in the decade up to 1914 has suggested that it was based on the erroneous assumption that the Royal Navy would engage in a close blockade of German North Sea ports and that the alternative, which was actually pursued, of a distant blockade was discounted. Expectations that British forces would be strung out all over the world omitted to take into consideration the use of such allies as France and Japan to police the Mediterranean and the Pacific while the main British forces were concentrated in the North Sea and Atlantic.[7]

Coastal Defence

As previously noted, the German Navy was dominated by Army planning concepts up to 1889. These relegated the Navy to a coastal defence role, protecting the seaward flanks in the North Sea against France and in the Baltic against Tsarist Russia. The first post-war Chief of the Naval Command, Admiral von Trotha, and his staff entertained rather illusory hopes in the months prior to May 1919 about how much could be salvaged from defeat, but the terms of the Versailles Peace were particularly savage in their reduction of the fleet. The bulk of the High Seas Fleet was ordered to be confiscated and the German Navy was left with only 36 vessels. Four old battle-cruisers were refitted and brought back into service between 1921 and 1925, together with two cruisers. Between 1919 and 1926, relatively little consultation between Army and Navy seems to have taken place, perhaps in part because General von Seeckt had suggested the creation of a supreme command, in which the Navy would have had no say to speak of. The civilian Defence Minister Gessler (1920 to 1928) indicated to naval officers in 1926 that war with Britain was obviously out of the question and that the most they could possibly cope with was war with either France or Poland. Gessler assumed as a matter of course that important tasks would be assigned to the Navy in the war on land. For the Army appears to have assumed that, since the Navy's warfighting capability at sea would be limited, its artillery could be transferred to the sea coast to extend the front line in ways similar to operations in Belgium in World War I. Gessler confirmed that even Admiral Behncke had agreed on at least one occasion that he was agreeable to the deployment of the Navy in this way.[8]

---

[6] A. von Tirpitz, *My Memoirs* (London: Hurst, n.d.), Vol. I, p. 113.

[7] P.M. Kennedy, "The Development of German Naval Operations Plans against England, 1896-1914," in *The War Plans of the Great Powers, 1880-1914*, ed. P.M. Kennedy (London: Allen & Unwin, 1979), pp. 171-198.

[8] See Oldekop memorandum *RWM/ML/BZ 1517/26 GKds* of July 18, 1926 to Admiral Kurt Zenker in *Marine Archiv: Marinekommandoamt: Akte AII-AIII, Heft 1: "Verschiedenes," (1923-1929)*.

Behncke's successor, Admiral Kurt Zenker (1924 to 1928), reacted to this particular exchange by seeking to involve the Defence Minister directly in naval affairs by bringing him into the post-mortem discussions of the 1926 autumn manoeuvres as a method of educating him. During the same winter, a naval staff working group was established to consider the problem of French use of Danish territorial waters in any plans the French Navy might have for supporting Poland in a war with either the U.S.S.R. or Germany. In 1927, the German Army Command and officers of the Defence Minister's Secretariat (*Ministeramt*) began pushing for the establishment of a National Security Council to co-ordinate not only Army-Navy plans, but also to bring civilian ministries and the governments of the *Länder* into co-operation with the efforts of the military to draw up joint operational plans for defence against Poland in the ensuing winter. The new Defence Minister, General Gröner (1928 to 1932), aided and abetted by General von Schleicher, encouraged both services to draw the Foreign Ministry in particular into such planning exercises. The prospect of the coming into fleet service of new light and armoured cruisers in this period increased the Navy's chances of denying the French fleet passage into the Baltic. Against this, however, had to be set the worsening of domestic economic, social, and political conditions in Germany following the onset of the Great Depression. These conditions raised the spectre of a Polish pre-emptive strike against East Prussia, a key area of food production that could save Germany from having to import food and expend large amounts of foreign exchange in order to do so. German balance-of-payments problems were particularly acute because of a steady withdrawal of U.S. and other foreign investments. The Navy's task was to protect the shipment of food from East Prussia and interdict possible Polish landings in the rear of the German Army.

In Army planning to 1932, tentative expectations were placed on possible Soviet intervention in the event of Polish aggression; the Navy had never been convinced of such links and almost totally avoided involvement in the Army's policy of helping to build up the strength of the Red Army. The wisdom of this approach appeared to be vindicated in the course of the first Soviet Five-Year Plan (1928 to 1932), when Stalin made it clear that there was nothing special about the relationship with Germany and used economic incentives during the Depression to persuade France and its allies of the value of signing non-aggression pacts with the U.S.S.R. Moreover, Soviet statements at times of German-Polish tension seemed to suggest a Soviet interest in encouraging confrontation, while interference in German domestic politics was suggested in the form of promoting conflict between the Communist and Social Democratic Parties.[9]

---

[9] The *SPD* had been roundly denounced by Radek and other Soviet spokesmen

The advent of Hitler to power in 1933 was taken by Admiral Raeder as a signal for unrestricted rearmament: the day after Hitler took office, for example, Raeder issued a set of general guidelines for Navy support of the German arms industry and staked out a claim for building up a strong competitive position for Germany in the international arms trade. Defence Minister von Blomberg (1932 to 1938), too, encouraged the Navy to concentrate on longer-term operational planning and to relegate previous short-term contingencies covering the Baltic to a lower level of priority in planning. The view was now that the Versailles restrictions, already visibly eroded during the Geneva Disarmament talks, would inevitably be phased out sooner or later; that equality could be demanded and no longer denied; and that the Navy could concentrate on the expansion of the fleet through the open acquisition of previously forbidden capital ships, aircraft-carriers, U-boats, and aircraft.[10]

Battle-Fleet Operations

Staff studies since 1928, when Germany first obtained full details of Franco-Polish operational plans, suggested that Denmark's ability to prevent the penetration of the Baltic Narrows was negligible. The need for Germany to ensure the uninterrupted flow of vital imports to North Sea ports dictated that more powerful naval forces would be essential, and in larger numbers, both to defend lines of communication round the north of the British Isles and to engage in economic warfare against the French west-coast ports. It was inevitable, however, that Raeder's fleet expansion plans would excite British suspicions, if not hostility. Hitler, mindful of the Anglo-German naval arms race before 1914, decided that Raeder's aspirations would have to be curbed for political reasons in 1935 in order to try to ensure at least benevolent neutrality by Britain in the event of a Franco-Soviet attack on Germany.

---

in December 1926 for exposing secret German military activities in the Soviet Union, but what had mainly touched it off was a dispute between General von Seeckt and Professor Hugo Junkers, who claimed that the Army had inveigled him into the projects in the Soviet Union, had failed to compensate his firm adequately for services rendered since 1922, and had forced him into bankruptcy. See the correspondence between the president of the Supreme Court, Dr. Simons, and Foreign Minister Stresemann in: *Auswärtiges Amt: Abteilung IV Russland: G.A.: Handakten: "Junkers," (1926-1927)* and the author's "The Far East in German Peacetime Planning for Crises," in *Proceedings of the British Association for Japanese Studies* VI/1, ed. J.W.M. Chapman (1981), pp. 49-72. On the role of non-aggression pacts, see the author's "The Polish Labyrinth and the Soviet Maze," in *International Studies* 1982/II, ed. I.H. Nish (London: ICERD/LSE), pp. 66-87; *Marine Archiv: AIIIc: "Osten," (1931-1934)* and *Auswärtiges Amt: Abteilung IV Russland: G.A.: Handakten: "Sicherheitspakt-Nichtangriffspakt," Bde.1-3, (1931-1932)*.

[10] Raeder-von Blomberg discussion of March 28, 1933, and Raeder memorandum *M I 376/33 GKdos* of January 31, 1933 in *Marine Archiv: Akte AI-IV; "Sammlung von Besprechungsniederschriften und Besprechungsergebnissen," (1929-1933); M-IV: "Attaché- und Auslandsangelegenheiten," Bd.2, (1936-1937)*.

This had already been a significant element in planning against France and Poland since the mid-1920s, when Zenker (as well as Hitler) had welcomed evidence of British hostility to the Soviet Union. Navy planners had even expressed the hope that French blockade measures against Germany might lead to Anglo-French and Franco-American frictions which could be exploited to German advantage. Benevolent Anglo-American neutrality was absolutely crucial for German economic access to overseas markets and sources of energy and raw materials in the event of war with Germany's European neighbours. This was forcibly brought home to Hitler during the economic crisis of 1934, when German currency reserves fell even more catastrophically as a result of a trade deficit mostly attributable to Hitler's determination to end all economic and military ties with the Soviet Union.

In the event, however, it was not Britain, but Japan and Italy which demonstrated the kind of toughness toward the Soviet Union and the Communist movements in Spain, China, and elsewhere, that won Hitler's plaudits. The German Navy had long since cultivated relations with Italy as a counter to French influence in the Mediterranean. In practice, however, Italian pressure was brought to bear against Britain in the Mediterranean and in East Africa more than on France. A most important element here lay in the irresolution of British policy, combined with attempts at bluff that failed to impress the Italians because of the laxity of British diplomatic and military code and cypher security, which had been thoroughly penetrated by both Italian and German cryptanalytical agencies. During the 1920s, the Germans became increasingly aware of the stout resistance of Soviet and Comintern codes and cyphers, and this had reinforced experiences of World War I in demonstrating the need to devise secure cryptological systems, which could—and did—help prevent other countries from initially observing German weaknesses, and then assisted Hitler in the launching of surprise moves and attacks.[11]

In the early years of his regime, Hitler does not appear to have confided many of his ideas and plans outside the circle of Party retainers, and on the military side, he relied particularly on the responses and resources of the network of interests round Göring, and to a lesser

[11] The evidence for decipherment of British and French cypher material during the Weimar Period is fairly full. See *Reichswehrministerium: Abwehr-Abteilung/Chiffrierstelle: "Entzifferungs-berichte," (1925-1933)*. Again, it is very full for the period 1939-1943 and much of this can be seen in the so-called *B-Berichte* and *X-Berichte* in National Archives, Washington, D.C.: R.G. 457, Records of the National Security Agency. There are much less systematic materials for the period 1933 to 1939 available, but it may be that more of this evidence will be released by the NSA in the United States and GCHQ in Britain. What material there is tends to be of Italian origin or arises in the context of German-Italian relations.

extent on Rosenberg and von Ribbentrop. In diplomacy up to 1936, Hitler operated a Bismarckean-style network of checks and balances designed to win Germany the breathing-space necessary to complete the basic programme of rearmament by 1940. Knowledge of his opponents' moves and estimates of the likely reactions abroad to German rearmament and expansionist aspirations came principally from Göring's own cryptanalytical agency, the *Forschungsamt*, which rapidly emerged as the largest single agency of its kind in Germany. National economic and military planning revolved round the Four-Year Plan office, headed by Göring from 1936, and the organization derived its initial ideas and inspiration from an outline of the Plan composed by Hitler himself and still—new "discoveries" notwithstanding—the sole major surviving document of the regime directly attributable to Hitler. The Plan provided no blueprint for external policy or strategy as such, and such indications as there are of Hitler's strategic thinking up to 1938 are not best illustrated or understood from the archives of the Foreign Ministry or the Armed Forces. The most important clues are to be gathered from an understanding of the "power base" developed in Prussia by Göring and his associates from the summer of 1932, however untidy an agglomeration of offices and powers it may appear.[12]

Foreign reactions to developments in Spain in 1936, where the Navy had long had close contacts and interests, were particularly crucial, as events there were seen by Hitler as an acid test of anti-Communist and anti-Soviet sincerity. Britain, much to Hitler's disappointment, failed to follow Hitler's crusade, and proof of British antipathy was quickly supplied by some of Göring's minions, while others, such as General Faupel, hurried off to Spain to lend air support to Franco's forces.[13] Though less desirable in Hitler's eyes as allies, Japan and Italy in various ways did respond positively to the clarion call, and the Navy was well-placed through its long-term contacts with the Japanese and Italian navies to respond to Hitler's express wishes for good relations with the two countries. But here again, the links with Göring and the Air Ministry are plain and probably inextricable because of the fact that the Air Force drew its early personnel from the naval

---

[12] In his immediate post-war interrogation, Ribbentrop complained that "the Führer . . . had various sources of information of his own, which were unknown to Ribbentrop, especially with regard to England and the United States." See De Witt C. Poole memorandum, "The Nazi Experience in Its Foreign Political Aspect," for James W. Riddleberger in National Archives, R.G. 59, State Decimal File 840.00116 E.W./12-745. For further information on the *Forschungsamt*, see *Breach of Security*, ed. David Irving (London: Kimber, 1968).

[13] Anthony Eden categorically stated to Japanese Ambassador Yoshida Shigeru that Britain would have no part "in a crusade against any ideology." Eden memorandum of November 16, 1936 in Public Record Office, Kew, FO 371/F7043/303/23.

and military aviation departments of the Weimar Navy and Army.[14] The Italians were quick to exploit the Spanish situation to gain German support, just as over China in 1937 the Japanese—and especially the Japanese Military Attaché, General Ōshima Hiroshi—confronted Ribbentrop and Hitler with an ultimatum to give up all assistance to the Kuomintang government, in which all three German services were involved, but the Air Force least.

Navy strategic planning right up to May 1939 was predicated on a Franco-Soviet encirclement, in which it became gradually ever more certain that Britain would participate on the side of Germany's enemies from the summer of 1938. Hitler was disappointed that neither Italy nor Japan displayed a firmness of resolve to commit themselves to battle similiar to his own, but at least it was clear that, by contrast with World War I, both countries were unlikely to be on the side of the enemy. In a situation where Britain was likely to be an enemy, the German Navy found itself, at the outbreak of war, in a position of much greater inferiority at sea than had been the case in August 1914. The one valuable asset it possessed, however, was that its communications systems were secure, whereas those of the British and French forces generally were not. In order to strengthen the fleet quickly, a crash programme of conversion of merchant vessels into armed merchant cruisers was initiated, and steps were taken to provide existing cruisers with adequate means of supply to keep them at sea for longer periods of operation, until the first of the large capital ships and more submarines could be completed.[15]

The sole occasion on which the German Navy engaged in operations involving the whole fleet was at the invasion of Denmark and

---

[14] The biographies of the leading officials in the *Technisches Amt* of the Air Ministry illustrate the point clearly: see Milch note *RdL P III Nr.675/34g* of August 20, 1934. (Source as n.4 above.) Göring and Rosenberg backed various schemes for barter deals with Manchukuo from 1932, the most important of which involved airships for soya beans. The Air Ministry sent Commodore Coeler and Commander Breithaupt to Japan to make appropriate contacts at the end of 1934. On one of these reports to the Navy in January 1935, Admiral Raeder noted, in the characteristic green pencil reserved for top officers and officials, "the Führer wishes good relations." See Wenneker (Tokyo) Report G 53 of January 9, 1935 to Naval Command in *Marine Archiv: M Att: "Attache-Berichte Tokio 1935"*.

[15] Before Munich the German Navy had hoped to be able to get its hands on Standard Oil tankers run by German crews and using the Danzig flag of convenience, but this was frustrated by the transfer of the flag to Panama. Lack of time and funds made it difficult to expand the tanker fleet before war broke out, and various stopgap measures were explored in extensive war games in early 1939. See *O.K.M.: 3.Skl.: Akte AIII-15: "Unterlagen für OKM Kriegsspiel," Bd.2, (1939)* and *1.Skl.IIa:Akte 2-3: "Handelskrieg," Bd.3, (1938-1939)*. Such considerations were subsumed in the main strategic planning document, *1.Skl.Ia Op 222/39 gKdos.Chefs.* of June 2, 1939, updated to August 1939, in *O.K.M.: 1.Skl.: KTB, Teil Ca: "Grundlegende Fragen der Kriegführung," (1939-1943)*.

Norway in April 1940. Losses were high, though the immediate objectives—denial of the Baltic to the enemy and the securing of vital imports of high-grade iron ore and nickel from Scandinavia—were achieved. Apart from the advantage of surprise, the German side had the advantage of strong support from land-based German air power, and although it was later pointed out by the British Naval Attaché in Japan that British losses could have been very much higher if the attacking aircraft had used torpedoes instead of bombs, nevertheless the German success strikingly demonstrated that a new era of naval warfare had arrived for the inferior surface fleet provided that it was assured of superiority in the air. The achievement was not lost on the Japanese and the Italians, though the impact on strategic thinking would probably have been immeasurably greater had it not been for the fact that, so soon after, Navy successes were overshadowed by the startling Army victories over the French. Losses, together with the slow bringing into service of new warships, ensured that it would be very difficult indeed for the Navy to put a major task force of this kind to sea against any of the offshore islands, from Spitzbergen in the north to the Cape Verde Islands in the south.[16] The failure to bring the aircraft-carrier *Graf Zeppelin* into service in place of the big battleships meant that the Navy lacked sufficient air cover beyond the range of operations of land-based units of the German Air Force.

From the outset of the war, and not just after the losses of the bulk of the surface fleet, the German Naval War Staff (*Seekriegsleitung*) saw Britain as the prime opponent, the war as an economic war, the main target as merchant shipping of all countries bringing the enemy material sustenance, and the main object of warfare to "destroy England's will to wage war and to compel her to be prepared to make peace in the shortest possible time." The means for conducting this economic warfare were "surface forces, submarines, aircraft, and the organs of politics, the economy and propaganda."[17] The Navy and Air Force were seen as the decisive weapons in this struggle, but from the beginning, the U-boat arm was seen as the principal weapon in the Navy's armoury. The Naval War Staff therefore called for German

---

[16] Göring made extravagant claims about the Air Force being able to occupy the Atlantic islands unaided, and unveiled plans for a long-range bomber, based on the Azores, which would provide Germany with its "sole opportunity" to put pressure on the United States and force it, in the event of U.S. entry into the war, to build up its own air defences and prevent it from exporting military aircraft to Britain. See *OKM/1.Skl.2088/40 Chefs* of September 7 and *1.Skl. Op I 2486/40 Chefs* of November 14, 1940 in *O.K.M.: Ob.d.M.: "Persönlich-Grossadmiral Raeder," Heft 3, (1940-1941)*.

[17] See, for example, the Naval War Staff study of October 14, 1939 on stepping up the war at sea against Britain in *Oberkommando der Wehrmacht: Wi-Rü-Amt: Wi Ia H:Akte Wi VIc, 244-1: "Sonderstab HWK," (1939-1942)*. This proposed a more extreme offensive than Hitler at this time, mainly for political reasons, wanted to follow.

war industry to make the construction of U-boats and the production of aircraft suited to the war at sea the two most important priorities. In the absence of a substantial German battle-fleet it made good sense to avoid the mistakes of World War I strategy and try to fight a superior enemy unaided. Admiral Raeder shrewdly calculated that his Italian and Japanese friends, with much more substantial battle-fleets than his, should be helped and encouraged to pursue offensive naval operations in order to tie down and distract the Allied Powers at least until such time as the German U-boat arm was powerful enough to deliver the *coup de grâce* to Britain.[18] Hitler, who had been greatly impressed by Lloyd George's account of the effects of submarine warfare in 1917 when they met in Berlin in 1936, was inclined to accept such an argument. The propaganda value attaching to the destruction of the *Graf Spee* in 1939, the fear of the loss of the *Deutschland*, the actual loss of the *Bismarck*, and the subsequent Japanese successes against British and U.S. battleships led Hitler to argue against any use of large capital ships. While it did become increasingly hazardous for such vessels to run the gauntlet of the passage into the open Atlantic, occasional and unpredictable sorties—such as those sent to attack the Arctic convoys—did lend support to the policy of co-ordinating Allied efforts to tie down substantial enemy forces that might have been used offensively elsewhere.[19]

One of the main weaknesses of the battle-fleet strategy, however, lay in the need to rely so heavily as it did on the availability of large quantities of fuel oil, especially at times when supplies of fuel could no longer be made good from available reserves. The German Navy had to suffer the frustration of seeing large quantities of its carefully stockpiled reserves being diverted by Göring and the so-called planners to the needs of the other services and the civilian economy, and not being replaced because of the failure to provide, as promised, home-produced fuel substitutes at more than half peace-time levels. In order to keep the Italian fleet at sea, Raeder had to transfer large quantities of his precious stocks of furnace oil in 1941, while opera-

---

[18] Raeder tried to press for some kind of "supreme war council" to make it possible to co-ordinate the strategies of the two Axis Powers and Japan in the light of Mussolini's unilateral attack on Greece in 1940. See *1.Skl.I Op 46/41 Chefs* of January 14, 1941, discussed with Hitler on February 4, 1941. The preponderance of German power, however, soon made such a proposal with reference to Italy largely redundant, and Hitler had little faith in being able to persuade the Japanese save by German action and the demonstration effect. Source as n.2 above, but *Bd.1, (1941)*.

[19] After the entry of Japan into the war the surface warships were seen as having acquired a new significance and the German Navy was expected to use them to reinforce the Japanese Navy's operational strategy. See *OKW/WFSt/Abt.L (Ik Op) Nr.442173/41 gKdos.Chefs* of December 14, 1941, source as n.15 above, final reference, but *Bd.2, (1941)*.

tions in the Indian and Pacific Oceans would not be covered by the Japanese on account of their own even larger requirements. Even after the seizure of the Dutch and Burma fields, the Japanese Navy objected to supplying oil to German armed merchant raiders and guaranteed supplies of fuel to the "Monsoon" group of U-boats operating from South-east Asian bases from the end of 1942 only if these were picked up from the refineries directly by German supply tankers. All larger surface warships used large quantities of fuel that could be more effectively employed by many more U-boats, and this was an important part of Hitler's rationale for limiting or ending battleship and cruiser operations. These constraints affected not only battle-fleet operations by the German Navy: in the end, the Italian fleet virtually ceased to put to sea and the Japanese fleet, like the German, had to husband the scarce fuel resources available to it for use only in dire and brief emergencies.[20]

Counter-Blockade

From 1889 to 1897, the Imperial German Navy moved from a strategy of coastal defence to one based on the idea of attacking enemy lines of communication, mainly by the employment of cruiser warfare in distant waters (*Ausfallsflotte*). The concept was best suited to a relatively weak fleet fighting a guerilla-style war of attrition from comparatively secure bases. This was probably a reasonable strategy so long as it was pitted against the less powerful fleets of the day, such as the French or the Russian. The strategy provided part of the rationale for the deployment of the German Cruiser Squadron in the Pacific from the late 1870s to 1914. But, as its fate at the Battle of the Falklands in December 1914 demonstrated, it was unlikely to be capable of putting up much resistance when employed as a single task force against a preponderant fleet like the Royal Navy of the day. For, apart from being able to afford a higher rate of attrition, a preponderant fleet could mount attacks not only on the local bases from which such a force operated, but above all it could attack its metropolitan bases in Europe as well.

Admiral von Tirpitz, who spent a year with the Cruiser Squadron in the Far East prior to becoming State-Secretary in the Navy Ministry, recognized the limitations of the *Ausfallsflotte* and became the driving force behind the creation of a battle-fleet that even a preponderant fleet's commander would think twice about attacking directly. In the

---

[20] See the Author's "Oil, Deviance and the Traditional World Order," in *Tradition and Modern Japan*, ed. P.G. O'Neill (Tenterden, Kent: Paul Norbury Publications, 1981), pp. 130-150. On September 5, 1942 the Japanese Navy indicated that "each drop of oil must be put to the utmost military use" and urged the German Navy to reconsider the value of continuing to use armed merchant cruisers in the Indian Ocean area. Source as n.2 above, SRGL Nos. 0523 and 0527.

event, the creation of the so-called *Risikoflotte* proved to be part of a highly defence-minded strategy which failed to achieve any significant weakening of the Royal Navy. It certainly made sense in a general war to withdraw the Cruiser Squadron in order to reinforce the High Seas Fleet, making use of the Navy's Supply Service (*Marineetappendienst*) to supply the Squadron with fuel and provisions needed to bring it safely to home ports. In the end, the isolated individual cruisers such as the *Emden* created many more problems for the enemy than the Cruiser Squadron itself, and German naval historians (including Erich Raeder and Otto Groos) who studied these events after 1919 came to the conclusion that such individual warships, if backed up by an efficient fuel and provisioning service operating from neutral countries, could inflict disproportionate damage on the enemy's economy and communications and tie down much larger tonnages of enemy warships in relation to the size of the threatening forces.[21]

Initially, the Navy leaders had hoped that Germany might even retain some of the old colonies and identified the new methods of world-wide communication by radio as a promising development for future naval strategy, but the Versailles settlement meant that they had to revert to the coastal defence posture accepted by Admiral Behncke until 1924. The loss of the colonies and the lack even of a network of naval attachés in the major capitals abroad greatly inhibited the prospects for cruiser warfare against even French or Polish sea communications. However, from an early stage, undercover contacts were established with former German naval officers working abroad for shipping lines, commercial organizations, and government agencies, and a world-wide intelligence net of sorts was established in the course of the 1920s. Naval officers sent on official trips overseas for training or contacts with foreign navies recruited suitable members of German communities overseas, and in the winter of 1924 Admiral Zenker decided to reinforce this policy by despatching warships abroad on training exercises and drawing members of the German community abroad into the supply and provisioning of these vessels from the spring of 1925. This enabled the Navy to identify the most valuable

---

[21] For a detailed summary of the activities of the Supply Service and of the German Navy in World War I, see the lecture "Preparations for War in Distant Waters" given to the Armed Forces Academy on October 21, 1936. *Marine Archiv: AIII MND: Akte III-1: "Etappenwesen-Allgemeines," Heft 5, (1935-1937)*. This lecture was given by Commander Werner Vermehren, who had served with Grand-Admiral Raeder at Jutland and returned to Germany from Mexico as a result of the world depression to become a long-standing member of the Supply Service during its period of growth during the 1930s. In 1942 he was despatched to the Far East and took over the service there as assistant German Naval Attaché in Japan. The author is grateful to Captain Vermehren and his daughter, Frau Maria Freitag, for information provided at their meeting at Lübeck in September 1982.

collaborators, who were subsequently to be recruited for a revived Naval Supply Service, which until 1938 formed a part of the Secret Military Intelligence Service (*Abwehr-Abteilung*) set up by General von Schleicher in the Defence Ministry against the Navy's wishes in 1928.[22]

In the end, this Service prospered in its new location because its existence was better secured by more powerful political backers after 1930, as it was handed over to Colonel von Bredow, a close political collaborator of von Schleicher. It prospered and expanded firstly because von Bredow was able to win the support of the Foreign Ministry in 1932, secondly because efforts to win the support of the German shipping lines were largely successful, and thirdly because the Foreign Ministry agreed at the end of 1932 to permit the re-establishment of naval attaché posts abroad. Once the Nazis took over, its central administration was expanded and a large network of contact people (*Versorgungsmänner*) were recruited all over the world. By 1938, the Service had been divided into three zones: the "Inner Zone," covering the Baltic and North Seas, which was mainly a ship-reporting service with contact people supplied with radio transmitters for direct contact with warships at sea, which was transferred to the covert espionage service (*Abwehr I Marine*) in the spring of 1939; the "Outer Zone," covering the Atlantic, which was seen as the main locus for cruiser warfare against the French, then against the French and British; and the "Overseas Zone," covering the Indian and Pacific Oceans, which was viewed primarily as an area from which supplies of fuel and provisions (as well as, eventually, raw materials for the German war economy) could be drawn and transferred for consumption in the other zones.[23]

The Supply Service was intimately linked with the Navy's operational planning system and its officers participated in fleet wargames and manoeuvres, while co-operation between cruiser captains and its central organs, as well as its overseas contacts, was close and regular. Compared to the days of coal-fired vessels, the Service encountered special problems of oil fuel supply, firstly because German warships burned a special fuel mixture instantly recognizable to foreign suppliers, and secondly because the fuel bunkering services across the world were dominated by Anglo-Dutch Shell and Standard Oil of New Jersey. The German tanker fleet in the 1920s was even smaller than the French, and a variety of methods were employed to build up the

---

[22] Von Schleicher letter *RWM/W Abt Nr.148/27 GKds* of March 14, 1928 to Naval Command Fleet Section reply, source as n.7 above.

[23] For a detailed description see the lecture given to the Naval Academy by Captain Werner Stoephasius, Head of the Naval Supply Service until 1943, in *OKW/Abwehr IVL Nr.83/38 g.Kdos* of March 11, 1938 in *Oberkommando der Wehrmacht: Ausland IV: Akte III-11, 2: "Niederschriften über Etappendienst," Bd.1 (1931-38)*.

Navy's oil reserves during the 1930s or to try to ensure that warships could be fuelled at sea in distant waters: subsidies were given to German tanker owners; arrangements were made for requisitioning oil on board German merchantmen directed to safe neutral ports in time of crisis or war; special ships were constructed to provide arms, fuel, and provisions (Z and V ships); and a Spanish oil company (CEPSA) was secretly acquired, which had a modern refinery on the Canary Islands, and to which oil could be delivered from Central America for transfer to U-boats and other warships under cover of Spanish neutrality.[24] At first, the Weimar Navy deployed training cruisers overseas (*Auslandskreuzer*) as its only instrument for the conduct of counter-blockade operations. Until the early 1930s, however, the fleet in home waters was too weak to risk deliberately sending cruisers out into the Atlantic to attack French lines of communication, guarded by a superior French Navy. However, when these vessels were increased in number and other vessel types were commissioned, and aircraft were built, the counter-blockade strategy began to take on a formidable character. The conversion of armed merchant cruisers was made necessary mainly because of the need to deal with the Anglo-French combination and to keep light cruisers in home waters.

A most important facet of the counter-blockade strategy in the early years of World War II was to avoid at all costs the mistake of World War I by alienating the United States through acts of sabotage and subversion there, and above all avoid incidents at sea that would undermine U.S. neutrality. As the most important of the neutrals, the policy line adopted by the U.S. was likely to be heeded by all the other neutrals, and it was hoped that British blockade measures would create far greater friction with the neutrals than German counter-blockade measures. This was a major reason for establishing a warning zone in the area round the British Isles, which tended to result in many neutral vessels discharging their cargoes outside the zone and then transferring them to ships of British or Allied registry to take them through the war zone.[25] In part, this formed part of Hitler's own political

---

[24] Cf. n.20 above.

[25] Admirals Schuster and Groos, appointed to head the Special Staff for Economic Warfare, were constantly seeking ways and means of furthering economic warfare against Britain, and were just as frequently restrained on legal, practical, and ethical grounds by General Thomas, Admiral Burkner, Admiral Canaris, and even the Foreign Ministry. Sabotage specialists were sent to the U.S. in 1939-40, but told to lie low until it looked as though the U.S. might enter the war. Canaris had to reassure all concerned that he had no immediate plans for sabotage, though it appears that later in the war agents were landed by U-boat in North America and the Secret Military Intelligence Service claimed to have connections with American communists willing to carry out acts of sabotage. See J.W.M. Chapman, *The Price of Admiralty — The War Diary of the German Naval Attaché in Japan, 1939-1943* (Ripe, E. Sussex: Saltire Press, 1982), Vol. I.,

strategy, designed to further the possibility he constantly entertained of persuading Britain to make peace, especially in October 1939 after the fall of Poland and in July 1940 after the fall of France. The creation of the Pan-American Security Zone, on the other hand, caused Raeder much frustration because the United States constantly permitted Canadian and British warships to operate in that Zone to intercept and eliminate German merchantmen, and even warships, prior to U.S. entry into the war. Hitler added to these frustrations by refusing to allow Raeder to lay mines off the Canadian coast; to attack the refineries in the Dutch West Indies in May 1940, because some were owned by Standard Oil; or to attack U.S. warships accompanying convoys to Iceland from April 1941 onward. Behind many of these restraints lay the advice of Göring, who had made claims in 1940 that air power alone was likely to be so effective that the involvement of the Navy would be redundant. The inability of aircraft to fight effectively in the bad weather conditions that affected the Atlantic and Arctic coasts confounded these claims, but Göring also was able to persuade Hitler that deals could be struck with U.S. oil majors and raw material suppliers if only the Americans were handled in the proper way. Göring went so far as to provide encouragement, if not funds, to business groups in the United States who favoured moves against the re-election of President Roosevelt in 1940.[26]

The failure to seize any of the off-shore Atlantic islands, the failure of the German Air Force to create large enough or effective enough units for promoting the war at sea soon enough, and the failure to provide adequately for the fuel supply of the German armed forces, meant that the Navy had to resort mainly to the U-boat arm as its central strategic force. The versatility of the U-boat was more than amply demonstrated during World War II against merchant and warship targets, and the characteristics incorporated in the most advanced German designs (high underwater speed and difficulty of detection when submerged) are among the features that have promoted it to the principal ship type for modern strategic forces at sea. After initial failures in operations off Norway, torpedo design and effectiveness were greatly improved by German technologists, and the acoustic torpedo was an important forerunner of modern torpedo

---

228-29; *Auswärtiges Amt: Inland IIg: Akte 413: "Verschiedene Meldungen betr.Ostasien," Bd.1, (1941-1944)*.

[26] Raeder's complaints to Hitler may be found in *O.K.M.: Ob.d.M. Persönlich: "Grossadmiral Raeder," Hefte 1-5, (1939-1942)*. On Göring's role, see Canaris letter *OKW/ Ausland Ig Nr.231/41 gKdos* of February 12, 1941 warning him that his connections with the U.S. oilman Davis, whom he had met in Berlin in September 1939, might now be revealed through Davis being summoned to appear before the House Un-American Activities Committee. *O.K.W.: Ausland III: Akte III-13: "Ölversorgung," Bd.4, (1938-1942)*.

weapons. Supply and tanker submarines were a logical extension of
the surface vessels which the Supply Service helped to operate, and
these together extended the range of operation of the U-boat arm to
all the world's oceans by 1942. Just when it seemed that the balance
had swung in favour of the counter-blockade, Allied anti-submarine
warfare measures in the form of the auxiliary carrier, ten-centimeter
radar on ships and aircraft, and task groups with more efficient underwater weapons, combined with the electronic advances that mastered
the solution of the "Enigma" cypher system to bring about the decisive
shift that effectively blunted the most deadly of the German Navy's
counter-blockade weapons.[27]

RELATIONSHIPS BETWEEN THE EUROPEAN CENTRE AND THE
PACIFIC PERIPHERY

THE COLLECTIVE German view of the Pacific had much in
common with that of the rest of Europe in the era of imperialism in
seeing the societies of East Asia as at the very periphery of their world.
But, whereas the British and French imperialists may have grabbed
all the best pieces of real estate, the Germans prided themselves in
dominating the metaphysical world of scientific ideas and culture, not
least because the products of their ancient universities and modern
Technische Hochschulen had migrated in such numbers to the ends of
the earth after 1848. The influence of German scientific and social
scientific thinking on East Asian societies was profound, not least in
Japan where they were all-pervasive in the new institutions of higher
learning and especially in the vocational and professional fields, such
as law, medicine, the applied sciences, and engineering. But unlike in
England, where enthusiasm for the energetic efforts of the Japanese
to catch up with the West waxed in direct proportion as respect for
Chinese traditions waned, German admiration for Chinese culture
remained profound throughout the nineteenth and early twentieth

---

[27] Information about both these developments was supplied to the German Navy
High Command by the Secret Military Intelligence Service in the memorandum *OKW/
Abwehr I M/T B.Nr.1663/43 gKdos* of August 18, 1943 from its representative in Switz-
erland, who obtained information from a Swiss-American working in the Navy Department in Washington via Colonel Masson, the head of the Swiss secret service. This
stated *inter alia:*

> The English have in their 'Intelligence Naval Office' [sic] a quite outstanding aid
> in the struggle against the U-boats. A special office since the outbreak of war has
> concerned itself exclusively with the decipherment of the German codes. For some
> months past, it has succeeded in reading all orders sent by the German Navy to
> the U-boat commanders, something that has tremendously simplified the hunt
> against the U-boats.

Oberkommando der Marine: 4.Abt.Skl.: "Operative Geheimhaltung," (1941-1944).

centuries, while Japanese culture was seen as a distinctly inferior variant of it.

The highly publicized role of William II in the Triple Intervention of 1895 markedly reflected these preferences within the ruling elite in Germany, and so alienated Japanese feelings as to exclude the possibility, much discussed at the time, of a triple alliance among Britain, Japan, and Germany against Russia in 1902. Despite this, a considerable degree of sympathy and support existed for Germany, especially within the Japanese Army and civil service, but it was not sufficient to detach Japan from the alliance with Britain before or during World War I. Although British influence within the Japanese Navy was considerable at least until 1923, it should be stressed that this was by no means exclusive: even before 1914, when interest in the Anglo-German naval rivalry was keen, tough competition had already emerged between British and German arms producers such as Vickers-Armstrong and Siemens-Schückert to supply the requirements of the Japanese fleet construction programme. A number of senior officers in the Japanese Navy were trained in Germany: these included Admiral Yamamoto Gonbei, Navy Minister from 1906 to 1908 and twice Prime Minister in 1912 to 1914 and 1922 to 1923, and Prince Fushimi, who spent several years in Berlin at the turn of the century, and served as President of the German-Japanese Society in Tokyo from 1928 to 1932, when he was appointed Chief of the Naval Staff as a way of helping to cool internal faction-fighting in the Navy.

It was repeatedly argued after World War I that, if the first Yamamoto administration had not been brought down by the Siemens-Schückert scandal in 1914, the chances of Japan remaining neutral in the war, or even of switching sides, would have been greatly enhanced.[28] It was a feature of government thinking in Germany during the war that they could, through German efforts alone, alter the global balance of power. But in a world of rapid technological change, the perception that Europe combined, let alone Germany unaided, could automatically remain at the hub of the world economy and politics has been shown to be quite false. Fundamentally, as is already evident from the decision to recall the Cruiser Squadron from the Pacific, the region was seen as peripheral to the outcome of the war. A victorious Germany in Europe, it was expected, would be in a position to dictate the terms of peace in the Far East as much as anywhere else. In other words, Germany did not really need Japan. Even after defeat in 1919, this attitude can be observed even in the

---

[28] See *Kokumin Shinbun*, January 23, 1914, and a Foreign Ministry briefing of an inter-departmental meeting of April 12, 1919 in *Marine Archiv: Etatsabteilung III: Akte 6006: "Schutzgebiet Kiautschou," (1917-1919)*, pp. 72-125.

statements of Germans with a good knowledge of conditions in Japan: the retired Commander Wolfram von Knorr, who had been Naval Attaché in Japan in 1914 and who returned there as a newspaper and business representative in 1920, wrote to the General Staff in Berlin to say that he did not believe that the experience of colonial warfare prevailing in East Asia would provide it with much of value for the conduct of warfare on the European continent. The views of Ambassador Solf on military matters in Japan displayed even shorter shrift: in response to a request from Major von Bötticher for information about the current state of the Japanese Army, Solf complained about having to expand the scope of his reporting to include material requested by the Ministry of Defence. It exposed the hollowness of Foreign Ministry claims that its representatives could collect military and naval information and that there was therefore no need for the Army and Navy to despatch attachés to diplomatic posts abroad.[29]

As the German Navy had, until 1933, no official permanent representative in Japan, it experienced difficulty in obtaining any systematic picture of developments there, let alone an accurate evaluation of these. If the German Navy at the zenith of its strength during the war had manifestly been unable to affect developments in the Pacific directly or indirectly through power politics, it was much less able to do so after the scuttling of the High Seas Fleet in 1919. Nevertheless, by analogy with the projection of German ideas, techniques and culture, possibilities existed for influencing the East Asian societies and elites in ways that could alter the balance of advantage more positively in Germany's favour than the mistaken policies and strategies of the past had done. For this to be accomplished, the German Navy had to arrange its channels of communication with and about the Pacific region effectively before it could think in terms of influencing local elites. First of all, however, in the absence of the power to coerce or threaten, it needed to have something of value that could be employed as an incentive or bargaining counter. The key to this lay in German industrial technology, for which there was already widespread regard in both China and Japan. Renewed Japanese interest in this field came in January 1919, when Japanese diplomatic representatives in Europe reported to Tokyo the keen flurry of interest and activity of representatives of the other Entente Powers sent to Berlin. The *Gaimushō* subsequently sent Tōgō Shigenori and Debushi Katsuji to Germany, and the Japanese armed forces despatched an Army mission under General Watanabe Yotarō and a Navy mission

---

[29] See von Bötticher letter *RWM/HL/Allg.TA/Statistische Abtlg.Br.B. Nr.8599/20 T3/IV* of September 30, 1920 to Foreign Ministry and Solf (Tokyo), J.No.2004 of December 14, 1920 enclosing an exchange of letters between von Knorr and Major Liebmann, source as n.8 above.

under Admiral Utsonomiya to Berlin in the summer of 1919. As part of the division of German spoils, the Japanese Navy was given six U-boats and access to German processes of relevance to military technology.[30]

From this point on, a variety of doors opened and channels of information and contact were established. These can be summarized in the following general categories: (1) middlemen employed to conduct business with foreign navies secretly so as to avoid the prying eyes of third parties; (2) front companies and industrial firms; (3) officers seconded for tasks of varying duration; and (4) permanently attached officers, officials, and commercial representatives. These categories were not mutually exclusive, nor were the channels of communication always separate or clear-cut, but often they stemmed from the asymmetric interaction of naval, bureaucratic, and business hierarchies operating in Germany and Japan simultaneously. For the Japanese Navy, for example, its officers and employees operating in Germany were peripheral to different central agencies of the Navy in Japan. Unlike in the Japanese case, however, the absence of permanently attached German naval personnel in Japan meant that clearly established hierarchies and lines of command or communication were far less evident.

Middlemen

A good example of the use of middlemen in relations between the two navies can be found in the small German firm of Schinzinger and Hack in Berlin. The senior partner in the firm, which arranged for the delivery of military equipment to the Japanese Navy which German industry was forbidden or discouraged from exporting or manufacturing, was Adolf Schinzinger, appointed as Imperial Japanese Consul in Berlin in 1919. He handled most of the direct contracts with the Japanese Embassy as senior partner, while the junior partner, Dr. Friedrich W. Hack, seems to have dealt mainly with German industrial firms and suppliers, as well as with officers of the Naval Command. Other German firms, particularly those with offices in Japan, such as

---

[30] Hioki (Stockholm) Telegram No. 189 of January 4, 1919 to *Gaimushō;* Colonel Satō (Paris) Telegram No. 479 of January 10, 1919; War Ministry memorandum of May 27, 1919 in *Gaimushō: 1.6.3. 29-2: "Ōshū Kyūsen go Teikoku Kanmin Tekkoku e Haken Ikken".* See also the memoranda of conversations between Tōgō, and Dr. Naumann and Dr. Eltzbacher, which will appear in the forthcoming biography of Tōgō by Hagihara Nobutoshi, in *Auswärtiges Amt: Büro RM: Akte 40: "Japan" (1920-1936)* and *Abtlg.A.: "Bolschewismus," Bd.6 (1919);* also the cables from Debuchi Katsuji, chargé in Berlin in 1920, to Foreign Minister Uchida in *Gaimushō: 1.6.3. 29-1: "Ōshū-Sensō Kankei Kakkoku Sengo no Taido Ikken."* The author wishes to thank Professor Hosoya Chihiro (Niigata), Mr. Hagihara (Tokyo), Frau Dr. Maria Keipert (Bonn), and Miss Kimura Saki (London) for their assistance with these materials.

Illies and Co., did not deal exclusively in arms, but the secrecy in which the arms brokers operated gave rise to suspicions that Schinzinger and Hack had cornered the market by bribing either German naval officers or Japanese officers in Berlin or both. A particular victim of the cosy relationship involved was Commander von Knorr, who complained bitterly that his firm, *Auslands GmbH*, was being prevented from having a fair chance to compete and was being squeezed out of business by the arms brokers. In practice, however, it was the secrecy surrounding these transactions that gave rise to many accusations of this kind, for in the early years at least, the Japanese were concerned lest their activities in Germany excite the annoyance of the other Entente Powers because of Japanese failure to support the Versailles controls. After a few years, however, controls became less strict and the Allied Naval Control Commission was one of the first to be withdrawn from Germany and it became common knowledge that German firms were involved in supplying technology to the Japanese Navy. The need for secrecy declined and the need for the services of such German firms also declined, particularly as the Japanese trading firms established themselves in Germany and could take over liaison with German manufacturers on behalf of the Naval Attaché's Bureau.[31]

Schinzinger and Hack's partnership seems to have broken up by the end of 1924 and Hack specialized increasingly in military aviation, where Allied controls tended to be a lot sharper. Initially, Hack worked with the Rohrbach company, which produced all-metal aircraft at a factory in Copenhagen for the Japanese Navy, which shipped them to Japan, tested them, and bought licences for manufacture from 1924. Hack maintained contact with officers in the Naval Command in charge of aviation and subsequently worked with Ernst Heinkel, who had extensive dealings with the Japanese Navy and who went to Japan during the 1920s, as did Professor Messerschmitt and other aero-engineers. Hack's connection with Heinkel and the Aichi Tokei works continued into the 1930s, when the He 118 dive-bomber was supplied to the Japanese Navy, and Hack played an important role in bringing von Ribbentrop in touch with General Ōshima in 1935.[32] Another

---

[31] See the file referred to in n.5 above for details of the role Schinsinger & Hack in the 1920s; the Hack Papers are in the University of Freiburg Library.

[32] For material on Heinkel, see Ernst Heinkel, *Stürmisches Leben* (Stuttgart: Europaischer Buchklub, n.d.); *Militärarchiv*, Freiburg, File RH 8/v.3679; Milch Papers Vol. 54, Imperial War Museum, London. On Rohrbach, see *Militärarchiv*, Freiburg: Files RH 8/v.3606, 3661-2 and correspondence with Dr. Erich Pauer (Bonn) and with Dr. Otto Dahlke (Oregon, U.S.A.), an employee and designer with Rohrbach in the 1920s and later with other firms such as Arado and Miag. For Junkers, see Speer Collection, Imperial War Museum, London, Files 5400/45 and 5665/45, Messerschmitt material in File 4355/44 and Focke-Wulf material in File 4856/45. For Dornier material, see *MA* Freiburg, File RH 8/v.3661-2. The author has been helped by Mr. Philip Read (London),

useful middleman of this kind was Dr. Ernst Prieger, who worked as an agent in Japan for the aircraft broking firm, Fokkes and Koch, and was for a time a member of the Navy Supply Service in Japan. In 1940, he put the German Naval Attaché in Japan, Admiral Wenneker, in touch with the Head of the Military Affairs Bureau in the Japanese War Ministry, General Muto, who offered the Army's assistance in acquiring raw materials for the German war economy without the knowledge of either the Japanese Navy or German economic agencies in Japan.[33]

Front Companies and Industrial Firms
An early example of the activity of German industrial firms in Japan can be found in the visit of retired Admiral von Hintze as a director of Siemens-Schückert to Japan in 1920 to sign a contract for the supply of electrical equipment and munitions to Fuji Electric. The firm's agents in the Far East were convinced of the likelihood of the outbreak of a war between Japan and the U.S. over China, and pressed for direct contacts with Japan in order to be in a position to exploit the possibility of being able to make a profit through the sale of arms and munitions to both sides, if it came about. A more important example of contact arose out of the handing over of U-boats to the Japanese Navy in 1919. The Japanese were impressed with the quality of these ships, which included a submarine cruiser suitable for operation at long range across the Pacific in the event of a war with the U.S. A problem for the Japanese Navy, however, was that it was obliged to scrap all six vessels after eighteen months, and it was very keen to acquire licence and production rights on the larger U-boat types, some of which were only just introduced at the very end of the war for operations off the U.S. east coast. The German Navy was interested in obtaining more information about the performance and handling characteristics of such vessels, some of which were minelayers, others of which had a pressurized chamber for keeping a catapult aircraft to undertake a reconnaissance of a chosen sea area in order to facilitate torpedo or gun attacks.

Contracts were signed for the supply of patents, designs, and parts for each of these U-boat types between the Kawasaki dockyard at Kobe and the German Navy front company, *Ingeneurskantoor voor*

Professor Hans-Joachim Braun (Hamburg), and Frl. Ingeborg Krag (Braünlingen), a former secretary in the German Air Ministry.

[33] For a personal impression of Prieger, the author is grateful to Rear-Admiral George C. Ross RN (Retd.), as well as for information on another middleman in the inter-war arms trade, the Austrian Gazda, who sold the Oerlikon rapid-fire anti-aircraft gun to the Royal Navy after failing to sell it in Japan. For material on Prieger and Fokkes & Koch see Speer Collection, Imperial War Museum, London, Files 4586/45, 5841/45, and 4856/45; and see *O.K.M.: M Att: "Japan-Mobilmachung,"* Bd.2 (1940).

Scheepsegebouw (IvS), which operated in the Netherlands in order to avoid Allied military controls. A team of engineers and technicians led by a former U-boat captain, Commander Bräutigam, was sent to Kobe in 1923 to supervise the assembly of the first vessel from parts supplied directly from Germany, and then to help the Japanese organize complete fabrication of the subsequent nine vessels from then until the end of 1928. Subsequently, two Japanese naval attachés involved in submarine construction and co-operation, Captain Araki Jirō (1920 to 1923) and Captain Nomura Naokuni (1929 to 1932), were promoted to rear-admiral and put in charge of naval bases where submarine flotillas were stationed. There were hopes that the influence of the submarine arm would grow within the Japanese Navy because of the general satisfaction expressed about the performance of the German-designed vessels, but as early as 1934 Nomura and a German engineer named Hashagen indicated that the operational philosophy surrounding the use of submarines in the Japanese Navy was quite different from that in the German Navy. Whereas the Germans saw the U-boat as part of economic warfare in the first instance and secondarily as a means of sinking warships, the Japanese view was that they were best employed on scouting missions to lead the main battle fleet against the enemy fleet, then for sinking enemy warships, but only lastly as a means of attacking enemy transports, preferably landing ships rather than merchantmen.[34]

Although the submarine was undoubtedly a versatile instrument in the war at sea, the Japanese Navy appears to have decided to make the aircraft its principal development priority. Its development of aircraft-carriers and carrier aircraft after World War I was largely the result of collaboration with the Royal Navy up to 1923, but the experience with both submarines and battleships as platforms for catapult aircraft was gained mainly thanks to collaboration with the German Navy and aircraft companies. All the main German military aircraft designers and engine manufacturers were involved in projects with the Japanese Army and Navy right up to 1945, when design plans and models of the Me 163B and Me 262 A1 jet aircraft were transported to Japan by U-boat.[35]

---

[34] For a more detailed analysis of German assistance to Japan in the submarine field, see the author's "The Transfer of German Underwater Weapons Technology to Japan, 1919-1976" in *European Studies on Japan*, ed. I.H. Nish and C.J. Dunn (Tenterden: Paul Norbury Publications, 1979), Chapter 26.

[35] For statistics of German aircraft and aero-engine supplies to Japan and Manchukuo, see the table in *Oberkommando der Luftwaffe: Generalquartiermeister/6.Abteilung: Akte 8a: "Ausland, Allgemein," (1941-1945)*. These cover the years 1936 to 1942 only. Göring was given the go-ahead to supply the Japanese with up-to-date information on jet and rocket aircraft, if they asked for it, in January 1944. After much hesitation and

Officers and Officials on Secondment

There was a regular two-way traffic of Japanese and German naval officers either passing through or on specific secondment in both countries. Most of the traffic tended to be from Japan to Germany. Only after 1926, when regular visits by German cruisers to Japanese ports began, did the flow from Germany significantly increase, reaching its peak during the period of blockade-running by surface and submarine vessels from 1941 to 1945. No active senior officer of the German Navy ever went to Japan, though numerous senior officers of the inter-war period had served in the Pacific before 1914. These included Admiral Otto Groos, who went as captain of the *Hamburg* in 1926 and subsequently served as Raeder's Chief of Staff in the early 1930s and as Head of the Special Staff for Economic Warfare (*Sonderstab HWK*) from 1940 to 1945, and Commander (later Admiral) Wilhelm Canaris, who was sent on a special mission to Japan in 1924 by Admiral Behncke, and who had been interned in Chile in 1914 after the Battle of the Falklands.

On the other hand, several senior Japanese naval officers at different times visited Germany during the inter-war period. In 1921, while *en route* to the Washington Naval Conference, Admiral Katō Kanji, Chief of Naval Staff in 1930, decided to seek out Grand-Admiral von Tirpitz, living in retirement in the quiet Black Forest town of St. Blasien, to pay his respects and to make proposals for future collaboration between the two navies. Unfortunately, he turned up in full dress uniform, which made it rather difficult to conceal the meeting from the world's press and to engage in the exchange of confidences. This was to be left later to the visit in 1923 of Captain Teramoto, who was sent to Tirpitz with an introduction from Admiral Yamamoto Gonbei. Tirpitz was urged by the Naval Command to give Teramoto full details of his experience with U-boat warfare and on the handling of large modern fleets at sea, something the Japanese Navy had not engaged in, in anger, since 1905.[36]

The Great Kantō Earthquake of 1923 intervened at this point, and the Japanese Navy's budget had large sums diverted from it for reconstruction. This may well have influenced the shift to naval aviation, because the development costs were so much lower than for submarines. Reports from Japan indicated the desirability of on-the-spot inspection to find out about apparent delays in Japan's responding to further German proposals for closer collaboration. Commander

changes of mind, Hitler finally agreed on the despatch of models and plans by U-boat in November 1944. See *O.K.L.: G.Qu./6.Abt.: Akte 8a: "Ausland, Japan"*.

[36] See unsigned memorandum of a discussion with Tirpitz on November 8, 1923 in *Marine Archiv: Marinekommandoamt: AIIc.1: "Marinepolitische Angelegenheiten," Heft 1, (1923-1929)*.

Canaris was despatched in the summer of 1924 and arrived to a cool reception because information about his visit had not been passed on. His report was received by Admiral Zenker, who already had doubts about the value of the relationship. The huge Japanese Navy technical questionnaire, the slowness of Japanese responses to German enquiries, and the devastatingly scathing report by Canaris about the Japanese seeming only to want to exploit German technology and give little or nothing in return, combined to bring about a distinct cooling in the relationship until it underwent something of a revival during Captain Nomura's tour of duty.[37] It was during this period that relations between Nomura and Admiral Groos were particularly warm and served as the basis for a renewal of their friendship when Nomura returned as head of the Japanese Naval Mission in 1941. Nomura was closely connected with Admirals Katō and Suetsugu in the period after 1932 and became chief-of-staff of the Combined Fleet in 1936.

In January 1935, Admiral Yamamoto Isoroku passed through Berlin on his way home from the preparatory London Naval Conference, but he was persuaded by Japanese diplomats in London not to accept an invitation from von Ribbentrop to meet in Berlin, he opted instead for a brief formal meeting with Admiral Behncke in his capacity as President of the German-Japanese Society in Berlin. When Admiral Nagano Osami passed through Berlin at the end of November 1935 on the way to the London Conference, a point was made of getting Admiral Canaris to pass on to Grand-Admiral Raeder the suggestion that he meet privately with Nagano for confidential discussions on disarmament and other matters.[38] Most of the German officers visiting Japan in the 1930s were technical and aviation specialists, and a small group of officers, including Admiral Förster and a senior naval engineering specialist, visited Japan in the summer of 1939. A proposed visit by the former Navy Minister, Admiral Osumi, to the Nuremberg Rally in 1939 was cancelled at the outbreak of war, though a parallel visit by General Terauchi went ahead thanks to the persistence of Generals Ōshima and Kawabe, which contrasted with the more lukewarm attitude of the Naval Attaché, Rear-Admiral Endō.

The largest and most important of the Japanese visits was that of the Naval Mission headed by Admirals Nomura and Abe, who were subsequently appointed as senior naval officers in Berlin and Rome respectively until 1943, when Abe moved to Berlin for the remainder of the war. As with other missions, its main purpose was to provide

[37] Canaris memorandum *AII 500/24 GStbs* of November 3, 1924 in Ibid., pp. 423-500.

[38] Canaris letter *Chef Abw. Abtlg. 30/35 g.Kdos* of November 12, 1935 in *O.K.M.: M-IV: "Attaché- und Auslandsangelegenheiten," Bd.1, (1934-1936)*, pp.-302-03.

access to the latest developments in naval technology, whether German
or foreign, and to update information on tactical and weapons development as applied to naval warfare in theory and practice. A small
German Navy and Air Force team was sent out to Japan in May 1941
in response to Japanese Navy willingness to provide detailed technical
information on Japanese aerial torpedoes, which were perhaps the
most advanced in the world at that date. Seventy torpedoes were
subsequently despatched to Europe by blockade-runner and German
Navy representatives in the Far East were later shown captured British
naval equipment seized at Hong Kong and Singapore.[39]

Another category of temporary visits was that of German and
Japanese warships to each other's ports. There were two such Japanese
visits to Germany. A training squadron led by Admiral Matsushita
Hajime stayed in Germany for two days in May 1934 and was received
by Hitler, von Blomberg, Raeder, and von Hindenburg. In the summer
of 1937, the training cruiser *Ashigara* stopped off in Germany in
conjunction with a visit to the Spithead Coronation Review for King
George VI. Its Chief of Staff, Commander Maeda Tadashi, had been
in charge of the German desk in the Naval Staff Intelligence Division
and was subsequently singled out for particularly cordial treatment
by the German authorities as a coming man with high-level social
connections within the Navy and Japanese society.[40] German visits to
Japan took place practically every other year between 1926 and 1937
and were resumed in the form of covert collaboration provided for
German armed merchant cruisers in sheltering places in the islands
of the South Seas from 1940 to 1942; subsequently base facilities were
provided from 1942 to 1945 at Penang, Singapore, Soerabaya, and
Djakarta, as well as at Kobe and Kamkura. This was reciprocated to
a limited extent on the German side following visits from Japanese
cruiser submarines at U-boat bases on the French west coast from
1942 to 1944.

---

[39] See *O.K.M.: 1.Skl: "Japan-Kommission,"* (1941); M Att: "Japan-Mobilmachung":
Bd.IV (1941); Milch Collection, Vol. 13, Items 81-87, Imperial War Museum, London.

[40] *Auswärtiges Amt: Abteilung IV Ostasien: Akte Po.14: "Marineangelegenheiten in Japan,"*
(1933-1936); Marine Archiv: M Att: "Attaché-Berichte Tokio, 1937". Maeda was a member
of the family of Marquis Maeda, who had served with the German Army before World
War I. His elder brother, Maeda Minoru, was head of the Naval Intelligence Division
in Japan at the outbreak of the Pacific War. Maeda Tadashi was later Japanese Naval
Attaché at The Hague (to 1940) and in Batavia, served under his brother in intelligence,
and was subsequently sent as officer commanding in Java, 1943 to 1945, where he
played an important part supplying the German U-boat squadron. The author is grateful to Mr. Louis Allen (Durham) and Mr. Oba Sadao (London) for Relevant information.

Permanent Representatives

Stop-gap Measures, 1919 to 1933

In the absence of German naval attachés, the appointment of which had been urged by the Japanese side at least as early as 1923, the main channel of contact lay through Japanese naval attachés in Berlin from 1920 onward. These alternated roughly every three years, though there were usually numerous assistant attachés and civilian employees continuously attached to the Bureau of the Naval Attaché. Some civilian employees seem to have been employed in Berlin for over twenty years, but this was a rare exception. When Anglo-Japanese relations cooled after 1923, Berlin became a much-sought-after posting for language officers and technical personnel, and the Navy Bureau swelled in numbers, few of which had diplomatic accreditation. None of the naval attachés in Berlin was as influential or impressive as the Military Attaché and subsequent Ambassador Ōshima, but probably the most effective of them were Admiral Nomura (1936 to 1939) and Rear-Admiral Kojima (1943 to 1945).

On the German side, reporting on naval matters by permanent diplomatic representatives before 1933 tended to be rather hit-and-miss. In 1921, Foreign Minister Rosen decided to appoint the retired Colonel Renner to the post of Counsellor of Embassy in Japan. Renner had served as his military attaché when Rosen was Minister at The Hague during World War I, had an English wife, and was credited with being opposed to unrestricted submarine warfare because of its likely impact on the U.S. His job was to monitor developments in U.S.-Japanese relations at a time of tension in the Pacific. In advance of his departure, he was briefed by Captain Gartzke, who was in charge of undercover naval intelligence, about the naval situation in the Pacific, and asked, together with the new Consul-General Ohrt at Kobe, to make suitable reports to Berlin for relay to the Naval Command.[41] The Head of the Intelligence Section of the General Staff, Major von Bötticher, made a parallel visit on secondment to the U.S. Army at the same time, apparently to observe the same situation from the other side of the Pacific. Since the anticipated clash failed to develop, Renner was replaced, along with Rosen. Occasionally, members of the diplomatic corps, such as Consuls Czibulinski and Bischoff, were either former naval officers or were interested in naval affairs, and this tended to result in a greater level of interest, though not necessarily any greater level of gratitude on the part of the Navy, for reporting on naval matters to Berlin.[42]

---

[41] Source as n.5 above.

[42] Bischoff, who was Consul at Kobe, then Consul-General at Dairen, displayed such an interest in the technical equipment of the cruiser *Köln* when visiting Japanese

In such circumstances, efforts were made by the central naval intelligence authorities in Berlin to organize networks of voluntary reporters, drawn from individuals in the German business community, on long-term contracts to provide information on naval developments in Japan in the 1920s. Some of these were former officers, others were employed by shipping lines and could pass on their information securely by the many German ships on the Far East routes, while others were reporters or in commerce. They were usually contacted by naval officers sent to Japan on secondment or on the training cruisers, and their eyewitness experience was passed on to the Naval Command directly in the form of individual reports, or indirectly in the numerous reports written by cruiser captains. One of the most useful such eyewitnesses was retired Command Bräutigam because of his contacts with Japanese yards working for the Japanese Navy. Bräutigam was rather dismissive of the technical and strategic capabilities of the Japanese Navy compared to the American, and saw no signs between 1923 and 1927 of the Japanese making the kind of all-out effort necessary to prepare for the "inevitable" showdown with the U.S. Japan's strongest point lay in its "absolutely outstanding" manpower, but Bräutigam refused to accept the commonly held view in Japan that men rather than weapons were decisive. "If the world war was a battle of technology," he argued, "this will be even more the case in any future conflict." He did not think such a conflict would come before 1937 and argued that the Japanese would have to make substantial improvements in their equipment, especially in the air arm, which he thought would play a significant, if not decisive, role in a future war. On current speculation about a Japanese knockout blow being launched at an American fleet on its way to the Far East, Bräutigam argued that the U.S. was unlikely to send a fleet or, at most, would be more likely to despatch older and more dispensable vessels, such as cruisers.[43]

The despatch of training cruisers to Japan was particularly important to the German Navy, for it offered good opportunities to display

---

ports in the autumn of 1933 that the first officer sent a letter of complaint back home implying that Bischoff might be a spy. Colonel Ott, who had just come back from Japan at the end of 1933, was asked for his opinion and confirmed that Bishoff had been behaving rather oddly. One reason for this was that his marriage was on the rocks; he subsequently was divorced.

[43] Most of Bräutigam's reports were conveyed by hand to the naval intelligence desks in Berlin or by statements made to cruiser captains. For the complete collection of these, see *Marine Archiv: Abteilung B-BU: Handakten Spindler: "Sammlung Japan," (1926-1929)*. Interestingly, Bräutigam's activity in Japan was raised by Soviet naval officers during the visit of Captain Spiess to Moscow in October 1932: *Marine Archiv: M II-1: "Auslands-Berichte," (1931-1933)*.

German equipment, to renew social and commercial links, and to
further acquaintance with known Germanophile officers. The visit of
the *Hamburg* in 1926, for example, offered Captain Groos the opportunity to make contact with Captain Viscount Inoue of the Naval Staff,
who then went to Berlin as Naval Attaché (1926 to 1929), Commander
Nomura Naokuni, Lieutenant Kojima Hideo (then serving on the
battleship *Nagato,* which was being fitted with Heinkel catapult planes),
and especially Admiral Katō Kanji. All these officers expressed their
hopes that technical co-operation between the two navies would become
closer again; Nomura gave indications of Japanese tactical and strategic views, while Katō went so far as to express the frank hope that
one day the next generation of officers in both navies would be fighting alongside each other to achieve victory against their common
enemies.[44]

Both Admirals Zenker and Raeder made efforts to persuade the
Foreign Ministry and the Reichstag to provide the means to implement
Foreign Minister Stresemann's agreement in principle, made in July
1927, to the re-introduction of naval attachés, but the economic climate
affecting the nation in the late 1920s was hardly conducive to expansion.[45] Admiral Raeder was keen to gain permanent professional
representatives in the capitals of the major naval powers, including
Japan. The best he could arrange as a stop-gap measure lay in promoting exchanges of officers for short periods. While the Army Command
remained in step with the Navy over this, it achieved a larger measure
of success—after much pressure—with the Japanese Army, which
accepted the secondment of Colonel Eugen Ott in 1933, than the Navy
did.[46] Although German technical specialists were allowed on board
warships, it was for specific purposes, and the Japanese Navy's passion
for 120 percent operational secrecy (as Admiral Nomura expressed
it in 1942) meant that acceptance of foreign officers on seagoing
warships would remain anathema. This proved to be the case right
up to the end of the war, when Grand-Admiral Dönitz suggested such
a scheme in late 1944.[47] What the Japanese Army and Navy did do,

---

[44] *Marineleitung/AIIc 512/26g* of October 22, 1926 to the Foreign Ministry enclosing a report by Captain Groos on the visit of the *Hamburg* to Japanese ports between
July 23 and August 19, 1926 in *Auswärtiges Amt: Abteilung IV Ostasien: Akte Po.2 Japan:
"Akten betreffend die politischen Beziehungen Japans zu Deutschland," Bd.3, (1924-1928).*
[45] For details, see *Auswärtiges Amt: Büro des Reichsministers: "Militärwesen," Bd.1,
(1920-1929).*
[46] *Der Reichswehrminister/T.A. Nr.1936/30 T3 III/Ia* of December 8, 1930 to the
Foreign Ministry in *Auswärtiges Amt: Abteilung IV Ostasien: Akte Po.13 Japan: "Militärische
Angelegenheiten Japans," Bd.2, (1927-1932).* Information about this and the proposal to
send a Navy officer on secondment to Japan was relayed by the Foreign Ministry to
the Foreign Policy Committee of the Reichstag in April 1931.
[47] See *M Att 1819/44* of December 14, 1944 to Tokyo, discussed between Dönitz

however, was to help create an atmosphere, through their resistance to budget cuts and disarmament in 1930 to 1932, for a much more sympathetic view to be adopted toward ending the manpower restrictions of the Versailles system, when these matters were raised at the Geneva Disarmament Conference of 1932. Domestic opposition to the military in Germany also changed, and when Admiral Raeder made a fresh submission in May 1932 for the re-introduction of naval attachés, it was accepted—with appropriate reservations—by the Foreign Ministry at the end of that year.[48]

Choosing Strategic Targets, 1933 to 1939
The choice as first German Naval Attaché to Japan since 1914 fell on Commander Paul Wenneker, a naval artillery specialist, whose excellent command of English owed much to his stay in a British prisoner-of-war camp following the loss of the *Mainz* at the Battle of the Dogger Bank on August 28, 1914. His departure for Tokyo was delayed until late 1933 through lack of space in the Tokyo Embassy. Ambassador Voretzsch, who was providing the space, was a diplomat of the old school who was hostile to the military in all countries, but especially those in Japan, which he diagnosed as suffering from a unique disease he termed *megalomania Japonica*. Nor was he more encouraging about the prospects for the new naval attaché to Tokyo when he made the following comment in his report to the Foreign Ministry in Berlin:

> It may interest the Defence Ministry to know that, so far as the assessment of the scale of business conducted by the naval attaché is concerned, we have been reliably informed through confidential conversations with other naval attachés, that, in view of the complete secrecy maintained by the Japanese about all matters of interest, the material accumulated by the attaché during his stay is likely to be practically nil.[49]

---

and Admiral Abe on December 13 and between Dönitz and Hitler on December 3. See source in n.1 above, but SRGL No. 1982, with German source in *O.K.M.; 1.Skl.: KTB Teil C XV: "Zusammenarbeit mit Japan," (1942-1944)*. Wenneker replied to an urgent reminder sent out again on January 5, 1945 by saying that he doubted if the Japanese Navy had ships available for such secondments. Admiral Abe gave a positive response on January 15, but on January 23 Wenneker argued:
> The answer conveyed by Admiral Abe is typically Japanese: it avoids a binding promise and means that the officers will get to see very little.
See SRGL Nos. 2221 and 2425.
    [48] See the memoranda *ML/AIc 1356/0 GKds* of August 25 and September 10, 1930; *M I 515/32 GKds* of March 1, 1932, *M I 330/33 GKds* of January 26, 1933, *M I 562/33 GKds* of February 7, 1933, and *M I 563/33 GKds* of February 7, 1933 in *Marine Archiv: M I: "Attache-, Verwaltungsund Personalangelegenheiten," (1930-1933)*.
    [49] Voretzsch (Toyko) J. No. 840 of March 20, 1933, a copy of which was not passed on to the Defence Ministry for fear it might cause offence according to Czibulinski minutes *zu I D 1676* of May 8, 1933. *Auswärtiges Amt: Abteilung IV Ostasien: Akte Po.10,*

Fortunately for Wenneker, Voretzsch was replaced in December 1933 by Herbert von Dirksen, whose relations with his attachés proved to be far more positive. Fortunately too, Wenneker was a likeable and sociable man who quickly made many friends in the diplomatic community, and never let slip the opportunity to speak highly and in public of the role of the Navy in Japanese society.[50] Although his Japanese language ability was to remain rather limited, he won respect from the Japanese Navy authorities and made close friendships with the many middle-ranking officers he regularly came into contact with during his first tour in Tokyo from December 1933 to July 1937. But this applied more particularly to those Japanese officers who had served already in Germany, and applied particularly to such officers as Rear-Admiral Nomura Naokuni, Commander Maeda, in charge of the German section in the Naval Intelligence Division, and Commander Kojima, who served as second adjutant to Navy Minister Osumi before being sent to Berlin at the end of 1936. Wenneker also made friends with Captain Sekine, who was the Navy Ministry's press spokesman, and who was to prove a useful contact when Wenneker returned to Tokyo in 1940, as he had retired from the Navy and was employed by a publishing firm which provided valuable outlets for German propaganda following the German victories in Europe.

During this first tour, Wenneker was instrumental in organizing a number of technical missions, the most successful of which was the one in the autumn of 1935 when a three-man team was allowed to inspect and study the construction of the Japanese aircraft carrier *Akagi*. This was of direct value to current German plans to build their own aircraft-carrier, the *Graf Zeppelin*, which, however, was never completed.[51] At this time, Wenneker met Navy Minister Osumi, and

---

Nr.2: *"Marine-Attachés in Japan,"* (*1926-1933*). Prior to his departure for Tokyo via the Trans-Siberian Railway, Commander Wenneker was briefed by State-Secretary von Bülow of the Foreign Ministry, in early October 1933: see minute *e.o. IIF 3351* of October 10, 1933 in *Auswärtiges Amt: Abt. II F-M: G.A.: "Militar-Attaché Moskau," Bd.1,* (*1933-1934*).

[50] I am indebted for their memories and reminiscences of Admiral Paul Wenneker and Vice-Admiral Joachim Lietzmann to Frau Irma Wenneker, Herr Ulrich Wenneker, Fraulein Ingeborg Krag, Captain Werner Vermehren, Frau Inge Lietzmann-Holland, Rear-Admirals Helmut Neuss and George Ross, General and Frau Matzky and the late Major-General Alfred Kretschmer, as well as the former German Journalist, Werner Crome, who at various times kindly agreed to answer questions by interview or correspondence. There is a brief view of Admiral Wenneker in an oral history interview given by Captain Henri Smiths-Hutton USN (Retd.) in the U.S. Navy Operational History Archives, together with three separate statements taken by U.S. officers from Admiral Wenneker between 1946 and 1948. The author is grateful to Dr. Dean Allard and Mrs. J. Koontz for their assistance.

[51] Commander Wenneker visited the carrier *Akagi* at the end of January 1935 and provided several reports on air force organization in the Japanese Navy in response

then Admiral Nagano, the chief Navy delegate to the London Naval Conference, prior to the latter's departure via Moscow and Berlin for London, and correctly indicated to him that the Japanese delegation would not be in a position to move a single hair's breadth in the direction of a compromise with the Anglo-American Powers over naval arms limitation.[52] When Nagano returned to Japan in the spring of 1936, he was appointed Navy Minister in the Hirota Cabinet, allowing Wenneker unusually ready permission to undertake extensive tours of Japanese Navy yards, bases, and warships, tours on a scale that went far beyond anything accorded to any other naval attaché in Japan at this time. From conversations with officers of the fleet, Wenneker learned a great deal about the background to the February Incident and about the initiatives being taken by the Navy Ministry for a dramatic expansion in the capabilities of the fleet.[53] Most of all, he received ample confirmation of the Navy's decisive opposition to the plans of factions in the Japanese Army for an early showdown with the Soviet Union, and also of its own drive for southward expansion. He learned that the Navy intended to concentrate on Britain in place of the United States as its primary future target, and confirmed his own findings

---

to questionnaires from Berlin. Proposals for exchanges of technical and tactical data were put forward early in June 1935 and the Roth-Czech-Ohlerich commission left for Japan via the U.S.A. in September, returning home at the end of December 1935. See *Marine Archiv: M Att: "Attaché-Berichte Tokio 1935"; O.K.M.: 1.Skl.: "Berichterstattung der Deutschen Japan-Kommission," (1935);* and *Auswärtiges Amt: Abteilung II F Luft: Akte Lu OA: "Luftverkehr Ostasien," Bd.6, (1934-1936).* Following the loss of four fleet carriers at the Battle of Midway in June 1942, the Japanese Navy made enquiries about the purchase of the *Graf Zeppelin,* but was told that it was needed for German use and that it would be impossible for it to be sailed to the Far East. Shortly after, negotiations were begun for the sale of the German liner *Scharnhorst,* which had been laid up in Japan since the outbreak of war, and it was subsequently converted into a Japanese aircraft-carrier.

[52] Wenneker (Tokyo) *B. Nr. 168/35g* of November 21, 1935 indicated that there had been no change in the Japanese opposition to ratios, and Nagano thought that the British government would seek to put the blame for the inevitable breakdown of the Conference on other countries. The British and U.S. Naval Attachés, with whom Wenneker was on friendly terms, had also indicated no concessions to the Japanese position. *Marine Archiv: M Att: "Attaché-Berichte Tokio 1935".*

[53] Wenneker indicated that the British and U.S. attachés had instructions to buy information about the Japanese building programmes "at any price." Admiral Ross has indicated to the author that he and Wenneker swapped reports about the Japanese Navy with each other, and Ross was amazed that the German Navy's compilation on the Japanese fleet was as large as it was. Wenneker claimed to have photographed a lengthy report on the development of Anglo-Japanese naval relations since World War I that Captain Vivian had compiled for the Admiralty prior to his departure for home. One of the most prominent mistakes in the report about the effectiveness of the Japanese Navy, according to Wenneker, was the low rating given to the Japanese Naval Air Force. See *M Att GKdos 207/35* of June 21, 1935 in: *O.K.M.: M-IV: "Attaché-und Auslandsangelegenheiten," Bd.1, (1934-1936),* pp. 211-34.

of a year before that the Japanese Navy entertained high hopes about the expansion of the German fleet and about the emergence of the German-Italian Axis because of the threat this could pose to British naval forces in the Atlantic and the Mediterranean, thus reducing the likelihood of British intervention in East Asia.[54]

In May 1936, all the German armed services produced staff studies of Japan as a military factor in world politics for War Minister von Blomberg, which were set in a context of Hitler's interest in proposals for a joint German-Japanese initiative against the U.S.S.R. These studies identified China as the country most immediately threatened by Japanese expansionism, but also recognized that this would affect the interests of Britain, the U.S., the U.S.S.R., and even of Germany, which was then supplying the Chinese with arms in exchange for strategic materials. It was argued that such a situation would lead to an encirclement of Japan and that an Anglo-American blockade could be instituted, which would fatally affect Japan's overseas sources of supply and access to foreign markets. The German Navy High Command estimated that such a prospect would ensure that no decisive offensive would be undertaken by Japan against the major naval powers in the near future, while the Army General Staff warned:

> In no case does it appear likely that a Russo-Japanese war should have a decisive effect on the power-political position of the Soviet Union in Europe, but rather it would bring any European ally of Japan into serious conflict with England and America.[55]

Following the signing of the Anti-Comintern Pact in November 1936, for which the Japanese Navy showed little outward enthusiasm, attempts were made by General Ōshima to persuade the War Ministry to enter into secret staff agreements against the Soviet Union. A parallel *démarche* was made by Captain Kojima to the German Navy in May 1937, which proposed an exchange of intelligence about various foreign navies, as well as a continuation of the exchange of tactical and technical data resumed in 1935.[56] While these proposals were being

---

[54] Cf. Chapman, *The Price of Admiralty*, I, xii ff., and see Wenneker *B.Nr.G 157* of September 4, 1935: source as n.52 above.

[55] Each of the three German services produced separate assessments of Japan's power-political position in the Far East in May 1936, and these were summarized by Colonel Scheller of the Foreign Section for submission to von Blomberg, Keitel, and Jodl prior to their likely discussion with Hitler. See *Reichskriegsministerium: Wehrmachtsamt: Abteilung Ausland: Akte Stein: "Geheime Kommandosachen — Japan und Sonstiges," (1936-1938)*.

[56] *OKM/M I 88 GKdos* of May 11, 1937 to War Ministry indicated that initially it was a personal initiative by Kojima, but a cable was received from Wenneker shortly before his departure to the effect that this had the support of the Navy Ministry. This was confirmed in Kiderlen minute *M 2210* of June 28, 1937. *O.K.M.: 1.Skl.Ic.: "Marinepolitische Angelegenheiten," Bd.1, (1929-1940)*, pp. 89-95.

discussed internally in Berlin, the war in China broke out and in August the Japanese Navy launched a repeat attack on Shanghai. These events coincided with the departure of Captain Wenneker for home. Consequently there was no German Navy representative in Japan at the time who could interpret the significance of the Japanese Navy's strategy on the basis of constant personal contact with Japanese staff officers. The new German Naval Attaché, Captain Joachim Lietzmann, did not arrive in Japan until the end of September 1937.[57] This meant that senior officers in Berlin had no very clear perspective on the situation, and were more influenced at this time by the ramifications for Sino-German relations and their relevance for differences of opinion arising over these among Göring, Hitler, and von Blomberg, which came to a head in early 1938.

The opinion of the technical departments in the German Navy about renewed collaboration with the Japanese was that they fully expected a one-way flow of German technology to Japan, and Grand-Admiral Raeder was asked to consider if the political and strategic benefits that might accrue to Germany would provide an adequate compensation in return. Raeder then saw Captain Kojima personally on August 27 to tell him that the German Navy was ready to exchange technical for tactical information on a case-by-case basis. The War Ministry approved an informal exchange of intelligence about the Soviet Navy, but shied away from a commitment to extend this to other navies.[58] Captain Lietzmann had a difficult task to perform in Tokyo trying to explain away evidence of the supply of German arms and equipment to China in spite of repeated German assurances to the contrary. Lietzmann's conversations with staff and front-line officers in Japan, however, made it clear that resentment against Germany, on the part of the Navy at least, was much less than resentment against

---

[57] Lietzmann had been taken prisoner at the Battle of the Falkland Islands in 1914 and spent the war in Britain. He was on Admiral Raeder's staff from 1931 to 1933, then went as Naval Attaché to Paris (and Madrid) until 1937, when he was particularly involved on the intelligence side. On returning home in 1940 he became chief of staff to Admiral Schuster, who became Admiral Commanding in the Low Countries, then France, after the occupation. In 1942 to 1943 Lietzmann was in command of the training fleet, with his flag in the cruiser *Leipzig,* until relieved on grounds of ill health, according to his statements to U.S. interrogators. However, he spent the rest of the war in the Adriatic and the Balkans, which he appears not to have wanted to talk much about, for he subsequently made his way over the Alps to Italy and went off to Argentina for a number of years. He returned to Germany and died at Hamelin in 1959. Lietzmann statements and correspondence: See n.50 above.

[58] *OKM/AIII 3186/37 gKdos* of July 14 suggested that there was no pressure on the German side for the conclusion of an agreement about an exchange of intelligence. Admiral Witzell stated on August 2 that Germany would be a unilateral donor in a technical exchange and urged Raeder to weigh carefully the question of whether political and strategic benefits would outweigh this. Ibid., pp. 96-98.

Britain, which was repeatedly accused of being the main obstacle in the way of persuading the Kuomintang government to make peace on Japanese terms.[59]

The crisis in the Far East deepened and encouraged Hitler to seize the opportunity to take the initiative against Austria and Czechoslovakia, thus posing the Western Powers with a major strategic dilemma of global proportions. The Japanese Army and the Nazi leaders were keen to follow up their separate successes with the formation of a triple alliance against Britain, France, and the Soviet Union, but the Japanese Navy adamantly refused to be drawn into an open-ended commitment to fight both the Western Powers and the U.S.S.R. simultaneously. Apart from the need to make the necessary preparations for war, the Japanese Navy was conscious of the desirability of bringing the war in China to an end, as well as of the vulnerability of the Japanese economy to American pressures, the first serious signs of which appeared with the denunciation of their trade treaty in July 1939. The prominence of the Japanese Army in Japanese policy making and the admiration of Hitler and Ribbentrop for General Ōshima heavily obscured, up to this point, the decisive character of the Japanese Navy's influence in foreign policy. Try as they might to shift the Japanese Navy from its opposition to an immediate alliance, the German Navy's efforts proved of no avail. Thinking that Captain Lietzmann did not have sufficient rank or influence, efforts were made to make use of Admiral Förster, a former German fleet commander, to make representations in Tokyo; but his efforts were no more successful than any of the repeated meetings held in Berlin with Rear-Admiral Endō, where Admiral Canaris, Captain Fricke, Captain Burkner, and Göring attempted to apply continual pressure.[60]

---

[59] Cf. Chapman, *The Price of Admiralty*, I, xxii ff.

[60] A written agreement for the exchange of intelligence about the USSR was signed by Kojima on July 7, 1938 and this was extended to France and Britain by Commander Menzel of the Secret Military Intelligence Service in Tokyo in April 1939. At the time of the Munich Crisis, Raeder had planned to go ahead with staff talks for Japanese and Italian support of Germany if it were to be involved in war on its own, but the Berchtesgaden talks intervened and Ribbentrop stepped in in October 1938 with his plans for the triple alliance. Admiral Förster agreed to stay on in Japan in June 1939, and Ribbentrop seems to have asked Raeder to consider transferring Wenneker back to Tokyo in order to put more pressure on the Japanese Navy. See Bürkner memorandum *OKW/Ausl.III Org Nr.726/39 gKdos* of August 2, 1939 on a conversation with Admiral Endō. A telling report by Colonel Matzky *B.Nr.31/39 gKdos* of July 3, 1939 was shown to Ribbentrop and Hitler, who seem to have been influenced by his statement that the Japanese Army could live without an alliance and would not welcome being dragged into a war for which it was unready.

The Failure of Deterrence

When the stalemate was eventually broken by the announcement of the Soviet-German pact in August 1939, there was a loud outcry from the Japanese Army and Foreign Ministry, not least because of the opportunity it provided for Stalin to smash the Japanese forces threatening allied Outer Mongolia. From the Japanese Navy's point of view, however, the situation that arose was seen as vindicating its long-held opposition to war with the Soviet Union and the Stalin-Hitler *rapprochement* opened up the possibility of German mediation between Japan and the Soviet Union. The idea of security in the rear was seen by the Japanese Navy as a fundamental prerequisite for launching any southward offensive, especially if, as seemed increasingly likely, there was a serious risk of U.S. intervention in Asia. Admiral Nomura Naokuni and other officers sympathetic to Germany made several unofficial approaches to Captain Lietzmann in the winter of 1939 to urge Berlin to try to persuade Stalin to reach an accommodation with Japan, and to encourage a shift in Soviet interests toward India and the Middle East against Britain.[61] Japanese expansionism in Asia, combined with the German Navy's strategy of seeking to cut Britain and France off from their external sources of supply, raised the danger of U.S. intervention in the war both in Europe and the Far East, which Raeder and Hitler did not want to see come about. Hitler's whole strategy lay in being able to launch a sudden major offensive in the West, to bring about a Western collapse and prevent the possibility of a shift to a war of attrition involving the United States. A parallel dilemma faced the Japanese Navy, which was made particularly aware of such a prospect in January 1940, when the trade treaty lapsed and the British had the temerity to underline the threat by stopping the Japanese liner, *Asama Maru*, just off the Japanese coast.[62]

It was at this point that Grand-Admiral Raeder summoned Rear-Admiral Wenneker from his successful captaincy of the armoured cruiser *Deutschland* to go back to Japan for a second tour as Naval Attaché. Wenneker's most important instructions were to impress on as many high-ranking Japanese officers as he could the vital importance of keeping the United States out of the war. These plans, however, were gravely undermined by the fact that the subsequent German victories in the West, colossal and astounding as they were, remained incomplete so long as Britain remained in the war. They also greatly alarmed the United States (as well as the Soviet Union) without eliminating the strategic possibilities open to either of them to intervene if they wished. Hitler's gestures to a defeated France and his offer of

---

[61] See Chapman, *The Price of Admiralty*, I, 15-16, 18-19, 23-25.
[62] Chapman, *The Price of Admiralty*, p. 82 ff.

peace to Britain in July failed to make up for the incomplete nature of the German military successes.[63] The reaction of the Japanese Navy to the German victories was also to have a crucial importance: Japanese observers concluded that, if Germany with a fleet only one-tenth the size of Britain's but with a strong air force, could repel a British landing in Norway, then how much more could the vastly stronger Japanese fleet accomplish even against Britain and the United States combined. Although senior officers were less carried away by such a prospect than were the middle-ranking and junior officers, they could not hold out for long, a second time, against national pressure to exploit the situation in Europe by moving into the power vacuum created in South-east Asia. In principle, the Tripartite Pact was seen as a gesture in favour of the new world order. But while some continued to argue that it would help deter U.S. entry into the war, others demanded immediate and decisive intervention against the West European Colonial Powers. In other words, the leading admirals in Japan dithered and were unable to come to a clear agreement about an offensive or defensive strategy against the U.S. in 1940.

Three moves by the German authorities helped the Japanese Navy resolve many of its dilemmas: Firstly, the capture of British Cabinet papers by the German armed merchant cruiser *Atlantis,* in the Indian Ocean, revealed for all to see that Britain had practically no forces to spare for the defence of Singapore. Copies of these papers were handed over to the Japanese Naval Staff by Wenneker on December 12, 1940, and these helped the Naval Staff and Combined Fleet to initiate planning for war against the United States as the sole significant opponent rather than against both powers, as in the past.[64] Secondly, Admiral Wenneker established good working relations with his Soviet colleagues in Tokyo, and this helped prepare the way for the various slow stages in the Soviet-Japanese *rapprochement* which culminated in the Neutrality Treaty of April 1941. The important third step was the despatch of the Japanese Naval Mission to Europe because this made it possible for full information about German (and Italian) experience in the conduct of war since September 1939 to be passed on to the Japanese Navy. Explanations by Japanese naval officers in Tokyo and Berlin,

---

[63] Captain Kojima stated to Wenneker that Japanese moves against French Indo-China would be seen as a particularly crucial test of Anglo-American reactions on June 25, 1940, and remarked on the following day on the mild nature of the terms for the French armistice. Chapman, *The Price of Admiralty,* p. 158.

[64] Cabinet papers intended for Duff Cooper at Singapore were taken from the SS *Automedon* by the *Atlantis* and brought to Japan. Vice-Admiral Kondo stated that no one in the Japanese Navy had surmized from external appearances that British defences east of Suez were in such a parlous state. Work on the Pearl Harbor plan began within weeks of the receipt of this material in Tokyo. Chapman, *The Price of Admiralty,* Vol. II, entry for December 12, 1940.

however, made it clear to Hitler that the security it would offer to the Japanese rear would be an additional argument in favour of launching the attack on the Soviet Union. The unleashing of Operation Barbarossa, about which Ambassador Ōshima was briefed on June 6, was of the greatest importance in impelling the Japanese Navy to abandon the cautious reserve that had overtaken its leaders after the British defeat of the Italians in North Africa in December 1940. Despite the obligation to render automatic assistance to German forces if these were attacked by the United States, Japanese Navy spokesmen left Admiral Wenneker in no doubt that an attack on the U.S. would be launched at their moment of choosing and not that of their ally. From the statements of Admiral Nomura in Berlin to Admirals Groos and Raeder, the Japanese Navy appeared to have adopted a wait-and-see attitude which was predicated on the possibility of an attack on the British Isles. This, it was claimed, would be the signal to advance on Singapore. If it came to a fight with the United States, which the Japanese Navy seemed not too keen on beginning unless this was forced upon them, members of the Nomura Mission made it very clear that Japan would be in a position to maintain the offensive only for about six months and, after that, expected Japan to be hit hard by Anglo-American forces employing blockade methods.[65] This point was reiterated to Wenneker in Tokyo by Vice-Admiral Kondō Nobutake, the Vice-Chief of Naval Staff and the most important high-level contact in Wenneker's second tour of duty thus far, who confirmed that it would be too dangerous to bypass the Philippines in order to attack Singapore, because these lay across Japan's north-south lines of communication, which could then be cut by U.S. submarines, aircraft, and cruisers. Kondō concluded that "Japan is still as dependent as ever on America for the supply of vital raw materials. Even if the area controlled from Singapore were to be added, supplies obtained from the East Asian area would be by no means adequate for complete self-reliance."[66]

The decision to move into southern Indo-China was taken in the wake of the German attack on the Soviet Union and, according to Admiral Wenneker, it was not seen in advance as likely to cause the sharp reaction it did in Washington. The U.S. decision to introduce a complete embargo on trade with Japan followed a freeze on German

[65] See *OKM/1.Skl.I op 335/41 Chefs* of March 17, 1941, Enclosure 3, source as in n.26 above. See also Wenneker-Takada discussion in which Takada expressed the view that his superiors would have to look at the specific circumstances of a German-American *casus belli* and make their own decision regardless of the treaty position, which called for immediate declaration of war. See Chapman, *The Price of Admiralty*, Vol. II, entry for June 10, 1941.

[66] Wenneker, *B.Nr.279/41 gKdos* of April 17, 1941 in *O.K.M.: M Att: "Japan-Mobilmachung," Bd.IV, (1941)*.

and Italian assets, which had evoked no response, while the Japanese move into southern Indo-China also followed a British move into French-controlled Syria and Lebanon. But it was undoubtedly this complete embargo that pushed the Japanese Navy into a corner from which no amount of negotiation could extricate it honourably. The long-drawn-out talks in Washington, and the apparent willingness of the Japanese negotiators to discuss such issues as withdrawal from the alliance with Germany, only served to deceive Secretary Hull, who was astounded to learn from intercepted cables about the Japanese initiative in Berlin stipulating the signing of an agreement not to enter into a separate peace with the Western Powers.[67] Had there not been a sense of lull in the second half of 1941, perhaps Britain and the U.S. might have been less generous toward the Soviet Union and employed these arms and equipment to improve Allied readiness in the Pacific against Japan.

Parallel Lines to Infinity, 1942 to 1945
The incomplete result of German operations in the East, contrary to Hitler's own initial expectations, was already evident to Japanese decision-makers by September or October 1941. The savage nature of the Soviet winter counter-offensive and British pressure in Cyrenaica made Hitler and Mussolini react to the unexpected attack on Pearl Harbor and in South-east Asia with a feeling that the Japanese contribution to their strategic relief was long overdue. Strategic surprise attacks undoubtedly provided considerable short-term benefits to all the Axis powers, but the signs of a lack of Japanese in-depth capabilities were already being reported back to Berlin from Tokyo and Bangkok within days of the attack on Pearl Harbor. What was noted immediately was the failure to catch U.S. carrier task forces at Hawaii and the Japanese shortage of shipping space became increasingly evident as Allied attacks on Japanese lines of communication began to bite. By the early summer of 1942, Admiral Wenneker was evidently appalled, during a trip to the conquered areas, to find Japanese forces were living off the fat of the land, apparently oblivious to the previous predictions by senior officers of the likelihood of tough battles to come in an Allied counter-offensive. Even without the U.S. victory at Midway, Admiral Wenneker was providing Berlin with evidence that the Japanese Navy was suffering, in early September 1942, from a severe shortage of tanker space and giving priority in the supply of oil to convoy escorts rather than to offensive naval operations.[68]

---

[67] The agreement was signed on December 11, 1941, but the drafts were sent to Ōshima by cable in late November and these were intercepted by "Magic."
[68] Wenneker cypher *Tel. Nr.2683/42 g.Kdos* of December 17, 1942, source as n.15 above, but *Bd.2, (1942-1944)*.

The underestimation of the enemy also extended to the planners in the Combined Fleet, who paid no serious attention to pleas by Raeder and Ribbentrop to make the Indian Ocean rather than the Pacific the principal area of Japanese fleet operations. In the strike against Midway, it was assumed that surprise would be a pre-condition of the attack, when in fact U.S. direction-finding, radar, and cryptanalytical systems were now operational in a way that had not been the case in December 1941.[69] From the spring of 1942, Allied decipherment of Axis operational signals was beginning to give the Allied Powers a more or less complete picture of the offensive preparations being made, right down to the courses being steamed by individual vessels. The Japanese Navy was rightly proud of its own tight security and believed it would be impossible for the enemy to decipher its main fleet code system. Without knowing it, however, the German Navy actually held the key to knowledge about Allied successes in the decipherment and recognition of Japanese fleet signals weeks before what turned out to be the crucial battle at Midway. Already in April 1941, the German Navy had pointed out to the Nomura Mission the vital importance of radio traffic analysis and decipherment, but had given the Japanese only limited information about the scale and scope of German successes in this field, as it was known that Japanese diplomatic codes at least were being resolved by the Allies since at least that date. On May 10, 1942, the German raider *Thor* captured the Australian steamer *Nankin* on passage from Sydney to Colombo. On board were large amounts of official mail, including material from Combined Headquarters at Wellington to the British C-in-C at Colombo, from which it was deduced that the Allies had made significant inroads into the Japanese Navy's communication systems. This stirred the Japanese Navy into tightening up its security arrangements, but unfortunately for the Japanese Navy, the correspondence in question was not examined by them until the end of August 1942, long after the decisive defeat had been delivered.[70] It is futile, though nevertheless tempting, to speculate on what

[69] There is a brief account of the role of cryptanalysis in the Midway campaign in H.F. Schorrek, "The Role of COMINT in the Battle of Midway," in National Archives, Washington, D.C., Record Group 457, Records of the NSA, File SRH-20. The account of events given by Commander J.J. Rochefort, USN in 1969 in the Oral History Collection, U.S. Navy Operational Archives, Washington, D.C. is rather more instructive and first-hand in character.

[70] Intercepted British signals were being relayed via Admiral Wenneker from Berlin for relay to the Japanese Naval Staff, and on June 17, 1942 the Japanese indication that they had found these signals valuable for operations in the Indian Ocean were intercepted and deciphered by Ultra. The *Nankin* reached Batavia on June 25 and was ordered to sail on to Yokohama, but did not arrive in Japan until late July. Although the Japanese Navy made enquiries about captured British merchant naval codes on August 9, they were not shown any captured mail or war diaries until the end

the outcome of that battle and the Pacific War would have been if such a prior warning had been received.

One of the major reasons for this significant failure in operational co-operation between the German and Japanese navies lay in the refusal of the Japanese authorities to permit Admiral Wenneker the right to make direct radio signals from the Embassy in Japan either to Europe or to German ships at sea on offensive or blockade-running missions. In the summer of 1941, the Japanese authorities had monitored such transmissions and demanded that they stop soon after the outbreak of war in December. They insisted that all German transmissions be sent via Japanese cable or radio stations, even though these had already proved to be inadequate, technically and in terms of load, in peace-time. Admiral Wenneker and German ships received permission to begin transmissions between Batavia and Tokyo only in September 1942, and failure to sort out these basic problems of communication (which had been identified on the German side at least as early as the spring of 1939) meant that the initiative that the German side had conferred on Axis policies as a whole up to 1941 was rapidly squandered by a basic inability to work together rapidly enough to stay ahead of the enemy. Especially in the light of their own victories, the Japanese rather resented having to accept assistance from their European allies and were far from happy about allowing German naval operations across the boundaries in the separate war zones allocated under the Axis Military Agreement of January 1942. The clear inability of the Japanese forces to deal with operational demands in the Indian Ocean in addition to coping with the U.S. counter-offensive finally led to their agreement, at the end of 1942, to German proposals for the use of Japanese bases in South-east Asia for U-boat operations.[71] Local German commanding officers found that they had to address all their requests to the Army headquarters at Singapore via representatives of the Japanese Navy, which meant that they were ineluctably drawn into well-known and ubiquitous Japanese inter-service rivalries. But even if no such difficulties had existed, we know

---

of August. On September 2 they indicated to Admiral Wenneker that information from mail to Colombo suggested that the enemy had been able to locate the movements of the Japanese fleet and that their own communications were not sufficiently secure. Only then did the two navies exchange notes about communications security and an agreement about communications was reached on December 16, 1942. Despite this, the German side continued to complain about difficulties in the Japanese-controlled radio services in traffic from Tokyo to both Europe and South-east Asia. Source as n.1 above.

[71] Admiral Wenneker was granted permission to relay cypher signals to ships in South-east Asia via the Japanese Navy radio stations in Tokyo and Batavia for three brief periods a day only on September 4, 1942 for the first time, source as n.1 above, SRGL 0520.

that from the end of 1943 all the operations of the Monsoon Group of German submarines were being closely monitored by Allied crypt-analytical agencies right up to the end of the war in Europe. As a member of Admiral King's staff commented after the war on the forces operating under Admiral Wenneker's overall control, "the plan was good and could have amounted to something if we hadn't been able to thwart it."[72]

CONCLUSIONS

The Cultural Impact

Influence can rarely be exerted overnight. It is more likely to be effective if it operates against a broader cultural background, similarity of ways of thinking or of implementation of ideas, and elements of shared values. We can demonstrate that, although these strata were laid down in the closing decades of the 19th century, German cultural influence was still strong in Japanese society. The two societies entered the so-called "stream of development" at about the same time, and both the Second and the Third Reich stressed the idea of Germany and Japan being young and vigorous nations, eager to compete with the managers of the status quo. The idea of some kind of international combination to counter the influence of the "Anglo-Saxons" and perhaps even overthrow it was bandied about before World War I in Germany, Japan, China, and even in France and Russia before the alliance systems rigidified. It had some support in the geopolitical ideas of the Haus-hofers, and in those countries which felt humiliated in the post–1919 peace settlements, especially Germany, China, and the Soviet Union. But individuals in Japan, such as Count Gotō Shumpei and Tōgō Shigenori, were responsive to such ideas, even though they could hardly be said to represent any mainstream political views in the 1920s. However, German cultural influences and contacts in Japanese academic and professional circles were renewed in the inter-war period, not least because during World War I there had not been the kind of bitterness and slaughter in East Asia that had marked intra-European relationships: German residents in Japan had not been interned nor was their property sequestered.

It was only after the war and a recognition of Japan's need to avoid isolation that the Japanese joined in the heaping of obloquy on German misdeeds and guilt, and the notion of "militarism" was denounced as a German characteristic and its manifestations in Japa-

---

[72] See signal by U.S. Navy C-in-C, Admiral King, of January 29, 1945 to C-in-C Pacific in File SRH-32 in National Archives, Washington, D.C., Record Group 457, Records of the NSA; and comment by Captain Smiths-Hutton, on Admiral King's staff, source as n.50 above.

nese society were likewise condemned. But the fact remained that so many of Japan's structural and constitutional arrangements had been modelled on the Bismarckean system and their maintenance was greatly affected by the legal and administrative ideas and institutions that underpinned the workings of the state in both societies. In both societies, a form of "white" revolution by a reforming, conservative elite had imposed order on a patchwork quilt of principalities and fief-doms, though the Japanese oligarchs adopted a much more radical, unitary state system than the federalist formula of the Prussian state. The Prussian state, on the other hand, already had something of a head start in terms of industrial and technological development, but both societies continued to be predominantly agrarian in character until World War I in the German case and until World War II in Japan's case. With mainly U.S. support, Japan's general level of technological development caught up with the rest of the industrialized world in the 1960s and 1970s, but until World War II the tendency was for the Japanese level to be about a generation behind the German.

Military Organization
Unlike the Anglo-American states, which have tended to favour a system of voluntary military recruitment wherever possible, Japan imposed a system of conscription comparable to that prevailing in the European continent. The bulk of conscripts went into the Army, whereas the Navy could usually pick and choose its recruits, though both services saw their task as one of education and training geared to lifetime loyalty and commitment to the prevailing social order. The Army was particularly linked to the rural social order and the officers and the N.C.O.'s reflected this as much as the conscripts, whereas the Navy was the more explicitly technological service, the more cosmopolitan and commercial in orientation, much as in Germany. The system of "dual control" applied to both Japanese services, much as in Imperial Germany, where there was substantial inter-service rivalry, too. Whereas in Germany this was considerably dampened down by the severe cuts in the Weimar Navy and assumed a tripartite character after 1933, the absence of a separate air force until the 1950s helps to emphasize and maintain the strong traditional inter-service rivalry in the dualist Japanese system up to 1945.[73] In some ways, therefore, the German system continued to function in Japan after it had been modified, or largely eliminated, in republican Germany, but these differences subsequently made it much more difficult to cope with when the two countries came into closer military relations with each other in the Nazi period.

---

[73] Cf. J.W.M. Chapman, I.T.M. Gow and R. Drifte, *Japan's Quest for Comprehensive Security* (New York: St. Martin's Press, 1983) for a discussion of this and other aspects of post-war Japanese security policy.

One of the major differences that emerged was the strong tendency towards civilian control of the armed forces under Hitler and away from the junta-like tendencies that had predominated during World War I and threatened to predominate once again in the years before 1933. What helped prevent this was the German Army's overthrow of the Social Democratic Party's control of Prussia in 1932 and the transfer of power to Göring and the Nazi Party, which then disposed of the resources of the most powerful German *Land* as its springboard to national power on January 30, 1933. But it enabled the Air Force to occupy a special position in German defence planning and organization which had no counterpart in Japan until the establishment of the Air Self-Defence Force in the 1950s. Until 1933 aviation in Germany had been suppressed by active control measures on the part of the Entente Powers, with separate military aviation elements in the Army and Navy, as in Japan, as well as within the civilian Ministry of Transport. All three parent bodies either condoned or supported ventures by German aircraft manufacturers, particularly Junkers, to set up military aircraft production and testing abroad.[74]

Technological Influence
The involvement of most of the leading German aircraft designers with the Japanese armed forces in often overlooked because its economic scale was so much more modest than in many other countries, and this tended to underrate its technological impact. A major contribution to Japanese interest in aero-technology came from the serious interruption to economic development with the impact of the 1923 earthquake, which came on top of the need to adjust to new patterns of international trade and to cut back on defence. The aircraft came to be seen as the most versatile weapons system with the kind of potential that was inspiring to countries which sought to forge weapons to fight against seemingly overwhelming odds. They were also comparatively cheap and easy to construct, especially by comparison with large capital ships, where very long lead times were critical in catching up with superior opponents. It was in these circumstances that the Japanese Navy's technological priorities came to be influenced away from the traditional gun-based offensive platforms and from the submarine-based counter-blockade strategy to the task force concept with the aircraft-carrier as the core offensive weapons system. The attempt of Behncke and Tirpitz to promote a German "school" of thinking and base of technological co-operation within the Japanese

---

[74] Junkers was supplying military aircraft to Turkey as early as 1919, and to Russia from 1922, despite the attempts of the Entente Powers to inhibit them. See *Auswärtiges Amt: Abt. II-Luft: "Junkers Flugzeugewerke," 8 Bd. (1920-1936)* and *G.A.: Abt.IV Russland, Handakten: "Junkers," (1926-1927)*.

Navy undoubtedly had some effect in the early 1920s because it built on an existing structure slowly nurtured since the late 1870s that prevented total Anglo-American domination of the Japanese naval officer corps.

After 1923, German avionics were incorporated in numerous applications of air capabilities to the Japanese Navy: initially, the use of aircraft in large ocean-going submarines, which had been incorporated in German U-boat experiments in the closing stages of the war against the United States; then the adoption of catapult aircraft on battleships and cruisers; and finally the ideas incorporated in the torpedo-, minelaying-, and the dive-bombing aircraft first developed by Heinkel and Junkers. But the central concept remained the aircraft-carrier; its origins and development were Anglo-American ideas which were passed on to the Japanese Navy initially by Britain in 1922-23. The German Air Force supplied the Japanese with the plans of the Ju-86 dive-bomber in 1935-36 in return for Japanese help with German carrier construction and development, but it was the one major area where both the German Navy and Air Force signally failed to have any significant influence over the Japanese Navy. It was also one of many areas of failure in co-operation between the German Navy and Air Force that were to have considerable importance for the outcome of World War II in Europe.

The German aircraft industry's approach to the transfer of its technology was very much more dynamic than that of the shipbuilding industry or the German Navy as a whole, which was negative and niggardly after 1924. The Behncke approach was flatly rejected by Admiral Zenker because it appeared to him to involve a completely one-sided handing over of German technology with little tangible to be received in return, especially in the short-term. Admiral Raeder, too, consistently demanded reciprocity on a case-by-case basis. When Captain Nomura Naokuni was Naval Attaché in Berlin, Raeder complained about the Japanese Navy failing to answer German counter-questions and Nomura "visibly responded." This seemed to suggest that this approach was the most appropriate to take with the Japanese. But, again, a lot of Japanese purchases at this period appear to have been from the German aviation industry and the revival of the technical exchange between the two navies in the mid-1930s stemmed from the initiatives of the Air Ministry rather than the Navy.[75] When Captain Kojima, who had been involved in the fitting of Heinkel aircraft

---

[75] See Bürkner minute *B.Nr. M I 54/35 gKdos* of February 14, 1935. The Construction Department did not regard despatch of an expert as urgent, but the chief of staff, Admiral Guse, supported the despatch of a naval flying officer, Commander Czech. Source as n.38 above, pp. 347-48.

on the battleship *Nagato* in 1925, suggested the continuation of the tactical and technical exchange in 1937, it was met by the all-too-familiar European assumption that the Japanese had nothing to offer of value to the Germans and that it would be a one-way traffic. When aircraft-carrier technology was made available to the German Navy, Japanese officers tried to emphasize how unjust such prejudices were by underlining the fact that something substantial was being offered to the German Navy. It was rather a case of looking a gift horse in the mouth, however, and this was emphasized by the opinion of the German Naval Attaché in Japan, Captain Wenneker, that the Japanese habit was to give a little and expect a lot in return.

By then, however, the Japanese Navy had become accustomed to using the issue of technology transfer as a critical indicator of political will and friendship (or lack of it) in their relations with other navies. The closure of formerly wide-open technological relations with Britain after 1923, for example, had been a traumatic watershed toward isolation in the world, and at first it had seemed in Tokyo that the German Navy under Behncke would provide access to technical innovations which opened up possibilities for German use of technology to win friends and influence the Japanese naval officer corps in spite of the weakness of the German fleet. Commander Canaris and Admiral Zenker had set their faces firmly against this in 1925, when a very large Japanese Navy questionnaire had been submitted including every question under the sun. The reaction of Admiral Raeder to the even larger Japanese questionnaire submitted in January 1941, in advance of the arrival of the Nomura Naval Mission, was in much the same vein as that of 1925. Billed as part of the Japanese desire to learn about German war experiences, the questionnaire was met behind closed doors with the tart response: "this has nothing to do with war experiences, it's an intellectual sell-out."[76] Outwardly, however, German naval personnel were instructed to express a positively helpful exterior, but any Japanese officer who expressed the view that he was entitled, as an ally under the Three Powers' Pact of September 1940, to expect open-handedness was to be firmly told that any requests that might interfere with the German war effort or that could be construed as "tantamount to industrial espionage or theft" would not be entertained. An important guideline at this time was whether or not a specific technology could meaningfully be incorporated in Japanese offensive capabilities soon enough to help defeat common enemies, but the ultimate principle was stated to be "the protection of German industry, its knowledge, and interests."[77]

---

[76] Handwritten note on the cover letter *OKM/M Att NR.1315/41g* of January 28, 1941 in *O.K.M.: 1.Skl.IIIa: "Japan-Kommission," (1941)*, 1.

[77] Fricke circular *OKM/1.Skl.Ic Nr.5359/41g* of February 11, 1941 in Ibid., 21-22.

Grand-Admiral Raeder sought to maintain a personal control over the transfer of German naval technology to Japan at this point, as did the other heads of the services, but over time the economic branch of the armed forces, headed by General Thomas, attempted to centralize the dealings of all three services with the Japanese attachés. The interests of German firms and of individual patent-holders had also to be taken into account, as was subsequently learned when Hitler tried to make a "gift" to Japan of two U-boats early in 1943. This also brought in the complexities of the civilian bureaucracy, to which was added the efforts of Foreign Minister von Ribbentrop to perform a co-ordinating role for all the civilian ministries. The war in Russia put a complete stop to the export of German equipment and machinery, especially to the sale of machine-tools, to Japan via the Trans-Siberian Railway, although after 1939 the Soviet authorities refused to accept any military equipment proper for transit. Everything, therefore, had to go by sea in the face of the perils of interception by hostile forces. When Japan entered the war in December 1941, the German side hoped that it would have at least a year to build up its fortified position in Europe (*Kriegsreich*), but the speed of the U.S. military build-up in the Far East, especially combined with German defeats after the end of 1942, made it increasingly important to seek to build up Japanese technological capabilities in order to tie down as many Allied resources in Asia as possible.

Consequently, many more German items of equipment were released from about January 1943, beginning with bazookas for the Japanese Army and U-boats for the Japanese Navy, and these began to accumulate in French Atlantic ports to await transport to the Pacific. Most of the few ships that left were sunk, and greater priority was given to German ships to bring raw materials from the Far East. This resulted in a growing deficit in the balance of trade and the restrictions on technology transfer were gradually eased in order to offset that deficit as a more acceptable alternative to paying in gold, which was needed sorely to pay for Rumanian oil and imports from neutral states in Europe. German firms remembered the losses they had suffered at Japanese hands during the Sino-Japanese war in the 1930s and were in no mood to be generous, so allied relations got into a fearful tangle. Grand-Admiral Dönitz appears to have taken the important initiative that cut the tangle and persuaded Hitler to agree to settlement of compensation after the war, which paved the way for a technical exchange agreement in March 1944.[78] Although much play was

---

[78] Details can be found in *OKM/M Att I Nr.211/44 g.Kdos.III* of March 18, 1944 from on board the surrendered U-234 at Portsmouth, New Hampshire in 1945. See Box No. 370, German Submarine Materials, Library of Congress, Manuscript Division, Washington, D.C.

made of the need for allies not to keep secrets from each other in the joint struggle, Hitler himself reserved the right to exclude numerous more advanced weapons systems from the exchange (acoustic torpedoes, the Walther U-boat design), and there was a long tug-of-war between Göring and Hitler throughout 1944 before the decision was finally implemented for transferring details of German jet and rocket aircraft by U-boat to Japan.[79] As war in Europe progressed, however, it became more and more a battle against time, and German policy only served to fritter more of it away. By the beginning of 1945, it was manifestly likely that German resistance would be crushed, and Japanese officials in Berlin constantly urged the Germans to release engineers, technical specialists, and scientists to go by U-boat to the Pacific and to form some kind of German Legion that would fight in a last stand alongside their Japanese allies. At first Grand-Admiral Dönitz appeared to favour the idea, but after receiving a negative recommendation from Admiral Wenneker, who saw the prospects for Japanese victory in equally negative terms, the idea was rejected. In this case, too, it would appear that Dönitz, like his two predecessors, was influenced to some extent in this instance by what he believed to be the Japanese Navy dragging its feet over his requests to them to provide secondments of German officers to Japanese fleet units in order to give them experience on which to build up the core of a new post-war navy.[80]

Tactical and Strategic Influence
The Kojima proposal of 1937 included the idea of an exchange about tactical questions, as well as about intelligence and technology. Since the technical specialists in the German Navy thought so little of Japanese technology, the decision taken by Raeder was that tactical ideas could be swapped for German technology. In practice, however, there is no surviving evidence to substantiate any argument that tactical data was received in Berlin between 1937 and 1941 in fulfillment of such an agreement. Intelligence about Western navies was exchanged annually in the years 1938 to 1940, with data about the United States being received from Japan from the second half of 1940 onwards, such as information on the construction of U.S. warships, the location of U.S. forces and the like. The main purpose of the 1941 naval mission was to obtain as much data as possible about the fighting capabilities and tactics of the Western navies and about German methods of countering these. But already the Japanese Navy had a very extensive network of attachés engaged in intelligence gathering, supplemented by reports from consular officials and by Japanese newspaper report-

---

[79] See n.35 above.
[80] See exchange of cables Berlin-Tokyo, April 5-27, 1945, source as n.1 above.

ers and businessmen, many of whom were actively working for the
armed services. Extensive briefings were given on a vast array of subjects
during the period from April to July 1941 in Berlin and Rome, including such events as the attack on Taranto Harbour and on the battleship
Bismarck at sea, which were to provide important elements of knowledge employed in the tactics of the Japanese Navy air force after
December 1941. German officers were instructed to ask numerous
counter-questions, most of which were answered quite fully in July
1941 by the Japanese side. Full information was provided to a specialized aero-technical team that was sent to Japan in May 1941 about
aerial torpedoes and their tactical use. Japanese torpedoes were tested
at Travemunde and specially trained groups of the German Air Force
were established in 1942, which proved quite effective in the attacks
on British convoys in the Arctic and the Mediterranean in the course
of that year. Assessments were made of the kinds of tactical questions
the Japanese Navy was particularly interested in and this was added
to what had already been gleaned by the staff of the Naval Attaché
in Japan and by Naval War Staff officers in Berlin over the years.

It had long been known that the Japanese Navy was building very
large battleships indeed, partly because German firms such as Krupps
had been supplying the Japanese Navy with heavy armour plating
and machinery for making it since the early 1930s.[81] Admiral Wenneker
complained about not being allowed to look at these vessels even though
Admiral Nomura was taken over the battleship *Tirpitz* being brought
to completion in Germany in 1941. It was not until the summer of
1942 that he was given details of some of their dimensions and not
until the summer of 1943 that he was finally promised an opportunity
to look more closely at the *Yamato*. Commander Bräutigam already
had a rather poor view of Japanese naval technology in the 1920s,
which he considered inferior to American, and argued on the need
for the Japanese to upgrade their air power in the coming decade.
Captain Wenneker reported that the British had an altogether too
dismissive view of the Japanese Navy air forces in 1935 and there had
been opportunities to observe these in action in China after 1937, but
the German Navy was not best informed about Japanese air power
because this was dealt with primarily by the rival German Air Force
and the air groups in the Secret Military Intelligence Service. An
awareness of the differences in tactical uses of submarines had been

---

[81] See Frohwein minute II M 46/34 of January 10, 1934 in *Auswärtiges Amt: Abt.
II F-M: Akte K 6: "Kommandierungen nach Ausland umgekehrt," (1929-1933)*. According
to the Tokyo correspondent of the *Neue Zürcher Zeitung* in 1965, reported in a conversation with the author, he was told of a giant German steel press in Hokkaido which
provided an excellent protection against Allied bombing attacks in the closing stage of
the Pacific War.

known since the 1920s and had been reiterated to Wenneker in the 1930s. The Germans were in a position to estimate Japanese capabilities better than perhaps any other European country or even the United States by the middle of 1941.

Aware of the precedent of U.S. intervention in World War I, Hitler and the heads of the Supreme Command (*O.K.W.*) sought to reduce frictions as much as possible with the United States. For one thing, the fact that the U.S. was the leading neutral meant that most other neutrals would take the lead from it, and the exclusion zone established round the British Isles effectively meant that the U.S. authorities avoided sending their vessels into the zone and no incidents could occur. Incidents could occur within the Pan-American Security Zone, however, and Raeder, in particular, made repeated complaints about the un-neutral behaviour of the U.S. in allowing British and Canadian warships freedom of movement within the Zone, making it more difficult for German merchantmen to escape Allied controls.[82] Frictions also increased in number and strength when U.S. warships began after April 1941 to convoy vessels bound for the British Isles and the Soviet Union across the Greenland-Iceland gap. The final straw was the U.S. takeover of the defence of Iceland from Britain in October 1941, when German reconnaissance aircraft encountered American forces. Up until this point, Hitler had to restrain Raeder repeatedly from taking counter-measures against the U.S., whether in the matter of laying mines off Halifax, or not attacking American-owned oil installations on the Dutch West Indies or U.S.-protected convoys. In the first case, up to 1941, it was a matter of delivering a decisive blow against the West European Powers before the U.S. had any chance of intervening. When Britain still resisted and Hitler turned on the Soviet Union, he asked Raeder to hold off until the middle of October 1941 in the hope that a decision would have been reached in the East and again that that would pre-empt U.S. intervention.

From the German Navy's point of view, Hitler's decision to accelerate the preparations for war to a point before its optimum target date of 1943 meant that it had to rely on allies to tie down enemy forces. The Italian surface fleet was at its best just by existing and cutting the Mediterranean strategically in half, but enough was known about the capabilities of the Japanese Navy to indicate that these were a substantially more serious threat to lend credibility to German naval strategy until such time as more U-boats and surface warships could be brought into operational readiness. The German air and naval successes in Scandinavia did more than any other single set of operations to convince the Germans that the Japanese fleet could accom-

---

[82] For an itemized list of these complaints, see *OKM/Skl.I Op 2486/40 Chefs.* of November 14, 1940, source as n.16 above.

plish so much more than the Germans at sea, as well as to convince
the Japanese Navy that a revolution in seapower had arisen through
the combination with airpower. Having been briefed both as captain
of the *Deutschland* and as Naval Attaché in Japan prior to February
1940 about the importance attached to keeping the U.S. out of the
war, Admiral Wenneker faithfully respresented Berlin's position until
the great victories in the West were completed. The more cautious
groups in the Japanese Navy still were worried about the possibility
of war with the United States if Japan tried to move into the Dutch
East Indies in particular, where the largest U.S. investments in Asia
were located, but the confidence of these groups who were moved by
the fear of missed opportunities was immeasurably strengthened to
a point where the decision-making apparatus of the Navy was all but
paralysed, unlike the situation in the summer of 1939.

The adhesion of Japan to the Three Powers' Pact on September
27, 1940, represented a broad commitment to the notion of a "community of fate" between the two countries: the more one succeeded, the
more likely it would be that the other would do so in a form of recip-
rocal demonstration effect, which also could work in a similar way to
their mutual disadvantage. The Naval War Staff characterized the
Pact as a recognition of the unity of interests of the two countries,
however diverse the separate interests might appear to be. It was felt
in Berlin that Japan on its own could not count on defeating both
Britain and the United States. Admiral Wenneker sought to boost the
confidence of the Japanese Navy even further by arguing in the weeks
after the signing of the Pact that, although an American entry into
the war would not be at all pleasant, nevertheless it would be far
outweighed by a Japanese entry. These views were put in the form
of statements of personal opinion to Japanese officers on the one
hand, while at the same time Wenneker was engaged in an active
correspondence with senior Navy officers on the other, putting forward
arguments and trying to obtain clearer strategic guidance from Berlin.
Hitler and Ribbentrop had been content to let the Japanese take the
bait of the colonies of South-east Asia, but Hitler was far from content
to let the Japanese or anyone else benefit from German victories. The
Italian reverses in Greece and then in North Africa demanded intervention in the Mediterranean because there was no way that the
German will could be enforced on Britain with the Air Force alone,
as Göring had boastfully promised. Neither Spain nor France could
be cast into the fray; the Soviet Union in November 1940 refused to
be cajoled into quarrels with Britain, which left only Japan to throw
onto the scales while the assault on the East was launched. What clinched
this was the revelations of British weakness provided by the *Atlantis*
in December 1940.

From the Japanese point of view this was particularly important evidence of how much less risk there would be to Japan from any combination of hostile forces than there had been in the past. The basic idea of a single massive strategic blow owed a great deal to observation of what the German armed forces had done with surprise on their side in 1940. It also lent greater credibility to Wenneker's argument of November 1940 that, even if the United States did enter the war, from the German point of view, the main burden would fall on Japan, and, in any case, Germany already was at this stage, in his view, to all intents and purposes at war with the United States.[83] This last argument went down well with Raeder but Hitler and the Supreme Command were not fully convinced by it. They wanted the Japanese to intervene against Britain but to try to avoid catapulting the United States into the war, because that could introduce too many uncertainties for comfort and calculation. Even after the immediate Japanese successes at the outbreak of war in the Pacific, Supreme Command planners argued that the Japanese and Americans were now about even in strength at least, but with the Japanese having the edge in the Western Pacific theatres much more clearly.[84] But at the beginning of 1941, what the Japanese would much have preferred was a German attack directly on the British Isles, as the acme would have been to win control of Singapore without any battle.

The point repeatedly made to the German side at this juncture was that, however things turned out, Japan's offensive capacity could last approximately only six months against the United States. Thereafter, the United States could initiate a long war of attrition, especially if it was allowed to retain control of the Philippines, Guam, and Wake, which lay astride the main axis of Japanese advance southward. Besides, the reaction of the Soviet Union to a Japanese move south was unpredictable and, even with the resources of South-east Asia, Japan would still not have control of all the resources its economy required.[85] One of Hitler's calculations was that an attack on the Soviet Union would help to release Japanese energies in some direction or other, but for

---

[83] Wenneker letter *553/40 gKdos* of November 22, 1940 to Admiral Schniewind, discussed with Ambassador Ritter of the Foreign Ministry and with Hitler on December 20 and 27, 1940. *O.K.M.: 1.Skl.I Op: Akte 29-1: "Zusammenarbeit Deutschland-Italien-Spanien-Janan-Russland-Ungarn-Rumänien," (1938-1941)*, p. 102. A handwritten reply by Admiral Dönitz to a letter of this date from Admiral Wenneker is in the possession of Frau Irma Wenneker, interview with the author, September 1982.

[84] *OKW/WFSt/Abt.L (Ik Op) Nr.442173/41 gKdos. Chefs.* of December 14, 1941, source as n.19 above.

[85] Conversation between Admiral Wenneker and Admiral Kondō Nobutake, Vice-Chief of Naval Staff, in *Wenneker B.Nr.279/41 g.Kdos* of April 17, 1941 in *O.K.M.: M Att: "Japan-Mobilmachung," Bd.4, (1941)*.

some time he was kept guessing about where they would be targeted. He did not want the Japanese to intervene in the Soviet Union like hyenas at a lion's feast, although Ribbentrop did his best to urge Matsuoka to persuade his government to attack the Soviet Union. Hitler's preference was a Japanese assault against South-east Asia and distracting or tying down the United States in Asia while he disposed of the Soviet Union. He did not share Ribbentrop's notion that it would be possible to influence Japanese behaviour by persuasion and diplomacy, and the value of a surprise attack that was a surprise to one's allies as well meant that it could possibly move them more visibly than words.[86] It can be demonstrated that the Japanese Navy's relish for action of any unilateral kind in the first six months of 1941 had cooled down considerably, whereas German interest in Japanese intervention steadily increased over the same period. In spite of the temptation to hit out at the United States, however, Hitler's position was that there must be no war with the U.S. without prior entry of Japan into the war against the United States.[87]

It cannot be argued that Germany caused the Japanese entry into World War II. What is clear, however, is that the German attack on the Soviet Union was a step that removed the last major uncertainty in Japanese strategic calculations and that the decision on July 2, 1941, was directly related (not just coincidental) to the German move. Japanese Navy officers indicated to Admiral Wenneker that they did not expect any serious reaction to the planned move into southern Indo-China, any more than there had been to the move into northern Indo-China in the summer and autumn of 1940, which was seen as a test case for U.S. firmness of purpose and resolve. The British move into French-controlled Lebanon and Syria in June 1941 was seen by the Japanese as a precedent for their own action, while the U.S. freezing of German and Italian assets at this time had had no tangible effect (save on U.S. investments there) and seemed a symbolic act of little greater importance in the case of Japan to many of those who advocated it. Whatever the truth of the matter of mutual perceptions, a chain reaction was set off by the German actions in the Soviet Union which had a very significant impact on the Pacific, and a threshold was crossed in July 1941 which posed an inescapable challenge to the Japanese state. The German action also had a powerful impact on the United States, and particularly on the Treasury, where Secretary Morgenthau had lumped Germany and Japan together even before the Three Powers' Pact was signed.

---

[86] This emerges from a fragment of Hitler's *Lagesbesprechungen*. See Operational Archives, U.S. Naval History Division, Miscellaneous Files, Enclosure 13.

[87] See final sentence of Fricke directive, n.77 above.

The failure of the assault on the Soviet Union became gradually clearer during August and September 1941, and the Soviet winter offensive of November and December 1941, when Siberian divisions began appearing on the Soviet western front in considerable numbers, created a sense of desperation in Hitler as he struggled to control the crisis. Added to this was the British offensive in the Western Desert which pushed German and Italian forces a considerable distance westwards. In Washington, the German Military Attaché, General von Bötticher, kept insisting to the Japanese and to his home authorities that the U.S. position was nothing but one of bluff and these views were relayed to Japanese military attachés in Berlin and elsewhere by the General Staff. Admirals Schniewind and Groos plied similar views to Admiral Nomura and his colleagues in Berlin in efforts to push the Japanese along.[88] But these views, although noted by the Japanese Naval Staff, in no way carried conviction for the Japanese Navy, who insisted that the United States should in no way be underestimated. On August 22 and 30, Admiral Wenneker indicated that there was confirmation that Japan would not attack the Soviet Union, that the Navy felt that a southward move was more advantageous than not, and that there was now no going back. Konoe's initiative toward Roosevelt was seen as the last hope for rescuing the situation. Right up until at least the first week of November, Admiral Schniewind did not believe Admiral Wenneker's advice that the Philippines and the United States would be the objects of a Japanese advance, and although Admiral Nomura insisted to Admiral Groos that the negotiations with the United States were just a bluff of a tactical kind, it was not until the draft agreement not to reach a separate peace with the Western Powers was submitted in Berlin at the end of November 1941 that Japanese intentions *vis-à-vis* the U.S. were more firmly clarified.

Since this information also reached the State Department at the same time through "Magic" intercepts, the shock to Cordell Hull was considerable after having been strung along for months in the belief that the Japanese were seriously prepared to negotiate withdrawal from the Three Powers' Pact. This belief had lulled the U.S. into a false sense of security and helped divert more resources away from the western Pacific to the Soviet Union than might otherwise have been the case. The timing of the Japanese strategic strike on Hawaii was substantially influenced by the weather patterns in the Pacific

---

[88] Bötticher Tel. No. 2672 of August 9, No. 3197 of September 15, No. 3217 of September 16, and No. 3169 of September 13, 1941 in *O.K.W.: Wi-Rü-Amt: Wi.Vc: Akte 32/44: "Attaché-Telegramme USA,"* (1940-1941); Groos-Nomura and Fricke-Nomura correspondence, especially Fricke letter of October 15, 1941, which was submitted in a reworked form as *OKM/1.Skl.Ib 25142/41 g.Kdos* of November 10, 1941 to Hitler and then relayed to the Foreign Ministry: source as n.2, but *Bd.1,* (1941).

region: it coincided with a period of severe winter weather on the frontiers of Korea and Manchuria, when the likelihood of Soviet inter- vention was negligible, even without German intervention in Europe. It was also intended to pre-empt the peaking of Anglo-American production of warships and munitions from 1943 onward, plans for which were widely canvassed in the autumn and winter of 1941. The attack on Pearl Harbor was a complete surprise to Japan's European allies: Admiral Wenneker guessed that war would come within three weeks, after informal discussions with friendly staff officers at the beginning of December. There was certainly no hint of an attack on Hawaii, only about the targets in the South. The impact on the German Supreme Command and on Hitler himself was very considerable indeed: coming as it did at a time of very severe pressure in Russia and Libya. It promised substantial strategic relief for Germany to hope to finish off the Russian problem within another year and to strengthen Europe's defences in time to cope with an Anglo-American buildup.

The need to sign an agreement abjuring a separate peace was indicative of the great anxiety felt in Japan about the possibility of the war in Europe finishing first. These anxieties were conveyed to Admiral Wenneker who could do little more than listen sympatheti- cally, and note how jumpy Japanese naval officers were about any rumour, however slight, of the possibility of an Anglo-German peace initiative. These doubts were greatly relieved by the German decla- ration of war on the United States, which was the product of relief and the evidence that Germany now appeared to have of Japanese superiority in the Pacific. It was calculated that Germany was as good as at war with the U.S. already and that the Japanese would be strong enough to hold off the U.S. long enough for Germany to prepare an effective defence of Europe, in which the U-boat fleet was earmarked to play a leading role.[89] Although both sides emphasized the need to link up in order to avoid the risk of being picked off separately, there does not in fact appear to have been any genuine desire to work hand in hand to achieve victory against the common foe, as Admiral Katō had envisaged in 1926. From the outset, the dividing line between the separate zones of operations of the Axis Powers and Japan at the 70° East line of longitude was a purely notional one on the German side, which insisted on suppressing German Army and Navy objections to this in order to preserve a superficial image of allied harmony.

There was no real joint plan of operations and Raeder's sugges- tion of January 1941 for some kind of supreme command to co-ordinate allied strategy was ignored, apart from subsequent approaches from the Japanese side in 1942 to send an Imperial delegation to Germany

---

[89] See n.84 above.

to provide a clearer picture of the deteriorating situation in the Pacific. Doubts about the effectiveness of the Germans in Russia, in the light of existing Japanese experience in China, were frequently adumbrated by Japanese Navy officers in Berlin and Tokyo. An explicit suggestion of Japanese willingness to mediate between Germany and the Soviet Union was put to Admiral Wenneker unofficially in October 1941 and briefly reported to Berlin at the beginning of November, but Wenneker expressed strong doubt about Berlin's receptiveness to such an idea. Other doubts were glossed over by a statement to the effect that the war would be decided in the Atlantic, whereas in fact Hitler saw the Eastern Front as the decisive one. The ease of the early victories in the Pacific made everyone forget the earlier injunctions about a six-month offensive at most. Admiral Wenneker had to lodge a strong protest with the Japanese Navy Ministry in the spring of 1942, when their press spokesman, Captain Hiraide Hideo, made an extremely unfavourable comparison between German failure to make the 24-mile Channel crossing and the 2,500-mile Japanese advance.[90] Although the Japanese Navy spearheaded a diplomatic effort to persuade the Germans to reach a truce with the Soviet Union in succeeding years and argued that the Mediterranean had a higher priority than Hitler accorded it, there seemed to be no genuine willingness in Japan to make the Indian Ocean the theatre with highest priority for the Japanese Navy.

Once the feeling of astonishment at Japanese successes had worn off in Berlin, traditional stereotyped views of Japan quickly began to re-assert themselves in the German Naval War Staff. In a briefing on the situation in the Indo-Pacific theatre for Grand-Admiral Dönitz in March 1943, Commander Rost stated:

> In all dealings with the Japanese, their mentality must be taken into account. They are very sensitive, sly, clever and adroit at changing tactics, and can only with difficulty overcome a certain sense of suspicion toward the white race, even in their dealings with allies . . . The arrogance they demonstrated in the first few months following their tremendous victories, which made life difficult for Admiral Wenneker, has in the meantime abated. It currently takes the form of liking to give free play to their criticisms of our conduct of the war in Europe.[91]

It took a long time before the Japanese Navy provided an honest explanation of events at Midway in June 1942, and it was difficult for

---

[90] Wenneker (Tokyo) Tel. No. 795 of March 13, 1942 to Raeder and Schniewind in *Auswärtiges Amt: Staatssekretär: "Japan," Bd.6, (1942)*. Hiraide was reprimanded, Wenneker received an oral apology from Admiral Oka and a written apology from Navy Minister Shimada.

[91] Rost lecture of March 2, 1943: source as n.2 above.

them to get across, consequently, the significance of the fighting in the Solomon Islands to their inability to despatch strike forces into the western Indian Ocean to interdict Anglo-American supplies to off-loading points in the Red Sea and Persian Gulf. Even when a clear statement was set out by Admiral Wenneker in an end-of-year summary of the situation in the Pacific, it was not believed by the head of the Supreme Command Staff, General Jodl, who rejected it thus:

> An end-of-year summary of the situation . . . must be submitted to the Führer in view of its significance. It must be kept free of all exaggerations, especially those of a negative character. Expressions such as "the situation is very serious", "the fate of the whole of South-east Asia stands or falls with the Solomon Islands", "the shipping situation is catastrophic", or "the decline in production is extremely worrying" are forms of expression that are psychologically dangerous and do not conform to a calm, military method of appraisal. Rather, it creates the impression that Japan no longer has any value to us as an ally and must be written off, whereas in reality it is one of the significant factors in our favour for a successful prosecution of the war. I request that attention be paid to this in future reports.[92]

On the enemy side, it was calculated that 85 percent of the world's economic resources were available to them collectively. In order to confound the odds, the Axis Powers and Japan felt constrained to employ the strategems of stealth and surprise attack, but the strategic blows they could muster were never strong enough to eliminate any one of their major opponents, let alone all four. Despite his lighthearted declaration of war on the United States, Hitler could not even muster a single aircraft capable of delivering the smallest bombload on the American mainland. While the Japanese Navy had a rather more sober appreciation of the tasks undertaken, nevertheless a fanatical love of their own country blinded the leaders of each of the three Axis states into believing that their collective acts of will must somehow prevail against all comers, as though it were an extension of natural and physical law. Even when attempting to rationalize this in strategic terms by a worst-case analysis, a fanatical nationalist can never contemplate inferiority nor organize more than a temporary coalition of forces to achieve his international goals. The Axis house was divided from the outset; its enemies knew that it was divided and had limited resources; the surprise is that it took so long to fall.

---

[92] See Jodl cable *OKW/WFSt/Op Nr.552243/42 Chefs.* of December 24, 1942, source as n.68 above.

JAPAN'S SEARCH FOR ITS NATIONAL IDENTITY: TOWARDS PEARL HARBOR

NOBUYA BAMBA

WHY DID Japan plunge itself into the suicidal Pacific War? Many answers can be advanced to this question. Marxists argue that Japan, without natural resources and coming late to the ruthless international competition for colonies and markets, had no alternative to aggression. Constitutionalists contend that it was due to the inherent defect of the Meiji Constitution, which eventually allowed aggressive militarists (though not all military men were aggressive) to dominate the government. Students of the decision-making approach propound that haphazard and chaotic decision-making had to be blamed; and sociologists stress that Japanese "feudal" mentality and social structure beneath Japan's superficial achievement of modernization drove it to the irrational and chauvinistic adventure; and so on. These interpretations reflect a certain amount of truth, but none of them explains the underlying psychology and dominant ideology intrinsic to Japanese aggression. Hence in this paper I would like to pursue the ideo-psychological path which led Japan to attack Pearl Harbor. In my analysis, I would like to pay special attention to the 1920s, for this period is considered to be the watershed between popular aspirations for democracy and modernity and those for the enhancement of ultra-nationalism.

Any nation has certain diplomatic goals. And the goals of diplomacy may roughly be classified into three categories: the fundamental, the intermediate, and the ultimate. The first goal includes such objectives as the guarantee of national survival, the defense of national independence, and the preservation of territorial integrity. The ultimate goal is to fulfill national aspirations and ideals; and *if* the nation has the capability to do so, it hopes to create an ideal world according to its world design. This tendency was particularly conspicuous among big powers in the nineteenth century until a little after the mid-twentieth century. Between these two goals, various intermediate objectives can be arranged in preferential hierarchical order. These may include the expansion of foreign markets, the security of strategic positions, and the protection of established rights and interests abroad. Although the fundamental goal is identical for all nations except self-abnegating ones, the ultimate and intermediate goals vary from nation to nation. To secure the fundamental goal is the main prerequisite for any nation.

However, a nation is not always exposed to the real danger of national survival. When the fundamental goal is secured, the nation aspires to a higher goal. In the goal hierarchy, to attain a lower end is a means for achieving a higher end. Conversely, obtaining the means for achieving a higher end becomes an end in itself for the immediate purpose. In the final analysis all intermediate goals are means for achieving the ultimate goal. Hence, the guiding principle of a nation's diplomacy is determined by what the nation's ultimate goal is. And the ultimate goal of each nation is largely determined by its cultural tradition, i.e., its beliefs and myths, primary values and norms, principles and ideologies, its ethos and idiosyncracies. Why does it become so in reality? In the final analysis, a nation's diplomacy is determined by its chief executive or its Minister of Foreign Affairs. But when these diplomats formulate policies, they do so in the light of achieving the ultimate goal. In other words, they choose appropriate intermediate goals in the hope of attaining that which their nation aspires to most. Even if a key diplomat's perception of the ultimate goal differs from that of the general population, the "deviation" will eventually be corrected and the nation's diplomacy returns to a "normality" reflecting its general cultural tradition. It is so because such a diplomat or a government will eventually be ousted from power by various means such as by a general election or recall, by public accusation, assassination, *coup d'état*, or even by revolution. Hence, a nation's diplomacy in a long historical perspective tends to reflect the nation's dominant values, principles, and *Weltanschauung*.

SPLIT NATIONAL-CULTURAL IDENTITY

BUT IF a nation's culture disintegrates, what will happen to the nation's diplomacy? In fact, this is a common phenomenon which can be observed in many non-Western nations. For example, the Japanese slogan of the Meiji Restoration, *"fukoku kyohei"* (enrich the nation and strengthen the army), and the Chinese echo of the same slogan clearly indicated this kind of "split national-cultural identity." To make the nation "rich and strong" in order to avoid being colonized, Japan had to adopt modern Western technology, science, knowledge, and a whole set of modern institutions. In other words, Japan's modernization must be understood as the process of its acculturation and assimilation to the modern culture which originated and developed in the West. Consequently, the more Japan inclined toward modern civilization, the more it had to experience the disintegration of its own cultural tradition. And the traditionalists vehemently opposed this trend. For instance, when Japan was forced to open the country, an influential leader of the Tokugawa regime strongly protested by claiming that "such decision would be most harmful to the good tradition of the divine nation." Hence, the Japanese nationalists were more or less divided into two opposing camps: the modernistic nationalists and the traditionalistic nationalists.

Modern Japanese nationalism began with the Meiji Restoration in 1868. From the outset, however, it has contained these two diametrically opposed forces, namely, restoration of the old (*fukko*) and reformation in a progressive spirit (*ishin*). The Charter Oath of March 1868 called for the abandonment of the evil customs of the past and the seeking of knowledge throughout the world on the one hand, and the strengthening of the foundations of Imperial polity on the other. Since then, Japan has constantly vacillated between modernity and traditionalism. Furthermore, interestingly enough, the general tendency of national aspirations has shifted in cycles of fifteen to twenty years.

The years 1872 to 1873 marked Japan's initiation into wholesale modernization. "Civilization and enlightenment" (*bummei kaika*) was on everybody's lips. In the 1880s Japan's craze for Westernization further increased. The *Rokumeikan*—a novel Western-style red brick building where foreign diplomats and Japanese officials were entertained by everything Western including music, dance, food, and drink—symbolized Japan's desire to westernize in the eighties. Then came repercussions from the traditionalists. A number of factors came into play. Some of the major ones were the popular awareness of things Japanese stimulated by the injection of foreign elements into the indigenous society; increased national consciousness due to economic progress, development of education, communication and transportation, and greater political centralization; the humiliating Triple Intervention after the first Sino-Japanese War (1894 to 1895)— the intervention by Russia, France, and Germany over Japan's claim on the Liaotung Peninsula; and the Russian threat on the continent. Hence, popular enthusiasm for the West gradually shifted to scepticism, and the traditionalistic leaders, taking advantage of this opportunity, strongly attacked superficial imitation of the West. Thus the "Japanism" movement (*nihonshugi*) began to grow.

Japan's victory over Tsarist Russia in 1905 marked another turning point. Although nationalistic exaltation still lingered for a few years thanks to the victory, Westernization was accelerated once again. This period was called the period of Taishō Democracy (1912 to 1926). However, Japan's learning about the West grew much more reflective than before. For the first time, "Westernization" and "modernization" were distinguished. Simultaneously, people in general became interested not only in Western technology but also in Western philosophy and culture. Hence, modernization and Westernization penetrated Japanese society much more deeply than in the period between 1872 and 1890. Proportionately the traditionalists's protests also increased. The transition from the Taishō to the Shōwa (1925 to 1927) was, as I stated previously, the watershed between the enthusiasm for modernization and the upsurge of traditionalism. Some extremists began to attack parliamentarism, which had swayed the minds of the "Taishō Liberals." As a consequence, the debate on "parliamentarism" versus "emperorism" became vocal between the two rival groups concerned with the future political system of Japan. This issue paralleled the contemporary diplomatic issue, "co-operative diplomacy with the "West" versus "autonomous diplomacy." Shidehara Kijūrō was an advocate of the former, as Tanaka Giichi was of the latter.

Eventually the traditionalists overcame their opponents, and Japan entered a period of "ultranationalism." Within the nation, parliamentarism was destroyed by a series of assassinations and *coups d'état*, while abroad Japan (the *Kantō-gun*) caused the Manchurian Incident in 1931, and Japan pursued its "autonomous diplomacy" by withdrawing from the League of Nations in March 1933. Japan continued further aggression to the continent staging the second Sino-Japanese War in 1937, and finally along this road toward the propagation of the "Imperial Way," which I shall explain shortly, Japan attacked Pearl Harbor.

TOWARDS THE MANCHURIAN INCIDENT

As SURVEYED above, Japan's search for its national identity constantly swung between modernity and traditionalism. But if one takes a long historical perspective, one realizes that in the final analysis Japan's struggle in search of its identity was directed toward the manifestation of *kokutai* (national polity) in domestic politics, and its external expression of *kōdō* (the imperial way). The foundation of this orthodoxy had already been laid by the Meiji Constitution (1889), the Imperial House Law (1889), and the Imperial Rescript on Education (1890). They proclaimed that Japan was founded by the divine ancestors, that it was to be governed eternally by a successive line of emperors (*bansei ikkei*), and that the imperial prerogatives were bestowed upon the imperial descendants by the will of divine ancestors. The *kokutai* also stressed such values as loyalty, filial piety, obedience, self-sacrifice, courage, frugality, and sincerity, which emanated from *bushidō* (the way of samurai). In the course of Japanese history from the Meiji Restoration to its initiation of the Pacific War, these ideologies had eventually become Japan's dominant *Weltanschauung* and *raison d'être*. According to the Hegelian concept of state and history, the prewar history of Japan may be regarded as the process of its "self-realization" of "national spirit."

In the light of the previously mentioned "three stages of diplo-matic goal-attainment," Japan's aspirations for "self-realization" in world history grew through the following process.

The period from Commodore Perry's arrival (1853) to Japan's victory in the first Sino-Japanese War was the period when Japan endeavoured to attain the fundamental goal, i.e., the attainment of national independence and territorial integrity. From the end of the first Sino-Japanese War to the end of World War I was the period in which Japan tried to satisfy its intermediate goals. In order to obtain more rights and privileges, markets, and strategic positions, Japan began to contemplate its "advancement" toward the continent. In this process the Russo-Japanese War (1904 to 1905) was fought, Korea was annexed to Japan in 1910, and the "Twenty-One Demands" were thrust upon China. Another important national goal to be achieved during this period was the abolition of unequal treaties with the West-ern Powers. This goal had also been attained by 1911. During the First World War, thanks to the "war-boom," Japan's capitalist economy made great progress, and Japan found itself to be one of the three biggest powers when the war ended. Thus, Japan gradually came to aspire to the attainment of its ultimate goal. From the Manchurian Incident to the Pacific War—often called the "period of fifteen-years war"—Japan staked itself to attest its "national destiny" by carrying out such slogans as "The Establishment of New Order in East Asia," "The Establishment of Greater East Asia Co-Prosperity Sphere," and "The Attainment of Eight Corners of the World Under One Roof."

In this process of Japan's "self-realization" in world history, disputes of Japan's major diplomatic lines with regard to the ascer-tainment of its national identity had gone through several stages: first the controversy over the issues of "open the country" versus "expel the barbarians," then over the issue of "the Korean expedition" in the early 1870s. Traditionalists such as Saigō Takamori advocated the policy partly in his hope to stir up the declining samurai spirit and partly to admonish the "impudent" Koreans who had refused to accept the Japanese mission to Korea. Saigō's opponents, such as Iwakura Tomomi and Ōkubo Toshimichi, asserted the priority of domestic modernization to the chauvinistic adventure. After Japan won the first Sino-Japanese War and in the period of Japanism, the argument that Japan had to become "the Lord of East Asia" and to take the leadership to restore Oriental culture against the Western encroachment became prevalent among traditionalists. Their pan-Asianism and their asser-tion of Japan's mission in Asia sounded like the American Monroe Doctrine which claimed the United States's leadership to establish a "new world" on the American continents against the old and corrupt world of Europe. However, these discussions had been confined in the domestic society as public opinions, and did not take concrete forms of diplomacy until the end of World War I. This was partly due to the fact that even chauvinistic traditionalists recognized the necessity for Japan to co-operate with the Western Powers for the maintenance of national security and independence, and partly due to the fact that Japanese diplomacy still had not reached the stage for attaining the ultimate goal.

Japanese diplomacy in the twenties was in a transition from the intermediate stage to the ultimate. In domestic politics, it was also the transitional period from the "Taishō Democracy" to the "Shōwa Restoration." After the Great War, world aspirations for peace were high, and anti-imperialism, a democratic order, and international co-operation were common goals among nations. The Wilsonian and Leninist attacks on imperialism continued to be strong, and China, which had been a major victim of imperialism, enthusiastically supported both American and Russian assertions. Wilson emphasized self-determination and the sovereign rights of all people. In Great Britain, Lloyd George advocated "diplomacy by conference," by which he hoped to bring about "open diplomacy" and the "mobilization of world opinion." All denounced the "old diplomacy" and agreed on the need of establishing a "new diplomacy." In addition to the dominant mood of a world seeking peaceful and democratic diplomacy, Japan was also regulated by the Washington treaties covering the security of the Pacific region.

Japanese modernizers more or less supported the co-operative policy with the West. The general social milieu in the first half of the twenties also inclined toward internationalism, modernization, and democracy. The diplomacy led by Foreign Ministers Uchida Kōsai and Matsui Keishirō reflected the domestic atmosphere; and Shidehara Kijūrō, who succeeded them (in June 1924), was the champion of "co-operative diplomacy." Against this kind of trend, traditionalists were anxious about Japan's future prospects. They thought that Japan and its indigenous culture would be submerged in, and eventually be destroyed by, the increasing Westernization. Hence, they began to stage the movement for the manifestation of *kokutai* at home, and advocated Japan's "autonomous diplomacy" abroad. Prime Minister and concurrently Foreign Minister Tanaka Giichi (the Tanaka Cabinet was established in April 1927) was the leader of this group. The political party of Kenseikai (later Minseitō) and the Ministry of Foreign Affairs tended to back up the former line, whereas the Seyūkai and the military in general were in favour of the latter course.

The diplomatic problems in which Japan was involved during this period were, first of all, its keen sense of isolation. The Anglo-Japanese Alliance was replaced by the Four Power Treaty at Washington, which lacked the meaning of an "alliance" in any sense. The Nine Power Treaty, which pledged the territorial integrity and equal opportunity for trade in China, was in fact aimed at Japan, in order to stop further aggression in China. Japan's pacts with Tsarist Russia between 1907 and 1916, which guaranteed it a special position in Korea and Manchuria, were now abrogated by the Soviet Union. Wilson's "New Diplomacy" denied the former American assurances based upon the Taft-Katsura Agreement of 1905 and the Lansing-Ishii Agreement of 1917, which had recognized Japan's special interest in China because of her "territorial propinquity."

Japan's isolation was not the only cause of its precarious position in international society. There was also the spread of Bolshevism in East Asia. In March 1919, the Communist International was organized and the First World Congress was held in Moscow. Four months later, the Soviets issued a manifesto proclaiming, "All people should have their independence and self-government and not to submit to being bound by other nations." The Chinese and the Korean nationalists rallied to this call. The Russians also kept sending missions to China and Japan. As a result, the First National Congress of the Chinese Communist Party was held at Shanghai in 1921, and a Kuomintang-Communist alliance was formed in January 1924. Already in July 1921, Outer Mongolia had fallen under the control of the Soviet Union. The Russians were equally ambitious in Manchuria, and in Japan they established close relations with the increasing number of Japanese communists.

In China, both nationalism and civil war endangered Japan's vested interests. Due to the political and economic modernization during and after the war, the enlightened Chinese were mobilized in a rights-recovery movement against imperialistic nations. In 1919 the May Fourth Movement spread over the major cities of China, and more than ten thousand students demonstrated in Peking against the Paris decision on the Shantung problem and the Chinese Government's humiliating policy toward Japan. The movement was soon supported by other intellectuals, merchants, industrialists, and workers. Merchants boycotted Japanese and Western goods, and workers carried out strikes. Sporadic strikes in 1922 became widespread by 1925, covering Tsing-tao, Canton, Hankow, Shanghai, and Hong Kong. And Sun Yat-sen denounced extraterritoriality, the unequal treaties, and foreign concessions. Sun's unfinished national unification campaign was continued by Chiang Kai-shek who carried out the northern expedition against the warlords. In June 1928, the Nationalists took over Peking, and in October of the same year the Nationalist Government of the Republic of China was inaugurated in Nanking. With Chiang's success in the northern expedition, the long period of civil war came to an end for the time being, though the struggle soon resumed between Chiang and the communists. Throughout these wars, the lives and property of Japanese residents in China were often in danger.

At home in Japan, soon after the Great War, the war-boom ended, and the Great Kantō Earthquake of September 1923 caused serious damage to the industrial centre. A chronic depression developed, and eventually Japan was involved in the world depression. In 1930, the total number of unemployed reached about 2.6 million. The population increase and food shortages were equally serious problems during this period. In the Fifty-first Diet in 1925, for example, a Dietman spoke: "How can we feed our population which is increasing by 600,000 every year, amounting to a six-million increase within ten years? While the population is rapidly increasing, our industry, our wealth, and our economic revenue are not sufficient to feed them . . . . We must find a countermeasure and solve the problem immediately."

Emigration might have been a solution to this problem. But the so-called "anti-Japanese immigration law" of the United States (1924) and the revision of the Lemieux Agreement with Canada, which limited the total number of Japanese immigrants to 150 a year, virtually shut out Japanese emigrants from coming into North America. These American and Canadian attitudes to Japanese immigration brought about serious consequences. First of all, strong anti-Western and simultaneously pan-Asian sentiments began to prevail among the more traditionalistic nationalists. Secondly, Japan became increasingly interested in seeking the solution for overpopulation and food shortages in Manchuria and Mongolia.

Under these domestic and international circumstances, Foreign Minister Shidehara in the Katō Takaaki Cabinet (established in June 1924) aspired to make Japan a highly industrialized democratic nation supported by economic progress. He thought that a co-operative policy with the Western Powers would be the best way to save Japan from its international isolation and to ensure Japan's security. Hence, he tried to support the Washington System and the League of Nations whole-heartedly. He was convinced that promotion of trade and enlargement of Japan's oversea markets and investments were the most desirable means to solve the nation's economic difficulties as well as the problems of food shortage and overpopulation. This is the reason why his policy is often labelled "economy-oriented diplomacy." From Shidehara's viewpoint, Japan had to assume friendly attitudes toward the United States and China as much as possible, for both countries were very important customers for Japanese trade. In fact, during that time, the United States absorbed about 40 percent of Japanese exports. Consequently, while the Japanese public was enraged by the American immigration law, Shidehara tried to settle the problem as peacefully as possible. With China, for the same reason, he pursued an appeasement policy and adhered to the policy of non-intervention. However, Shidehara was strongly accused by his opponents saying that he was too conciliatory to the United States and "weak-kneed" to rampant Chinese nationalism. Moreover, the Wakatsuki Cabinet, which succeeded the Katō Cabinet after Katō's death, and in which Shidehara continued to be Foreign Minister, failed to manage the financial crisis, and the Cabinet resigned *en masse* on April 17, 1927.

The new Premier and Foreign Minister, Tanaka Giichi, had been asserting that Japan had to carry out a more "positive diplomacy," and that Japan had to recognize its leadership as the "Lord of East Asia." He also felt that his predecessor's policy of non-intervention in Chinese affairs was nothing but a policy of "non-resistance," and that because of such "weak-kneed policy" the Chinese were making light of the Japanese Empire. Thus, he was convinced that Japan's military might had to be demonstrated to the Chinese when necessary. Tanaka, furthermore, regarded Manchuria and Mongolia as Japan's "special position." Believing that Japan could never disregard the upheaval in the region, he sent Japanese troops three times into Shantung in order to intervene in Chiang Kai-shek's attempt to incorporate the Three Eastern Provinces into the rest of China. Tanaka's intention was to make Manchuria and Mongolia Japan's "special position" by using Chang Tso-lin, the warlord in the area, whom Tanaka regarded as his "younger brother." In his traditionalistic *"oyabun-kobun"* mentality, Tanaka did not seem to have a clear understanding of democratic rules in modern international relations such as the notions of national sovereignty and territorial integrity. Chang Tso-lin's assassination in June 1928 doomed Tanaka's ambitions in Manchuria. Moreover, Chang Hsüeh-liang, the son of Chang Tso-lin, brought the Three Eastern Provinces into political union with the rest of China under the Nationalist regime toward the end of 1928. Thus, Tanaka's "positive policy" toward China resulted in complete failure, and the Tanaka Cabinet toppled on July 2, 1929.

One can detect the fact that Japan's ultranationalism was already in embryo in the Tanaka administration. First of all, Tanaka often stated that Japan was the "Lord of East Asia," and that Japan and China were like family members; Japan of course was the older brother and China the younger brother. He believed that Japan's mission was to secure peace in the Far East and to attain the "co-prosperity" of Japan and China. He was firmly convinced that Japan's *kokutai* was "the best in the world," and that no nation could match this splendid tradition of the Japanese Empire. In the Fifty-fifth Diet of 1928, he emphasized the need for Japanese people's "absolute loyalty to the

Imperial Household and zealous patriotism." According to this conviction, Tanaka carried out ruthless purges of communists and anarch-
ists, changed the peace-preservation law so as to include the death
penalty for those who attempted to threaten the *kokutai,* and strengthened the special police force. Tanaka aimed to make Manchuria and
Mongolia "Japan's special position" so that the region would serve as
the "buffer zone" against communist infiltration into Asia from Russia.
Furthermore, Mori Kaku, Vice-Minister of Foreign and Political Affairs
in the Tanaka administration, was of the opinion that because the
Washington Treaties intended to put Japan into a cage, Japan would
have to overturn the Washington System. According to Mori, Japan's
"divine mission" was to work for the stabilization of Asian people's
life against Western domination and exploitation.

JAPAN'S ASSERTION OF *RAISON D'ÊTRE*

THE HAMAGUCHI Osachi (Yūkō) Minseitō Cabinet succeeded the
Tanaka administration, and Shidehara once again became Foreign
Minister. However, by this time, the real management of Manchurian
affairs was already under the control of the *Kantō-gun,* and not Tokyo.
Although Tanaka never contemplated taking the Three Eastern Provinces by military means, Chang Tso-lin's assassin, Kōmoto Daisaku,
and some more radical elements of the *Kantō-gun* did. They had
described even Tanaka's Manchurian policy as "weak-kneed" and "not
tough enough." When the *rapprochement* between Chiang Kai-shek and
Chang Hsüeh-liang was established and the latter started to build railways parallel to Japan's South Manchurian Railway, the radicals of
the *Kantō-gun* were convinced that there was no other alternative but
Japan's control of the region. For them, according to traditional military ideas, Manchuria was Japan's "life line," and the railways were
the "blood veins" of that life line.

Ever since the early Meiji period there had been a dominant argument in terms of traditional strategy that Japan, as a small insular
country, could maintain its national security only by expansion beyond
the four major islands. According to this argument, Japanese territory
proper was called the "sovereignty-zone," and its vicinity the "interest-
zone." The Army had maintained the view that in order to defend
Japan's sovereignty-zone, the interest-zone also had to be protected.
Based upon such logic, Japan had incorporated Ryūkyū, Taiwan, South
Sakhalin, and Korea into its territory step by step; and all those areas
came to be considered part of Japan's sovereignty-zone. Thus, in the
first decade of the twentieth century Manchuria became Japan's
interest-zone to protect the enlarged sovereignty-zone. By the end of
the twenties, most of militarists had even been convinced that Manchu-

ria was no longer just the interest-zone but Japan's life line itself. The Manchurian Incident broke out just when Japanese diplomacy had reached the ultimate stage, the time for Japan to assert its *raison d'être* in the world.

The Incident was welcomed by most Japanese at home. During that time, Japan was suffering serious economic depression, unemployment, agrarian-tenant disputes, and increasing crimes and suicides. A decadent and nihilistic atmosphere prevailed over big cities. *Ero fafue* (erotic cafés) and *ero baa* (erotic bars) thrived. In those bars, cafés, and dance halls, obscene and nonsensical conversations went on. In theatres, idiotic talks and dramas (*acharaka*) won popularity. In women's journals and magazines, the "disclosure" (*bakurokiji*) of divorces and triangular relationships became popular. It was the period of the so-called *"ero-guro-nansensu"* (eroticism, grotesquesness, and nonsense). A journalist described the situation by saying that the whole society looked like a cell without any exit in which people were being suffocated. Under such circumstances, the Manchurian Incident looked to many Japanese like an "outlet" which was suddenly opened to rescue them. Ishiwara Kanji, who was a Staff Officer and a chief promoter of the Incident, thought that the state of affairs in the Japanese Empire had come to a deadlock. Therefore, to own Manchuria and Mongolia was the only way left for Japan to solve overpopulation, food shortages, and other problems. A survey shows that nearly all the newspapers hailed the Incident, and people were told that Japan was fighting for the "establishment of a paradise based upon the Imperial Way" (*ōdō rakudo*) and the realization of "co-prosperity and co-existence of Japanese, Chinese, Koreans and Mongolians." Thus, Manchuria became Japan's Utopia.

Ishiwara asserted that the next war would be the final war of mankind. In order to win the war, a system of general national mobilization had to be built, and for that purpose Japan's control of Manchuria and Mongolia was absolutely necessary. However, a remarkable phenomenon was the fact that Manchuria and Mongolia were regarded not only as the vital areas for Japan's security and for its procurement of food and natural resources, but also as the symbol of the development of Oriental civilization. The war was to realize the "Great ideal of the Imperial Nation." The chief of staff of the *Kantō-gun* declared that since the foundation of the Japanese Empire, the nation's goal had been to bring "the eight corners of the world under one roof" based upon the way of *kami;* and that Japan had to establish a concrete plan by which it could spread the Imperial Way over all of China. This was the ideological background of the Manchurian Incident. In other words, the Incident was Japan's initiation for putting forth the realization of its ultimate goal, which had been aimed at "ever since the foundation of the Japanese empire." "The final war of the world will come," Ishiwara professed, "when Japan has firmly established its central position in the Oriental civilization and when the United States has accomplished the same position in the Western civilization."

The ideological backbone of the second Sino-Japanese War and ultimately that of the Pacific War must be understood as the further development of this kind of belief system. Hence, the *Draft of Basic Plan for Establishment of Greater Asia Co-Prosperity Sphere* declared:

> The Japanese Empire is a manifestation of morality and its special characteristic is the propagation of the Imperial Way. It strives but for the achievement of *Hakkō Ichiu* . . . . It is necessary to foster the increased power of the Empire, to cause East Asia to return to its original form of independence and co-prosperity by shaking off the yoke of Europe and America, and to let its countries and peoples develop their respective abilities in peaceful co-operation and secure livelihood . . . .
>
> The ultimate aim in thought construction in East Asia is to make East Asiatic people revere the Imperial influence by propagating the Imperial Way based on the spirit of construction, and to establish the belief that uniting solely under this influence is the one and only way to the eternal growth and development of East Asia . . . .

And the *Imperial Rescript Declaring War on the United States and British Empire* asserted: "Now that we have risen up in arms, we must accomplish our ultimate end. Herein lies the core of our theory. In Nippon resides a destiny to become the Light of Greater East Asia and to become ultimately the Light of the World . . . ."

PSYCHOLOGY OF JAPAN'S ULTRANATIONALISM

SINCE THE Manchurian Incident, as Japanese aggression was escalated through the Shanghai Incident, the second Sino-Japanese War, and the Pacific War, the whole nation was involved in the whirlpool of ultranationalism. But Japan's "mission" had already been set forth by the Meiji Constitution, the Imperial House Law, and the Imperial Rescript of Education. The myths and beliefs described in them justified Japanese aggressions. General Araki Sadao in 1933 asserted:

> Needless to say, the Imperial Army's spirit lies in exalting the Imperial Way and spreading the National Virtue. Every single bullet must be charged with the Imperial Way and the end of every bayonet must have the National Virtue burnt into it. If there are any who oppose the Imperial Way or the National Virtue, we shall give them an injection with this bullet and this bayonet.

Lacking an understanding of transcendence and ecclesiastical authorities to assert the supremacy of the other world, Japanese looked to the Emperor as the symbolic head of justice and good; the nation over which he reigned for that reason alone became virtuous. Hence, the basis for Japanese aggression differed fundamentally, say, from that of the Germans. In the divine-human continuum of the traditional Japanese *Weltanschauung,* there was no absolute, transcendental judge to chastise evil acts; rather, the deeds of the self-righteous nation in the name of the divine Emperor were considered just without question. In this kind of politico-religious society, only Christians and socialists rejected the existing order by demythologizing the Emperor. The following statement in *Akahata* (The Red Flag), the socialist-communist organ, illustrates the socialists's attitude toward the Emperor and war. On October 5, 1931, it advocated: "Through the people's struggle against imperialistic wars, through their struggle for the protection of the Soviet League and of the Chinese Revolution, let us destroy the Emperor and the Buddhist priests who instigate imperialism!" Here the Emperor was regarded as far from virtuous. He was, on the contrary, considered the symbol of evil and the source of imperialism. Christians, on the other hand, exalted the kingdom of God as the only true justice, and from this standard they too asserted that Japan's military expansion in glorification of the divine rule was sinful. However, Christians and socialists were only minorities in Japan.

After the war, many people defended their co-operation with the militarists in the pre-war period by the claim that there was no room for dissent because the Law for the Maintenance of Public Peace (*Chian Ijihō*) was so rigid and the government so autocratic. This is true to a certain extent. But perhaps the most important factor was that the war and jubilant nationalism gave the people of sense of "positive" meaning and identity. The *kokutai,* belief in the imperial way, and society as a whole had assumed profound religious implications for most pre-war Japanese.

Further explanation is required. As we have said, from the beginning of the modern age Japan was a politico-religious nation without a popular understanding of transcendental dualism. After 1890, the chanting of the Imperial Rescript on Education was required at all schools, and the people were taught to "revere the Emperor" and to "perform self-sacrifice in the interests of the state" from kindergarten on to university. As time passed, the people began to feel a sense of divine mission: the Japanese were a "chosen race" which alone could save exploited Asians, restore the Oriental culture despoiled by the West, and bring "the eight corners of the world under one roof." To many Japanese, these slogans were not simply empty cant, as Maruyama Masao, a prominent Japanese political scientist pointed out, but

a real source of meaningful life and existence. In the midst of "collective effervescence," akin to a Japanese drunken festivity, the people
became totally dependent upon one another. They were elevated to
a religious realm in which the Japanese state itself became divine, and
the state's acts were totally virtuous. The Emperor and the flag of the
rising sun were exalted as totemic symbols of the greater sanctity and
national identity.

Even under normal circumstances man must relate himself to
society to "live"; even more is this true of a situation of collective
effervescence. For social forces work upon us not merely from outside.
The collective spiritual force penetrates us and acts upon us from
within. As Emile Durkheim put it, "it becomes an integral part of our
being." Had Buddhism with its logic of negation maintained its original spiritual vitality, Japan might have been a somewhat different
society. It might have had something to oppose political power and
authority. But Buddhism had long been subjugated by political rulers
and incorporated into the dominant order of society, as the editors
of *Akahata* realized. Buddhism had lost not only its original quality of
transcendence, but also that of spiritual salvation. Buddha had been
dead in Japan long before God appeared to die in many Christian
societies. In the place of Buddhism, the Emperor and flag had been
elevated as symbols of "civil religion," and society thereby assumed a
religious character as the only source of "meaningful life" and the
"reality of existence." When an exclusive nationalism becomes the self-
righteous civil religion of a society, as in Japan through 1945, that
society endangers not only others but itself. During World War II
the rulers of both Germany and Japan went to great lengths to define
the *raison d'être* of their regimes in history, yet their machinations
resulted only in the frustration of the contribution to historical progress which they had promised. Blind patriotism, indeed, becomes easily
"the last refuge of a scoundrel."

AMERICAN STRATEGY IN THE PACIFIC: ITS PHILOSOPHY AND PRACTICE

THOMAS B. BUELL

A CENTURY ago two deep-thinking naval officers, Steven B. Luce and Alfred Thayer Mahan, inspired the genesis of the American strategy that achieved victory in the Pacific during the Second World War. The navy of their time had begun to rejuvenate its fleet after years of decay following the Civil War. Scientific and technical developments that made warships larger and more powerful had begun to arouse naval minds long dormant. But little thought was given to envisioning how the new fleet would be used. Heretofore coastal defence seemed to have been the Navy's prime mission, but by the late nineteenth century America was looking beyond its shores. How then could the Navy best serve the national interests? Where should the fleet be concentrated, in one ocean or both? Such questions were rarely answered or even asked. The technology embodied in the warships was an end in itself.

Admiral Luce deplored the Navy's intellectual vacuum. To remedy things he persuaded Congress in 1884 to establish the Naval War College at Newport, Rhode Island, despite opposition from his reactionary colleagues. Its mission was to study strategy and the principles of naval warfare. These were unfamiliar and abstract concepts for officers accustomed to dealing solely with such so-called "practical matters" as engineering and gunnery. Captain Alfred Thayer Mahan soon joined the staff to deliver lectures that were to become the basis of his famous book, *The Influence of Sea Power Upon History* (1890), which established the foundations of strategic thought in the United States Navy.

The War College of Luce and Mahan survived early tribulations and in time achieved service acceptance. Most naval officers who made strategy in the Second World War had been students there, and many had served on the faculty, notably Raymond Spruance and Kelly Turner. Courses in strategy and tactics in the pre-war years were intense. Students read, heard lectures, and wrote papers, but the principal method of instruction was the war game. The games began with hypothesized scenarios. The students drew up estimates of the situation, developed strategies and plans, and fought abstract battles between opposing fleets. The enemy was always Japan.

Realism was stressed by representing actual ships and bases on the game boards. The geography of the Pacific theatre necessarily became familiar. From all this, a vision of a future war developed. It was generally believed that war would begin with a surprise Japanese attack on the Philippines, putting the Army garrison there under siege. Meanwhile the Pacific Fleet would fight its way across the ocean, advancing to the rescue. The Japanese Navy would fight a delaying action, weakening the Americans through attrition and extended lines of communication. When the two sides were of equal strength, a great fleet action would decide the war.[1]

This vision of the future was wrong in several respects. It was expected that battleships would dominate. They never did, of course. The supposedly more vulnerable aircraft-carriers, it was thought, would provide secondary support from the rear. In reality they were the very core of the American naval power in the Pacific. While amphibious warfare in the 1930s was conceded as necessary to seize bases leading to the Philippines, it was never intensively studied—except by the Marine Corps. In practice it became a sophisticated—albeit hazardous—method of assault that overwhelmed the Japanese at every turn.

Logistical support was treated superficially in those pre-war days, as it was thought that a supply train of perhaps twenty or thirty auxiliary ships would be sufficient for provisioning a fleet remote from its bases. Yet after the war began thousands of specialized ships from oilers to floating drydocks were developed and constructed that maintained the Pacific Fleet at sea almost indefinitely.

Submarines, so the pre-war thinking went, were principally for reconnaissance and harbour defence. There was no doctrine for using them against Japan's merchant marine. But after the shooting started the submarines devastated the Japanese merchant fleet, and many warships as well.

Despite such pre-war misconceptions, students did benefit significantly from the War College experience. They learned how to think logically and systematically. They developed a common vocabulary, together with a common perspective of the huge expanse of the Pacific Ocean and of the strategic relationships of its principal island groups. In other words, they knew what strategy was, and they understood the principles of naval warfare.

Strategic planning outside the College, however, was largely inactive, given the pacifism of the 1920s combined with the economic depression of the 1930s. The Navy Department finally began to stir with the advent of war in Europe and the Far East. When Harold R. Stark became Chief of Naval Operations (CNO) in August 1939, planning activity intensified. The new CNO assumed that the United States

---

[1] This, by the way, was the view held by the Japanese as well.

and Great Britain would become allies inevitably. So he began clandestine discussions with the Royal Navy. This task had a special urgency for Stark because during the First World War President Wilson had enforced American neutrality and had forbidden any war planning until the United States had become a belligerent. The result had been chaos. Stark wanted to be ready this time, and he was at least partially successful. The so-called ABC Agreements and the policy of Germany First were jointly developed before the attack on Pearl Harbor. Given their preoccupation with Great Britain and the Atlantic theatre, Navy planners simply reaffirmed the school solution for a war in the Pacific when considering Japan.

Stark's staff included some of the best brains in the Navy. Among them was the assistant CNO, Rear-Admiral Royal Ingersoll, formerly the chief war planner and destined to be Commander-in-Chief, Atlantic Fleet, throughout most of the war. The intellectually domineering Rear-Admiral Kelly Turner directed the Navy's war planning after service at the Naval War College, where his teaching of strategy had become legendary. Turner went on to become the Navy's principal amphibious commander in the Pacific. Other top-notch planners included Harry Hill, later an amphibious commander in the Pacific; Charles "Savvy" Cooke, who would become Admiral King's chief planner and strategist during the war; Charles M. "Carl" Moore, who later became Spruance's chief-of-staff in the Pacific theatre; and Forrest Sherman, who would become Nimitz's plans officer during the war and eventually became a CNO.

Stark and his staff were an elite and rather aloof group who discouraged recommendations from the fleet, in large measure because of Kelly Turner's self-esteem and his belief that only the Navy Department had the big picture. As a result, the fleet commanders were frequently unaware of plans affecting them that were being developed in Washington. The Pacific Fleet commander, J.O. Richardson, as well as his successor Kimmel, were in effect expected to follow orders as they were issued and not to ask questions. Ironically, much of Stark's own strategic planning was undercut by President Roosevelt who was making his own strategy based upon counsel not from Stark, but from the Department of State. The latter's advice persuaded the President to stand the fleet in Hawaii—over Navy objections—on the wishful premise that it would deter Japanese aggression. Meanwhile his political initiatives seemed to Japan a cause for war.

By mid-1941, however, the voice of a commander at sea had begun to be heard in Washington. It was that of Admiral Ernest J. King, who commanded the Atlantic Fleet. As his forces were confronting U-boats and helping Great Britain to survive, King frequently went to the capital to consult with the Navy Department and the President. In this way, Roosevelt and Secretary of the Navy Frank Knox discovered what the Navy already knew: King was a premier strategist, an incisive thinker with a towering intellect, and a fighter. He earlier had been passed over because of his arrogance and his enemies, but Stark had been smart enough to give him a second chance, and King made the most of it. When the Japanese attacked Pearl Harbor, Roosevelt and Knox summoned King to Washington to run the Navy. Legend has it that when King heard the news, his reaction was, "When they get into trouble, they send for the sons of bitches."

King's appointment as Commander-in-Chief, U.S. Fleet (COMINCH) created an awkward situation. Stark and his staff had been responsible for strategy until King's arrival, and Stark had remained King's nominal superior as Chief of Naval Operations. King acted decisively—if not ruthlessly—to establish his personal authority. His first order after having become COMINCH on December 30, 1941, was a strategic directive to the new commander in the Pacific, Chester Nimitz. The Pacific Fleet, said King, had as its primary objective the protection of the lines of communication from Hawaii to Australia and to Midway. Meanwhile King stripped Stark of his entire planning staff, taking some into his own office and sending others to sea. Nevertheless, uncertainty persisted as to who made naval strategy and who advised the President. Roosevelt solved that predicament by transferring Stark to London in early March 1942, and giving King both hats to wear. He had become the most powerful man in the history of the United States Navy.

In the first weeks of the war the Japanese advanced rapidly into Malaysia, overwhelming the disorganized western defenders. Meeting at the First Washington Conference during the unfolding disaster in the Far East, the American and British chiefs of staff decided to establish an unified command there (known as ABDA, for American, British Dutch, Australian) under the British General Archibald Wavell, in an effort to bolster the Allied defences. The question then arose as to who would give Wavell his orders. It was decided eventually that the combined American and British Chiefs of Staff would give strategic direction not only to Wavell, but to all American and British theatre commanders. The other Allied participants, for example the Canadians, Australians, Dutch, New Zealanders, and Chinese, would not be included in strategic deliberations even if their armed forces were involved. The next step was to define the strategic areas of responsibility. Quite properly the Pacific theatre came under American jurisdiction.

The Combined Chiefs of Staff (CCS) wanted their supreme status made legitimate, so they drafted a charter and submitted it to Roosevelt and Churchill in February 1942 for approval and signatures. Roosevelt finally initialled it in late April. Churchill never did sign it.

The absence of a charter notwithstanding, the CCS went on to become the finest example of coalition leadership in history.

The status of the American Joint Chiefs of Staff (JCS) was murkier still. They sought formal recognition and authority as a body, but Roosevelt refused to grant it either by executive order or by legislation, reasoning that with nothing in writing the Joint Chiefs would have the broadest possible latitude in running the war. Hence the JCS functioned in a legal limbo. While their supremacy in the armed forces hierarchy was unchallenged, the JCS were without authority over the civilian administrators responsible for industrial mobilization. They likewise resented receiving unfair criticism stemming from Roosevelt's deliberate ambiguity about their tasks and functions.

But such matters were essentially political and, however irritating, did not prevent the JCS from getting on with the war. In the Pacific they were still faced with one final organizational decision concerning the status of Admiral Nimitz and General MacArthur. Army Chief-of-Staff General George C. Marshall, ever the advocate of unity of command, asserted that there should be only one Pacific commander. King agreed, but only if Admiral Chester Nimitz was in charge, arguing it would be a naval war given the large ocean areas and small land masses. Moreover, King had conceded European war direction to Marshall, and he expected Marshall to reciprocate in the Pacific.

But what were they to do with General Douglas MacArthur? He had to remain in the Pacific if for no other reason than that Roosevelt and the JCS wanted MacArthur to stay away from Washington. King would never allow the General to control naval forces, but on the other hand, MacArthur by his seniority would never subordinate himself to Nimitz. The solution was a compromise. MacArthur would command the South-west Pacific Area, essentially Australia, New Zealand, New Guinea, and the Philippines. Nimitz was given command of everything else, the so-called Pacific Ocean Area. Both reported directly to the JCS, Nimitz through King and MacArthur through Marshall. So, in effect, the war in the Pacific was run by committee. So much for Marshall's theory of unity of command.

There followed an interesting contrast in their personal relationships. King and Nimitz met frequently to discuss and resolve a host of issues, some said because King did not entirely trust Nimitz's judgement.[2] By comparison, Marshall and MacArthur (who I think did not like each other very much) got together only once, when Marshall was passing through the Pacific on a roundabout return from an overseas

---

[2] On the other hand, King never conferred with his Atlantic Fleet commander, Royal Ingersoll, even though Norfolk was but a few hours away from Washington, and Ingersoll's fleet was fighting the Battle of the Atlantic. King often ignored Ingersoll and dealt directly with his subordinate commanders.

conference. Otherwise they communicated in writing or through emissaries. Marshall did invite MacArthur to Washington on several occasions, but MacArthur always declined on the grounds he could not leave his headquarters. His absence often worked against MacArthur during showdowns in Washington to resolve Pacific strategy, as King and his colleagues usually prevailed over MacArthur's recommendations presented *in absentia.*

Although the American wartime leaders had dissimilar personalities that often clashed, they all possessed one distinguishing characteristic that made them winners. It was their fighting spirit and their profound confidence that victory was inevitable. They sought to win the war as quickly as possible, by a direct approach that came to grips with the enemy.[3] This explains, for example, why Marshall wanted a cross-Channel amphibious assault in 1942, and why King wanted to move aggressively in the Pacific.

But the realities of logistics tempered such ambitious goals, such that the greatest problem facing Allied strategists was how best to allocate limited resources. As the Allies at first lacked men and materiel for a two-front war, they were guided by their pre-war policy of Germany first and then Japan. As a consequence, the European theatre received about 85 percent of their resources, the Pacific the remaining 15 percent. The question was how that small allocation was to be used against Japan. The British and Marshall advocated a passive defence, even to the extent of yielding even more territory if the Japanese pressed, as there was still plenty of ocean to fall back upon, or so they reasoned.

King scorned such ideas. They were heresy, he said. They would allow the Japanese to dig in, to consolidate their gains, and to exploit the resources they had conquered. Defeating Germany could take years, he reasoned, and the Japanese, if left unmolested, would be getting stronger all the time, lengthening the war and causing higher casualties. Hence, King would argue, there had to be at least a limited offensive in the Pacific to keep pressure on the Japanese.

It was certainly sound strategy, but at first it was also premature. In early 1942 King and his Navy by necessity were on the defensive, forced into reacting to Japanese initiatives. A small number of American aircraft-carriers seemed to be the only barrier between the Japanese and the West Coast. Hysterical public officials beseeched King to return the fleet to California. To a lesser degree, some of Nimitz's staff advocated holding the carriers in Hawaii as a fleet in being. King ignored such cries of alarm and despatched the carriers on raids that made great publicity but hardly scratched the Japanese.

---

[3] By contrast, the British advocated a peripheral approach and the strategy of exploiting opportunities as they developed.

Then the Navy got lucky. Cryptographers learned of Japanese intentions to seize Port Moresby in New Guinea, threatening the lines of communication to Australia that King had ordered Nimitz to protect. Thus forewarned, American carriers turned back the Japanese invasion forces in the Battle of the Coral Sea in May 1942. Similarly, the Americans won at Midway the following month, yet another instance of a battle fought to conform to King's very first strategic directive.

King passionately wanted to exploit the American victories before the Japanese could recover. The best opportunity seemed to be an amphibious assault in the Solomon Islands, where the Japanese had been advancing and threatening the line of communication between Hawaii and Australia. But Marshall balked. He needed every resource he could get for Europe, or as it turned out, for the invasion of North Africa. He and King haggled for nearly all of June. King threatened to go it alone, if necessary, with whatever force of ships and Marines he could muster. By the end of June Marshall finally agreed to an assault against Guadalcanal, but in spirit only. The Army would contribute nothing.

It was a terrible gamble without Army help. There were too few men, ships, and aircraft and too little time (six weeks) to plan, train, and organize. Vice-Admiral Robert Ghormley, the theatre commander, was pessimistic, almost defeatist. But King would not tolerate delay. The assault had to go on. The Marines went ashore on August 7, 1942. The Japanese counter-attacked within days and smashed four cruisers at the Battle of Savo Island. Through an act of providence the helpless transports supporting the Marines ashore were unharmed. King was stricken. He later said it was his blackest day of the war.

Yet the Navy and the Marines hung on in a see-saw war of attrition which they finally won after months of killing struggles. They had halted the Japanese offensive momentum, once and for all. Although King fretted for months afterwards that the Japanese might again attempt a major offensive, they never did. They had squandered their best pilots in the Solomons, while the Americans had been able both to fight and to assemble forces for a 1943 offensive. The initiative passed wholly to the Americans for the remainder of the war.

Even so, why had King, with forces so unprepared, taken such a risk? For had the Japanese not committed their forces piecemeal, they could have driven the Americans from the Solomons. Such a setback, in all likelihood, would have ended King's career and profoundly changed the course of the war. No successor could possibly have wielded the influence that King possessed and exercized.

I believe that King's obsession to attack the Solomons was his most important strategic decision of the war. It involved American forces for the first time in an offensive campaign in the Pacific, and it gave King a precedent to maintain the offensive momentum in that theatre, in lieu of a passive defence favoured by others. Given such a visible commitment, Roosevelt and Marshall, whether they liked it or not, were obligated in the eyes of the public to help make it succeed. Although King never publicly admitted it, one can speculate that he may well have wanted to get on Guadalcanal in advance of the November elections to put Roosevelt on the spot. Those were desperate days.

It is not possible here to address in detail King's advocacy, before the CCS in various 1943 conferences, of a strategy of offence in the Pacific. Several words, however, are in order. Under CCS rules the Americans and the British had to agree on the grand strategy for a given theatre before any major operations in that theatre could be authorized. While British forces did not operate in the Pacific until the waning months of the war, the British Chiefs of Staff nevertheless indirectly influenced Pacific strategy by their persistent opposition to King's proposals. The policy of "Germany First" was taken literally— every man, every weapon sent to the Pacific, reasoned the British, was one less of each to use against Hitler. But King, having forced his JCS colleagues into line, advanced his Pacific strategy as non-negotiable. The British were neither expected nor allowed to question its merits, although King thoroughly explained it, much like a school teacher, frequently citing Naval War College antecedents for his strategy. What King asked for and eventually got—after considerable arm twisting— was British acquiescence to allocating adequate resources to the Pacific.

It would also be well to acknowledge one important facet of King's Pacific strategy that did require active British participation, and that was in Burma. King wanted the British to reopen supply lines to the Chinese armies via the Burma Road. The reason was that King looked to China as a source of vast manpower, which, when properly equipped, could engage the bulk of the Japanese Army and so divert it from opposing the American forces coming across the Pacific. The British, however, were wary of both the Burma theatre and of helping the Chinese. Hence progress was slow until the latter part of the war when Mountbatten and Slim successfully invigorated the campaign.

Following the Trident Conference in May 1943, the strategic concept of offensive operations in the Pacific had been established, at least from the CCS view. King had received what he wanted, and thereafter it was a matter of working through the JCS to get it implemented. The Allied conferences of 1944 and 1945 were directed increasingly to political issues, and the JCS, concerned only with military developments, became progressively less involved in their deliberations.

It is also not possible to address here the implementation of the strategy that evolved once the American offensive kicked off with the assault of the Gilbert Islands in November 1943. Most military and naval scholars are aware of the mutually supporting dual advance across the Pacific, MacArthur leading the southern thrust across New Guinea to the Philippines, while Spruance's central forces advanced through the Gilberts, the Marshalls, and the Marianas to Iwo Jima and Okinawa. This grand strategy, as it developed, began as a compromise to keep both Nimitz and MacArthur usefully employed, but in the end it worked remarkably well because it applied pressure on the Japanese on two fronts, and it was more than they could handle.

Let me conclude with several comments on those I term the practitioners. King was without question the prime mover in terms of American strategy in the Pacific. Had the Navy been led by a lesser man the war against Japan could have lasted years longer than it did. It was King alone who convinced Roosevelt and Marshall to get moving in the Pacific and to negotiate with a united front when dealing with the British. Otherwise the Pacific theatre would have been quiescent; all major resources would have gone to Europe.

King's shrewdest procedural achievement was his insistence that all JCS strategic decisions had to be unanimous. He would never agree to decisions by majority vote because he would have lost on issues he considered vital. Hence, when there was disagreement, decisions were deferred, usually to the distress of impatient theatre commanders wondering what to do next. Nor would the JCS refer a dispute to the President because, in my opinion, they did not trust Roosevelt's judgement in matters of strategy. Hence the JCS would often be stalemated for months, but King was willing to wait and to debate as long as necessary to achieve unanimity.

While King was very often obstinate in getting his way with the JCS and CCS, on the whole he sought a consensus from his naval colleagues on how to implement the Pacific strategy once Roosevelt and Churchill had approved it in principle. There were two major exceptions: his advocacy of the assault on Guadalcanal in August 1942, and of the invasion of the Mariana Islands in June 1944. In both cases he overruled the objections of his principal subordinates. Otherwise King listened to the advice of such people as Chester Nimitz, Raymond Spruance, Kelly Turner, their staffs in the Pacific, and of course his own planning staff under Savvy Cooke. It was their opposition, for example, that finally persuaded King to abandon one of his favourite plans, an assault against Formosa.

The United States Army, led by George C. Marshall, had as its primary focus the war in Europe. Although Marshall was not a student of sea power, nevertheless the Army did influence Pacific strategy because its forces fought in nearly every major Pacific campaign. The dominant Army presence was, of course, Douglas MacArthur. As with most theatre commanders, his strategic vision was limited to his own domain, and in his view all available forces in the Pacific should have been assigned to his command. He consistently opposed the Navy's plan for a central Pacific offensive, mistakenly asserting that the fleet would be vulnerable to Japanese land-based air power, and that amphibious assaults against heavily defended atolls would be suicidal. In the early years of the war, by contrast, MacArthur would bypass and isolate entrenched Japanese forces, and he normally operated within range of his own Army aircraft. His thinking had completely changed, however, by the time of the assault against the Philippines, for by then he had learned to appreciate what sea power could do.

MacArthur, interestingly enough, was able to win the respect of many of those flag officers in the Pacific Fleet who had come to know him personally. He was a charmer. MacArthur even managed to persuade Nimitz and his staff that the Marianas should be bypassed and every resource brought to bear upon the Philippines. King, not surprisingly, was furious when he learned of Nimitz's defection, and he quickly brought Nimitz back into line.

The greatest strategic issue to MacArthur was his return to the Philippines. His reasons were both moral and military: the Filipino people had to be freed from the Japanese invader, and the Philippines, when once again in American control, would isolate Japan from its conquests in Malaysia, the source of the raw materials for which it had gone to war. King at first was ambivalent about the Philippines, but as the war progressed he was less and less in favour of recapturing them. He regarded them as a diversion, as they were not in a direct line to Japan. Seizing them would delay other operations, as indeed they did. For example, the assault on the Philippines allowed the Japanese extra time to fortify Iwo Jima and increased Marine Corps casualties there.

The war finally ended as it had been envisioned by the Naval War College years before, with Japan blockaded by American forces which had fought their way across the Pacific, although no one could have predicted the atomic bomb. While the Navy's basic strategic concept envisioned before the war had remained intact, the means of implementing that strategy had been profoundly changed. The four keys to victory were carrier air warfare, amphibious warfare, submarine warfare, and logistical support. None of these had been extensively developed before the war by the Navy as an institution. Fortunately, the Navy had learned fast once the shooting started.

CANADIAN VIEWS OF UNITED STATES POLICY TOWARDS JAPAN, 1945-1952

A.R. MENZIES

CANADIAN VIEWS of American policy towards Japan during the war, occupation, and the negotiation of the Japanese Peace Treaty were moulded by an awareness of our junior partnership with the United States in the defence of North America, recognition of the need to defeat Japanese militarists while keeping Japan in the Western orbit, an optimistically liberal approach to Japanese politics and economic management, and a determination to preserve the North Pacific fisheries east of the date-line primarily for Canadian-American exploitation.

It is not the purpose of this paper to describe the development and expression of Canada's international identity in the inter-war years. Although a Canadian legation was opened in Japan in 1928, it did not provide broad strategic analyses of the situation in the Pacific; Ottawa continued to look to British reports for these. Nevertheless, papers prepared by Canadian academics for the Yosemite Conference of the Institute of Pacific Relations (IPR) in 1936 provided thoughtful perspectives on Japan's aggressive posture and activities in the Western Pacific.[1] The Canadian Institute of International Affairs (CIIA) commissioned William Strange to write a book entitled *Canada, the Pacific and War,* published in 1937, which contained prophetic predictions about the inevitability of Canadian involvement in any American-Japanese War. The young academics—Hugh Keenleyside, Lester Pearson, Hume Wrong, and Norman Robertson—that Dr. O.D. Skelton had been bringing into the Department of External Affairs were influenced by and had a continuing interaction with academics who contributed to the CIIA and IPR conferences and publications.

When World War II broke out in Europe in September 1939 Canadian attention was focused on Hitler's armies overrunning Western Europe. For two years the Commonwealth countries—Canada, Australia, New Zealand, and South Africa—were the principal allies

---

[1] Canadian papers prepared for the Yosemite Conference of the Institute of Pacific Relations: Henry F. Angus, *Responsibility for Peace and War in the Pacific* (Toronto: CIIA, 1936); N.A.M. MacKenzie, *Canada and the Changing Balance of Power in the Pacific* (Toronto: CIIA, 1936); J.W. Pickersgill, *International Machinery for the Maintenance of Peace in the Pacific Area* (Toronto: CIIA, 1936).

157

in the defence of Britain and its empire overseas. Canada's armed forces were built up progressively, the Commonwealth Air Training Plan was launched, and Canadian war production grew quickly. Canada's importance in the Commonwealth war effort was considerable.

In keeping with this collective war effort, the Canadian government responded favourably to a British request of September 19, 1941, to send two battalions (totalling 1,973 men), the Winnipeg Grenadiers and the Royal Rifles of Canada, to Hong Kong.[2] In order to strengthen North American defences, President Roosevelt invited Prime Minister Mackenzie King to meet him in northern New York State where they signed the Ogdensburg Agreement on August 17, 1940, establishing the Canadian-United States Permanent Joint Board on Defence (PJBD). Three meetings of the Board were held on the Pacific coast in September to review defences and to plan the Northwest Staging Route by which aircraft could be moved by a safe inland route to Alaska.[3] The Edmonton-Whitehorse portion of the route was open by December 1941, complete with radio aids and runway lighting. On April 20, 1941, the Hyde Park Declaration erected a framework for the co-ordination of the production of war materials by Canada and the United States for hemisphere defence and assistance to Britain and the other democracies.[4] Furthermore, a series of joint economic committees were established, including the Joint Production Committee.

WAR AGAINST JAPAN

THE JAPANESE attack on Pearl Harbor on December 7, 1941, ushered in a new phase of World War II. Canada declared war on Japan even before the United States and other allies.[5] It regarded the threat from the Axis as world-wide and one to be met by collective action on the part of all the democracies. The Canadian contribution was made primarily on the Atlantic, in Europe, and through the production of war materiel.

The most immediate effect felt was the loss of the 1,973 men of the Royal Rifles of Canada and the Winnipeg Grenadiers when the Japanese attacked Hong Kong. The garrison surrendered on Christmas Day. Altogether 555 Canadians lost their lives in the defence of

---

[2] C.P. Stacey, *The Canadian Army 1939-45* (Ottawa, 1948) pp. 273-74.
[3] C.C. Lingard and R.G. Trotter, *Canada in World Affairs, Sept. 1941 to May 1944* (Toronto: Oxford University Press, 1950), p. 29.
[4] Lingard and Trotter, p. 4.
[5] Lingard and Trotter, p. 50. Also *Documents on Canadian External Relations, 1939 to 1941* (Ottawa: Department of External Affairs) Part II, Vol. 8, 1558-59.

the Hong Kong colony and in prison camps thereafter. The June 4, 1942, Report of the Royal Commissioner, Chief Justice Sir Lyman Duff, indicated that the force had been despatched in good faith on the basis of erroneous information from British sources that "war in the Far East was unlikely" at the time. There was criticism of the failure of the Canadians to despatch equipment and vehicles with their forces.[6] Generally this was an episode which strengthened the resolve of Prime Minister Mackenzie King that Canadian forces should not be used in the defence of, or reconquest of, colonial territories. This resolve influenced the War Cabinet against accepting the assignment of Canadian forces to Britain's South-east Asia Command in the final months of the Pacific War.

We have already seen that, before the United States entry into the war, the PJBD had been reviewing Pacific coast defences and the construction of the Northwest Staging Route to Alaska for aircraft. In meetings on February 25-26, 1942, the PJBD recommended the construction of the Alaska Highway linking the airfields of the Northwest Staging Route. This was approved by the two governments on March 6 and recorded in an exchange of notes on March 16-17.[7] The 1,523 mile highway was completed in November 1943. The Canol Pipeline Project, which was to supply 3,000 barrels of oil a day from Norman Wells to a refinery in Whitehorse, was undertaken. Work on the Alaska Highway and ancillary projects by the U.S. Army Corps of Engineers and contractors gave rise to some friction due to higher U.S. pay scales. However, Canada avoided long-term effects by offering better facilities with provision for the removal of movable U.S. equipment and the turnover of non-movable equipment within one year of the termination of hostilities.[8]

These infrastructure facilities were designed to fill a strategic void in North America's shortest great circle route to Japan. In June 1942, Japanese forces landed on Attu and Kiska Islands in the Aleutian chain, some 700 and 1,000 miles respectively from Shumushu in Japan's Kuril chain. Canadian aircraft and ships were despatched immediately to reinforce U.S. defences in Alaska. On August 15, a 4,800-man Canadian Army brigade landed with U.S. forces on Kiska, only to find

[6] Statement by the Minister of National Defence, Hon. J.L. Ralston, *House of Commons Debates*, January 21, 1942, 4470. Sir Lyman Duff, Royal Commissioner, *Report on the Canadian Expeditionary Forces to the Crown Colony of Hong Kong* (Ottawa, June 4, 1942). This report was debated in the House of Commons on July 10, 1942, 4096-97; July 15, 1942, 4254; and February 24, 1948, 1549-51.

[7] *Canada Treaty Series*, 1942, No. 13 (Ottawa, 1944). Canadian *House of Commons Debates*, March 6, 1942, 1091.

[8] Lingard and Trotter, p. 160; C.P. Stacey, *The Canadian Army 1939-45*, pp. 289-90.

that the Japanese had withdrawn a few days earlier under cover of fog.[9] The Canadian brigade, using U.S. equipment for the first time, stayed three months on Kiska before withdrawing.

It is interesting to speculate on what would have been the course of the Pacific War and its effect on Canada if the Japanese had persisted in their thrust along the Aleutian Island chain rather than concentrating on pushing south through the Philippines, Malaysia, Singapore, Indonesia, New Guinea, and the Solomon Islands. Then, again, if the United States had decided to attack Japan by the North Pacific route it would have had a very different impact on Canada than the South Pacific island route chosen. So far as the writer has been able to ascertain, Canadian views on this aspect of Pacific strategy were neither sought nor proferred.

Indeed, after U.S. entry into the war, Allied war policy was dictated by President Roosevelt and Prime Minister Churchill, and their Combined Chiefs of Staff and Combined Economic Boards.[10] Canada, which had been Britain's principal ally before Pearl Harbor, found itself very much a secondary power, excluded from real policy decision-making.[11] Perhaps to ease the appearance of firm Anglo-American control of high war policy, and to respond to complaints from Australia in particular, the British government announced on February 9, 1942, the establishment of a Pacific Council at ministerial level, representing the U.K., Australia, New Zealand, and the Netherlands, to co-ordinate defence in the South Pacific. As Canada had not been included, Prime Minister King reported to the House of Commons on February 16 that Prime Minister Churchill had informed him that "as at present constituted, [the Council's] duties are directly related to questions of regional defence of the areas in the South-west Pacific and South-western Asia against which Japanese offensive action is now directed." Mr. King went on to say that Canada's immediate sector of the Pacific Front was one it held jointly with the United States with whom arrangements for common defence were being worked out. Should future strategic requirements make it desirable to enlarge the scope of the Pacific Council to include the whole Pacific area, Mr. King declared that Canada would certainly be represented.[12]

On March 17, 1942, General Douglas MacArthur arrived in Australia from the Philippines and was appointed, by the U.S.,

[9] Lingard and Trotter, pp. 109, 159-60; C.P. Stacey, *The Canadian Army 1939-45*, pp. 289-90.
[10] C.P. Stacey, *Canada and the Age of Conflict*, Vol. 2, 1921 to 1948 (Toronto: University of Toronto Press, 1981) p. 360.
[11] Lingard and Trotter, p. 129.
[12] Canadian *House of Commons Debates*, February 16, 1942, p. 598.

Australia, and New Zealand governments, Supreme Commander in the South-west Pacific. Shortly thereafter, on March 30, a Pacific War Council was established in Washington to provide a common meeting ground for all the United Nations actively engaged in the Pacific conflict. Its first meeting on April 1, over which President Roosevelt presided, included British, Chinese, Australian, New Zealand, Netherlands, and Canadian representatives. Prime Minister King attended the third meeting on April 15.[13] India and the Philippines were represented on the Council later.

The Pacific Council in London ceased to exist, but provision was made for a counterpart of the Washington Pacific War Council to meet in London to inform the other governments about the policies decided on by the U.S. and U.K. The Canadian Cabinet War Committee had agreed on March 26 that Canadian representatives should attend the meetings in both Washington and London. The effectiveness of the Washington meetings was limited because the U.S. chiefs of staff did not attend. The Canadian High Commissioner in London reported that the meetings in the British capital were just make-believe.

The Pacific War Council might have provided a suitable grouping for Allied discussion of post-hostilities plans for the occupation of Japan and the peace settlement with Japan. But this does not appear to have been done, perhaps because internal discussion of these subjects by the Americans was still at an early stage.

The writer's experience is that post-war planning for Japan was a subject on which the Canadian government was not formally asked for views by the U.S. government, and the Canadians did not proffer any. Such consultation as there was, was informal. Dr. E.H. Norman, the well-known Canadian diplomat and historian of Japan, went to Washington two or three times, after his repatriation from Japan on the *Gripsholm* in August 1942, to give his views informally on the structure of Japanese society. In 1943 and 1944 the writer was invited on three occasions by Dr. Nathaniel Peffer, author of *Prerequisites to Peace in the Far East,* to give a series of lectures on Japan to U.S. Navy Civil Affairs courses conducted at Columbia University in New York. On these occasions there was much informal discussion of occupation and peace treaty objectives.

The Institute of Pacific Relations held a conference from January 6 to 17, 1945, at Hot Springs, Virginia, where a dozen national delegations composed of academics, civil servants, and military officers discussed the future of Japan, among other subjects. The writer attended that conference and found that the discussion provided a broad spectrum of views on occupation policies, the role of the

---

[13] Lingard and Trotter, p. 136.

Emperor, disarmament, reparations, the direction of the Japanese economy, and the nature of the peace treaty. The views expressed indicated considerable divergence on occupation policy. At the time the writer recorded this observation: "no doubt as time goes on a compromise of sorts will be worked out between those who advocate a radical re-examination of the structure of Japanese society and those who feel it may be necessary, at the outset at least, to work with whatever Japanese government is in power."[14]

Because of Canadian parallels with U.S. policies and their postwar impact on Japan, some mention should be made in this paper of Canada's harsh treatment of persons of Japanese ethnic origin who were living on the West Coast of Canada when the Pacific War broke out. Although there was no evidence of subversive activity in Canada, pressure from British Columbia politicians caused Prime Minister Mackenzie King to toughen an initial moderate policy and, on February 26, 1942, order the evacuation of all persons of the Japanese race from the Pacific coast. On March 4 the British Columbia Security Commission was created to take charge of the evacuation of 21,000 Japanese Canadians. The sale of their properties at low prices caused both emotional and real hardship. After the war Japanese nationals and their Canadian-born children were encouraged to return to Japan: 3,964 returned, including 200 Canadian-born.[15] In their tough handling of West Coast people of Japanese origin in Canada, Canadian politicians felt that they were acting in general conformity with American practice.

Canada considered that its contribution in the Atlantic, in Europe, and in the production of war supplies should be given full credit in the cumulative Allied war effort. Britain and the United States understood the position. Australia, after initial disappointment over the Canadian government's failure to accept the recommendation of the Canadian High Commissioner, Major-General Victor W. Odlum, that a Canadian division be sent to defend Australia in the early months of 1942, was somewhat mollified eventually by the provision of twenty million dollars in Canadian Mutual Aid.[16] Altogether Canada provided about two billion dollars in Mutual Aid, as well as compensating the United States for war construction in Canada.

Prior to the surrender of Germany on May 8-9, 1945, the Canadian government had been discussing with the American and British governments the allocation of forces it might make to the final stages

---

[14] Extract from diary copy of weekly letter by A.R. Menzies, January 21, 1945.

[15] Lingard and Trotter, p. 6.

[16] Canadian Department of External Affairs *Memorandum* No. 14, December 16, 1945.

of the war against Japan. Prime Minister King, recalling the Hong Kong disaster and other British requests for the supply of garrison forces as far away as the Falkland Islands, made it clear that Canadian forces would not be available for the reconquest of former colonial territories in South-east Asia. Domestic and international credit would be gained through participation in the direct assault on the Japanese Home Islands. Eventually it was announced in July 1945 that approximately 200,000 Canadian service personnel would be given the opportunity to volunteer for service in the war against Japan. The Royal Canadian Navy would have 37,000 men, with 13,500 at sea under Royal Navy command, for the assault on Japan. The Canadian Army would field 30,000, grouped on the 6th Division under Major-General Bert Hoffmeister, who would serve under U.S. Army command. The Royal Canadian Air Force would have 100,000 for Pacific duty.

These Canadian plans for an active role in the final stages of the assault on the Japanese Home Islands were curtailed by the effects on the Japanese will to continue the struggle after the dropping of the atomic bombs on Hiroshima and Nagasaki on August 6 and 9, 1945, and the entry of the Soviet Union into the war on August 8. Canada did not play a high-profile national role in the war with Japan, so there was not the same public interest in Canada, as in Australia, that it should be active in the elimination of Japan's post-war ability to commit aggression. The lessons for Canada were recognition of its North American strategic identity, awareness of the enormous military power of the United States, and a desire for a global system to manage the post-war world.

When the Japanese Instrument of Surrender was signed on board the *U.S.S. Missouri* in Tokyo Bay on September 2, 1945, Colonel L. Moore Cosgrave, Canadian Military Attaché in Australia, signed for Canada with nine other national representatives.

OCCUPATION OF JAPAN

CANADA WAS not consulted about the understandings concerning Japan contained in the Cairo Conference Declaration released on December 1, 1943, the Yalta Agreement of February 11, 1945, or the Potsdam Proclamation defining the terms for Japanese surrender of July 26, 1945. Between the Japanese acceptance of the Potsdam Proclamation on August 14, 1945, and the signature of the Instrument of Surrender on September 2, the U.S. State, War, Navy, Co-ordinating Committee (SWNCC) reached agreement on an United States Initial post-Surrender Policy for Japan, which was cabled to General MacArthur on August 29 and approved by President Truman on

September 6. This latter document envisaged that the Supreme Commander for the Allied Powers (SCAP) would "exercise his authority through Japanese governmental machinery" in order to reduce the commitment of U.S. forces for occupation purposes.The broad thrust of U.S. occupation policy was already outlined.

The Canadian government declined to send a force to join in the occupation of Japan as it had done for some months in Germany. Non-participation in the British Commonwealth Occupation Force (BCOF), commanded by the outspoken Australian Lt. Gen. Sir Horace (Red Robbie) Robertson, probably curtailed Canadian influence in the early period of the occupation, but also safeguarded the Canadians from friction with the Americans and the Japanese.

An immediate post-surrender concern of Canada was the release of Canadian prisoners of war, mainly from the force which had surrendered in Hong Kong and had been transferred to Japan. Canada decided to take an active part in the major and minor war crimes tribunals. On August 21, 1945, the United States proposed to Britain, China, and the Soviet Union that a Far Eastern Advisory Commission (FEAC) be established in which countries that had taken part in the war against Japan would make recommendations "on the formulation of policies, principles and standards by which the fulfillment by Japan of its obligations under the instrument of surrender may be determined." The other Allies, including Canada, were informed later. All accepted, except the Soviet Union, which balked at the advisory role assigned to the FEAC and wanted a control commission to operate in Japan.

At the Moscow Conference of Foreign Ministers of the U.K., U.S.A., and U.S.S.R. a formula acceptable to Stalin was worked out replacing the FEAC with a Far Eastern Commission (FEC) with the same composition and responsibility "to formulate the policies, principles, and standards in conformity with which the fulfillment by Japan of its obligations under the terms of surrender may be accomplished." The United States government was to prepare the actual directives to SCAP setting out the policy decisions of the FEC. Although the Soviet Union secured veto powers like the other major powers in the FEC, the provision whereby the United States might issue interim directives to SCAP gave it final control. Canada accepted the terms of reference for the FEC without substantive comment and designated its Ambassador to the United States, Mr. L.B. Pearson, as its representative. Initially, Dr. E.H. Norman and Ralph Collins served as Canadian alternates. The latter was a regular working-level attender of the FEC when it began meeting regularly early in 1946.

The Moscow Conference of Foreign Ministers on December 27, 1945, also decided to establish an Allied Council for Japan (ACJ) with its seat in Tokyo, "for the purpose of consulting with and advising the Supreme Commander in regard to the implementation of the Terms of Surrender, the occupation and control of Japan, and of the directives supplementary thereto." Among the four members was one popularly called the British Commonwealth member; although the Moscow Agreement spelled out that there would be "a member representing jointly the United Kingdom, Australia, New Zealand, and India," this member was in fact nominated by Australia. Canada did not think that joint Commonwealth representation in an international body like the Allied Council for Japan was a practical measure. Enquiry indicates that Mr. MacMahon Ball, the Australian member of the Allied Council, in addition to forcefully expressing his own views about the need for tough measures, received instructions from the Australian Minister for External Affairs, Dr. H.V. Evatt, who was less than punctillious about consulting other Commonwealth governments. The Soviet member, General Derevyanko, used the ACJ as a public platform to criticize U.S. policies. The U.S. members, George Acheson and later William Sebald, replied in kind. Canada was well off, then, to have declined to be represented in the ACJ by the British Commonwealth member.

Canadian views on occupation policy for Japan were largely expressed through the Canadian representatives on the Far Eastern Commission meeting in Washington. Canada has used international organizations as a means of augmenting the volume of its voice when joined in an international chorus. Through the Far Eastern Commission, Canada was challenged to think about a wide range of occupation policies and to formulate views to be stated in the FEC and its committees. As Head of the Far Eastern Section from May 1946 to April 1948 and then Head of the Far Eastern Division until a posting to Japan in November 1950, the writer, with assistance from J.R. Maybee and later D.W. Wilson, devoted considerable time to the drafting of instructions for the Canadian representative on the FEC. Information for the preparation of guidance directives was drawn from a number of sources, such as information exchanges of views with other FEC delegations in Washington; reports and advice from Dr. E.H. Norman, who left Ottawa on July 22, 1946 to become Head of the Canadian Liaison Mission in Japan; comments of Canadian businessmen and missionaries who had lived in Japan; articles and books by experienced observers; and comparative Canadian experiences in the European post-war settlements.

Through the FEC Canada learnt much about the policies and tactics of other countries about Japan. Although the details of instructions were drafted by relatively junior officers and signed off by a Section or Division Head, it should be noted that in a department of less than fifty officers it was relatively easy to obtain oral guidance from senior officers, including a judgement about any ministerial statement that might be required in Parliament. However, questions were rarely asked in the House of Commons on matters under consideration in the FEC. Canada recognized that the United States carried the major responsibility for the defeat and occupation of Japan; and it would have to shoulder further burdens if anything went wrong.

Frequently Canadian ideas would be tried informally on American officials before they were put forward in the FEC. This is a typical Canadian practice: first, discuss a proposal confidentially bilaterally with the responsible American officials; then second, put on the record of an international organization a carefully crafted Canadian statement that recognizes the realities of American power, but nevertheless expresses a distinct Canadian view. Work of the Far East Commission was conducted mainly in seven working committees composed of all eleven members. Ralph Collins was deputy chairman of Committee No. 3 on constitutional and legal reform, so there was a special expectation that he would be well briefed on such problems as the status of the Emperor, the Diet, the Cabinet, and the drafting of a new constitution. Generally, Canada took an active part in all committees except for that on Aliens in Japan. Priority was given initially to the disarmament of Japan and to measures that would inhibit Japan from committing aggression again. Dr. Norman argued that it was more important to try to destroy the spirit of militarism in Japan, expressed by the ultranationalist societies and certain cliques in the Japanese armed forces, than to destroy military equipment and the war industries. Japanese politicans and bureaucrats who had experienced the usurpation of power by the military could be expected to go along with such measures. Publicity about the war-crimes trials could be helpful. There was also a need to rewrite school textbooks. By 1947 Japan had been physically disarmed, but when the Chief of the Canadian General Staff, General H.D.G. Crerar, visited Japan in August 1947 as a guest of General MacArthur, he doubted that there had been much change in Japanese thinking.[17]

British diplomats in Japan, like Sir Alvary Gascoigne and Sir George Sansom, seemed to cling to pre-war views of Japan, and were inclined to be sceptical about the prospects of modifying the traditional Japanese social structure and thought patterns. It was the Canadian view, derived from the assessments of Canadian missionaries, and the historical and sociological research of Dr. Norman, that some moderate liberal and democratic thinkers had survived the militarist

---

[17] Letter from General H.D.G. Crerar to Hon. Brooke Claxton, August 10, 1947, Department of External Affairs file 50051-40-3.

period in Japan, and would speak out in terms that would evoke popular support, provided encouragement was given by sound occupation policies.[18] In this respect Canadian views supported statements by General MacArthur which claimed successes in democratization in order to encourage such trends.

Agrarian reform had occupied the attention of SCAP Headquarters from the outset and was vigorously supported by Australia. An FEC policy decision of April 18, 1949, stated that the three main goals of the land-reform programme would be: (a) elimination of exorbitant rents usually payable in kind; (b) sale of land from large landlords to tenant farmers; and (c) establishment of a government-backed agricultural credit scheme by which small farmers could amortize the purchase of land over a period of many years.[19] Russian attempts to derive propaganda advantage from advocating free land distribution did not have much impact among the conservative small farmers.

The British Labour government, supported by the Australian Labour government, took an active interest in pushing through an early Far Eastern policy decision on December 6, 1946, on Principles for Japanese Trade Unions.[20] Indeed this subject drew general support in the FEC. Much of the time was taken up in the FEC in the discussion of reparations. The Chinese and Philippine delegations made extensive demands. Canada sided with the United States in arguing that the FEC should determine reasonable peace-time levels of Japanese economic activity, and from these determine Japan's margin of ability to pay reparations. For reasons of social stability and a desire to see normal trade restored, Canada opposed reparations payments which would have hindered the revival of reasonable economic health in Japan.[21]

In the early years of the occupation the United States had to ship to Japan large quantities of food and other relief supplies. It also provided equipment and materials for the repair of the essential

---

[18] Michael Fry, *The Occupation of Japan: The MacArthur-Norman Years,* 12, to be published in the *Proceedings* of a Symposium on "The Occupation of Japan: The International Context," held at Old Dominion University, Norfolk, Virginia, October 21-22, 1982.

[19] Agrarian Reform in Japan," Far Eastern Commission Policy Decision April 28, 1947, *Third Report by the Secretary General,* Far Eastern Commission, December 24, 1948 to June 30, 1950, p. 18.

[20] "Principles for Japanese Trade Unions," Far Eastern Commission Policy Decision December 6, 1946, *First Report by the Secretary General,* Far Eastern Commission, February 26, 1946 to July 10, 1947, pp. 91-93.

[21] *Documents on Canadian External Relations,* Vol. XII, Interdepartmental Committee on Japanese Reparations meetings and correspondence, pp. 303-17. Also DEA file 8364-C-40.

infrastructure and basic industries. Much of this came from U.S. war production surpluses funded by the Department of Defense. Japan became dependent on the United States for seventy percent of its imports, although the U.S. had little interest in purchasing Japanese exports. Other countries were required to balance their trade with Japan annually on a bilateral basis. Canadians sought liberalization of Japan's foreign trade as well as an improvement in pre-war trade practices in which trade marks and trade names had been abused.

Economic reconstruction was slow in Japan. The Dodge Mission sent by the United States in 1949 to examine the economy and make recommendations had some effect, but the real boost to the Japanese economy came from contracting for the U.S. forces during the Korean War.

It was the Canadian view that the military occupation of Japan, like that of other occupied countries, achieved as much of a positive character as could be expected in about three years. After that, co-operation from those accepting occupation "medicine" would fall off and the occupation would become counter-productive. An additional factor was the deterioration of relations between the Soviet Union and the Western countries, which gradually brought the work of the FEC to a standstill.

THE JAPANESE PEACE TREATY

BY THE summer of 1947 the United States had decided that the time had come to begin the negotiation of the Japanese Peace Treaty. Canada welcomed the invitation issued on July 11 to member governments of the FEC to meet in a preliminary conference on August 19. The U.S.S.R. replied that the Council of Foreign Ministers of the Great Powers should draft the treaty.

In anticipation of these negotiations an additional officer was assigned to the Far Eastern Section of the Department of External Affairs. Dr. H.V. Evatt, Minister of External Affairs for Australia, proposed that interested Commonwealth governments should meet in Canberra from August 26 to September 2 to exchange views on the Japanese Peace Treaty. This would be the first major Commonwealth foreign policy conference outside the United Kingdom and would include India, Pakistan, and Burma. In a statement in the House of Commons on July 10, Prime Minister Mackenzie King emphasized that the Canberra Conference was for an exchange of views "in an exploratory and non-commital way."

A substantial effort was made in putting together a briefing book for the Canadian delegation[22] led by the Honourable Brooke Claxton

---

[22] *Time* (Canadian edition) August 18, 1947, p. 15. Also DEA file 50051-40-1.

and including Dr. E.H. Norman from Japan and Ralph Collins, responsible for FEC matters in Washington. Mr. Claxton made a statement at the opening session of the Canberra Conference emphasizing "Canada's strategic position as a Pacific Power," and the need for an early peace treaty with Japan to avoid uncertainty and instability. He listed basic objectives of the settlement as a guarantee of security against any further Japanese aggression and the need to return to economic normalcy and trade.[23] These were broad and generalized objectives. Mr. Claxton evidently did not wish to be too precise or to give the impression that the Commonwealth countries would be reaching agreement on common terms.

Dr. Evatt, on the other hand, fearing a resurgence of Japanese aggression, wanted a post-war control commission to ensure that the Japanese armed forces were not revived and that the level of Japanese industry was kept much lower than the United States thought necessary. In the final negotiations Australia accepted a security guarantee from the United States in the form of the ANZUS Pact, in place of rigid post-war controls on Japan. Canada, of course, already had such an U.S. security guarantee in the Ogdensburg Agreement.

Procedural differences continued to put off the negotiation of the Peace Treaty. Canada and Britain consistently advocated that the United States should take the lead in negotiating a multilateral peace treaty. And even if the U.S.S.R. should refuse to join in, an effort should be made to accommodate legitimate Soviet interests. Canada and Britain opposed suggestions for a series of bilateral instruments to end the state of war, or for freeing Japan incrementally from occupation controls.

Nevertheless there was a mounting awareness in Western countries of the deterioration of relations with the Soviet Union in Europe, and the extension of communist control in Asia through the civil war in China. It may be recalled that anti-communist sentiment had been stimulated in Canada by the June 27, 1946, report of the Royal Commission on the Gouzenko revelations about the extent and methods of Soviet espionage.[24] After the Soviet takeover in Czechoslovakia in February 1948, the Berlin blockade, and the conclusion in March 1949 of a defensive alliance by five West European countries in the Treaty of Brussels, Prime Minister King stated that Canada would

---

[23] Statement by the Hon. Brooke Claxton at the opening of the Canberra Conference, August 26, 1947, *Current Notes*, August 1947, pp. 437-49.

[24] J.W. Pickersgill and D.F. Forster, *The Mackenzie King Record*, Vol. 3: 1945 to 1945 (Toronto, 1970), Ch. 2. Also the *Report of the Royal Commission Appointed to Investigate the Communication of Secret and Confidential Information to Agents of a Foreign Power* (Ottawa, 1946).

play its part in a regional security pact under the United Nations Charter.[25] Mr. Louis St. Laurent, then Secretary of State for External Affairs, immediately set about preparing public opinion for Canadian participation in the North Atlantic Treaty signed on April 4, 1949. These developments across the Atlantic in Europe inevitably influenced Canadian thinking about the Pacific and the importance of preventing the trained manpower and industries of Japan from slipping into the Soviet or Chinese Communist orbits.

In January 1950 the writer accompanied Mr. L.B. Pearson, then Secretary of State for External Affairs, to the first conference of Commonwealth Foreign Ministers in Colombo, Ceylon, where questions about the Japanese Peace Treaty and recognition of the Communist government which had been installed in Peking on October 1, 1949, were discussed at length. There was general agreement that a peace treaty for Japan should be negotiated as soon as possible, but new problems arose regarding which government of China should be invited to attend the conference and to whom Japan should cede Taiwan. The Commonwealth countries were divided: Britain, India, Pakistan, and Ceylon had recognized the new Communist government, while Canada, Australia, New Zealand, and South Africa recognized the Nationalist government which had fled to Taiwan. It was agreed that a Commonwealth working party should meet in London to discuss peace treaty issues in greater detail.[26]

Mr. Pearson went on to make his first visit to Japan where he held talks with General MacArthur. In reporting to the House of Commons on January 22, 1950, Mr. Pearson said:

> It is clear that the Japanese have fulfilled pretty well the requirements that have been imposed upon them by the occupation, and it seems to me that from here on we must give them some incentive to maintain and strengthen the democratic way of life, and to wish to maintain close and friendly relations with the western world.

The outbreak of war in Korea on June 25, 1950, strengthened the arguments for an early peace treaty with Japan. On September 14 President Truman announced that he had authorized the State Department to begin informal discussions with other member governments of the FEC. Mr. John Foster Dulles, a Republican, was named by the U.S. Secretary of State, Dean Acheson, as his deputy for the negotiation of the Japanese Peace Treaty; and Dulles immediately

---

[25] C.P. Stacey, *Canada and the Age of Conflict*, Vol. 2: 1921 to 1948 (Toronto: University of Toronto Press, 1981), p. 416.

[26] W.E. Harrison, *Canada in World Affairs 1949-50* (Toronto: Oxford University Press, 1957), pp. 239-40. Also *Report of the Department of External Affairs 1950*, p. 19.

began a round of discussions on the basis of a memorandum outlining American views.

Mr. Dulles visited Japan three times for discussions with the Japanese government. The writer was given personal reports on two of these occasions by Mr. Dulles. To resolve the question of divided recognition of the government of China, Mr. Dulles proposed that there be no Chinese representative at the Peace Conference. Subsequently, the Japanese government would decide with which Chinese government it wished to sign. In fact Mr. Dulles had already received assurance from Prime Minister Yoshida that he would sign a bilateral treaty with the Nationalist government in Taiwan.

Because of the special concerns of the U.S. Department of Defense that base facilities in Japan should remain available to the United States for the defence of Korea and to defend Japan itself, Mr. Dulles persuaded Prime Minister Yoshida, during his January-February 1951 visit, to agree to sign a Security Treaty with the United States in connection with the Peace Treaty. Mr. Yoshida also agreed to modest Japanese rearmament through the creation of a 50,000 man Japanese Self-defence Force.

The Japanese Ministry of Foreign Affairs submitted informally to the Diplomatic Section of SCAP a series of memoranda setting forth Japanese views on a variety of peace settlement issues.[27] However, copies of these memoranda were not given to other interested governments by the Japanese or the Americans.

Canada was concerned that, in conjunction with the peace settlement, a convention should be negotiated which would bind Japanese fishermen to abstain from fishing salmon, halibut, and herring east of the international date-line, where Canada and the United States claimed that they were managing the stocks of these fish on the basis of maximum sustainable yield.[28] The Minister and Deputy Minister of Fisheries went to Washington in the early spring of 1951 to discuss this subject with Mr. Dulles, who agreed that it was in the interest of the United States and Canada that assurances be sought from the Japanese that a mutually satisfactory convention would be concluded. The North Pacific Fishers Convention between Canada, Japan, and the United States was therefore negotiated in 1951 to 1952 and signed separately, but regarded as part of the peace settlement package.

---

[27] Statement by Ambassador Akira Matsui, formerly secretary to Prime Minister Yoshida, to be published in the *Proceedings* of a Symposium on "The Occupation of Japan: The International Context," held at Old Dominion University, Norfolk, Virginia, October 21-22, 1982.

[28] Speech by Prime Minister Louis St. Laurent to the Women's Canadian Club in Victoria, B.C., September 5, 1952.

Canada sent a strong delegation headed by the Secretary of State for External Affairs, Mr. L.B. Pearson, to San Francisco to sign the Japanese Peace Treaty on September 8, 1951.[29] Fifty-four countries were invited to attend. India, Burma, and Yugoslavia did not attend. Neither Chinese government was invited. The U.S.S.R., Czechoslovakia, and Poland attended, but did not sign. Forty-eight countries signed. In his report to the House of Commons on October 22, 1951, Mr. Pearson expressed general satisfaction with the Treaty.

CONCLUSION

IN PRESENTING Canadian views of United States policy towards Japan during the war, the occupation, and the negotiation of the Japanese Peace Treaty, this paper has been largely restricted to describing Canadian views and activities during these periods. Specific comments on American policies have often not been expressed but may be conjectured. Events have been selected because of the availability of information. An exhaustive search of primary sources has not yet been completed. It may be concluded, however, that during the period 1941 to 1952 Canada's awareness of its common interest with the United States in the defence of North America was heightened, but in responding to the apprehended threat from Japan, the Canadian government was determined to maintain control of its own territory. With the demilitarization of Japan and progress in destroying its militaristic ideology, Canada took an optimistic and liberal view of Japanese democratic reforms and welcomed the economic reconstruction of Japan. Removal of the fisheries issue strengthened support for the Japanese Peace Treaty, especially in British Columbia. The outbreak of the Korean War underlined the importance of keeping Japan in the Western orbit. Canada respected primary American responsibility for Japan, yet sought to express distinct national views where these existed.

---

[29] *External Affairs*, October 1951, p. 331.

INDEX

ABDA, 28, 29, 148
Abe, Admiral, 94
Abyssinian Crisis, 50
Acheson, George, 165
Aichi Tokei works, 90
Akagi, 100
Alaska Highway, 158-159
Aleutian chain, 159
Allied ABC-1 discussions, 53
Allied Council for Japan (ACJ), 165
Allied Naval Control Commission, 90
Allied Occupation of Japan, 3, 6, 17, 33
American Joint Chiefs of Staff, 53, 149, 153
Anglo-Dutch Shell, 83
Anglo-Japanese Alliance, 4, 12-13, 25, 47, 54, 60, 71, 134
Anti-Comintern Pact, 102
Araki, Captain Jirō, 92
Araki, General Sadao, 140
Arita Hachiro, 58-59
Asama Maru, 105
Atlantic, 31, 125, 147
Atlantic First strategy, 27, 30, 32, 83, 85
Atlantis, 106, 120
atomic bombings, 163
Australia, 5, 7, 28, 29, 42, 47-48, 51, 53, 65, 148, 150, 157, 160-161, 164-165, 167, 170
Austria, 104
Axis Military Agreement (1942), 110

Ball, MacMahon, 165
Baltic, 74-75, 79, 83
Bastogne, 42
Batavia, 110
Behncke, Admiral Paul, 71, 73, 93-94, 113-114
Belgium, 73
Bismarck, 80, 118
Blomberg, von, 72, 75, 95, 102
Bolshevik Revolution, 6
Bond, General Lionel, 61-62
Bötticher, Major von, 88, 96, 123
Bräutigam, Commander, 92, 97, 116
Bredow, von, 72, 83
Britain, Battle of, 52
Britain, see Great Britain,
British Commonwealth Occupation Force, 164

Bruk Report, 3
Bulge, Battle of, 42
Bullock, 9
Burkner, Captain, 104
Burma, 172; campaign, 10; Road, 51-52, 57-59, 152
bushido, 132

Cabinet Foreign Policy Committee, 51
Canada, 16; and Pacific, 3-7, 16, 18-19, 29, 66; and Occupation of Japan, 6, 18; awareness of German threat, 65; Japanese threat, 66; coast, 85; Navy in Atlantic, 119; and American policy toward Japan, 157-171
Canada-United States Permanent Joint Board on Defence (PJBD), 158-159
Canadian Institute of International Affairs, 157
Canaris, Admiral Wilhelm, 93-94, 103, 115
Canberra Conference, 168
Canol Pipeline Project, 159
Casablanca, 30
Chamberlain, Neville, 49-50, 52, 58
Chang Hsüeh-liang, 137-138
Chang Tso-lin, 137
Charter Oath (1868), 131
Chatfield, Lord, 50
Chiang Kai-shek, 23, 25, 33, 37, 135, 137
Chiefs of Staff Committee, 47, 50-51
China Aid Act (1948), 34
China Incident, see Sino-Japanese War (1937-1945),
China, 25-26, 47-48, 51, 70, 104, 111, 118, 122, 125, 134-137; Nationalist, 10, 12-13, 135, 170-171; Peoples Republic of, 5, 7; and Korean War, 35; territorial integrity, 24-26, 36
Chinese Communist Party, 33, 155
Churchill, Winston, 27, 51, 59, 148, 153, 160
Clausewitzian-Jominian models, 17
Claxton, Brooke, 168-169
Cold War in Asia, 7
Collins, Ralph, 164, 166, 169
Colombo, 109
Combined Chiefs of Staff, 148, 153, 160